Big House on the Prairie

Big House on the Prairie

Rise of the Rural Ghetto and Prison Proliferation

JOHN M. EASON

The University of Chicago Press
Chicago and London

The University of Chicago Press, Chicago 60637
The University of Chicago Press, Ltd., London
© 2017 by The University of Chicago
Published 2017.

Printed in the United States of America

26 25 24 23 22 21 20 19 18 17   1 2 3 4 5

ISBN-13: 978-0-226-41020-3 (cloth)
ISBN-13: 978-0-226-41034-0 (paper)
ISBN-13: 978-0-226-41048-7 (e-book)
DOI: 10.7208/chicago/9780226410487.001.0001

Names: Eason, John Major, author.
Title: Big house on the prairie : rise of the rural ghetto and prison
    proliferation / John M. Eason.
Description: Chicago ; London : The University of Chicago Press, 2017. |
    Includes bibliographical references and index.
Identifiers: LCCN 2016023253 | ISBN 9780226410203 (cloth : alk. paper) |
    ISBN 9780226410340 (pbk. : alk. paper) | ISBN 9780226410487 (e-book)
Subjects: LCSH: Prisons—Location—United States. | Prisons—Social
    aspects—United States. | Forrest City Federal Correctional Facility. | Forrest
    City (Ark.)—Social conditions. | United States—Rural conditions—20th
    century. | Sociology, Rural.
Classification: LCC HV8827 .E273 2017 | DDC 365/.973—dc23 LC record
    available at https://lccn.loc.gov/2016023253

⊛ This paper meets the requirements of ANSI/NISO Z39.48-1992
(Permanence of Paper).

To "Coach," Norma, and Junior

CONTENTS

PREFACE

Big House on the Prairie represents a new approach to the study of punishment in the United States. This inquiry explains the causes and consequences of the prison boom—the rapid expansion from 511 to 1,663 prisons in the United States in roughly thirty-five years. I argue that the prison boom is best understood from the perspective of the rural southern towns most directly affected by their placement, as opposed to the northern urban centers whose residents are believed to fill prison cells. This radically different perspective will deepen our understanding of what theorist David Garland refers to as the new iron cage, where justifications for prison building have been replaced "with the system taking on a life of its own, giving rise to adaptive behavior serving secondary interests." The most insidious form of this new iron cage is the penal-industrial complex— "the set of bureaucratic and private institutions that produce and manage jobs around prison building." This book argues that the self-fulfilling mandate of the so-called prison-industrial complex (PIC) is best understood not as a by-product of either late industrial capitalism or racism, but rather as a last-ditch effort of stigma management in avoiding continued decline by rural towns suffering from the rise of the rural ghetto.

The research questions explored in this manuscript emerged as I served as a community and political organizer in one of the neighborhoods that sends a disproportionate number of its residents to rural prisons—the South Side of Chicago. My experience as a community organizer in Chicago provided me with a new way of thinking about the importance of race in shaping criminal justice policies and practices. As my mentor, then–state Senator Barack Obama taught me to temper passion for social change with rationality in implementing public policy initiatives. As I soon found out, local initiatives to reduce crime can have unintended consequences.

The community group I was working with had partnered with elected and appointed city officials, including the police, to combat drug dealing in the neighborhood. Using surveys conducted at community meetings, we identified drug dealing "hot spots." We used secret ballots, because we wanted to inform the elected officials but protect residents' anonymity. We decided to hold a march to heighten neighborhood awareness of our new campaign, "Operation Holy Ground." This would be the first in a series of marches that resulted in the closure of drug houses. Before we left the Catholic church basement to embark on the march, the core group of ten leaders organizing this action stood together holding hands in a prayer circle, led by a deaconess from a neighboring United Church of Christ congregation. During minute eight of her ten-minute prayer, as she repeatedly belted out, "In the name of Jesus," a lay leader from the Catholic church nudged me, opened one eye, and whispered across his tilted, cottony, gray afro and furrowed gray brow, "she's gonna pray the birds out the trees!" Despite their proximity (the two churches were separated by fewer than four city blocks), these congregations rarely engaged in activities together before they joined the community organization. Since then, they have occasionally worshiped together and have shut down drug dealing operations in a dozen or so homes within the neighborhood—in the process sending scores of young black men and women to prison.

That night the march included over a hundred residents, the alderman, the Chicago Police district commander, and three three patrol cars with lights flashing and loudspeakers in operation. As we made our way from the Catholic church, we stopped to pray at several homes where we had previously shut down drug-selling operations, leaving signs in the front lawns that read, "This Property Has Been Reclaimed as Holy Ground." This march was led by half a dozen clergy dressed in full clerical garb, including collars, colorful headgear, and even robes. The clergy represented the Catholic, Presbyterian, United Church of Christ, and United Methodist Church denominations, but that evening they prayed, sang, and preached with a single mind and spirit. Accompanied by several squad cars, clergy locked arms with the alderman and police commander, taking up the entire width of the street. When we reached our final stop, we sang and prayed, after which a priest sprinkled holy water and recited biblical verses announcing that the property in question was indeed reclaimed as holy ground. As we departed, we staked our "This Property Has Been Reclaimed as Holy Ground" sign in the front lawn. We knew, however, that our performance would not stop the drug dealer's operations. That would take his arrest, which typically followed within a week after the march.

Afterward, we held an evaluation in the church basement to learn how to better address and resolve the tensions in our work. As I went around the room, I asked each of the leaders how they felt about their specific performance in their duties and how well the action was executed overall. They were all excited! Many felt powerful as they stood up for their values in a way they never thought possible. The church leaders expressed outrage at the ubiquity of drugs and gangs in their middle-class black neighborhood. This righteous anger fueled our work. It motivated lay leaders to give up evenings and weekends to plan activities like marches, to meet with city officials, and to mobilize friends/neighbors for community engagement. However, the feeling of victory from the march, including police support to close the drug house, was short-lived—there was a human cost to our actions. The drug dealer in question, it turned out, was the son of a church member. Our triumph had yielded losses for families within the ranks of our own organization, as the police would have to arrest the perpetrator and several other young black men to fulfill their commitment to the marchers that night.

At the end of the evaluation, I asked if there were any political lessons to take away from the events of that evening. Several rather modest, reserved, Catholic lay leaders provided insightful answers. One lay leader who had earlier expressed fear of potential retaliation by drug dealers balked at the prospect of their imprisonment. He explained, "I know we're standing up for our neighborhood, but we are having our black children arrested here in the city for what? *White folks downstate to get jobs!*" Another leader responded in a low, monotone voice, "*You either get a job, or you become a job!*" Still others argued, "Black folks don't grow drugs or import them into our neighborhood, so why are we imprisoned the most for selling drugs?" The sobering reflections shared by church leaders on local drug trafficking and the broader implications of drug supply and demand, linked to the different levels of employment inside and outside the neighborhood, forever changed how I viewed the relationship between race, disadvantage, and the criminal justice system. Our group had effectively mobilized hundreds of residents to close a dozen drug houses, but our efforts seemed paltry in the grand scheme of things. Even more troubling was the realization that we were sending the children of fellow African American congregates to prison. We were fully aware that some young blacks turn to drug trafficking in the informal economy because legitimate means of achieving the American dream are stymied by racism. That night, the leadership questioned whether we were unwittingly contributing to an inherently racist prison system.

Soon after this march, I left organizing to enter graduate school at the University of Chicago. My plan was to study the "prison-industrial complex" in hopes of dismantling this behemoth of racial oppression. But in completing my master's thesis, I discovered that—in contrast to the commonly held belief among PIC activists that prisons are built in small, overwhelmingly white communities with high unemployment—prison building is most likely to occur in larger rural southern towns with higher proportions of blacks and Latinos. These findings[1] further honed my thinking on the causes and consequences of the prison boom.

On the basis of these initial findings, I decided to relocate with my family to rural Arkansas to uncover the challenges facing a community that pursued and secured a prison facility. As a student of communities and criminal justice, I believed the conventional wisdom that no good could come from prison building, and I questioned why any community wanted one. Within a week of being in Forrest City I was disavowed of this notion. Each person I encountered ardently supported building the facility.

Prison placement is often oversimplified as a dubious choice for rural community leaders; either as a way to secure jobs or as a way to stigmatize their communities. Some rural leaders see attracting a prison as a way to achieve order in a world that seems to be rapidly changing in ways that are increasingly beyond their control. I learned that collective memory and a shared sense of community are also vital in differentiating the instrumental purposes of a prison (jobs) from its symbolism. In Forrest City, racial violence and stigma marred residents' collective memory and shared meanings of community. Given the legacy of shame associated with prisons, the need to overcome stigma often plays the most important role in seeing a prison as a viable solution for a town's problems. This led me to reevaluate prison demand as nuanced, multifaceted, and dependent on context.

What follows is, in part, an exploration of the causes and consequences of the prison boom. But more importantly, this book will provide a broader and deeper analysis of the new iron cage by rethinking the penal-industrial complex. By unraveling why leaders in Forrest City, Arkansas, pursued and secured placement of the Forrest City Federal Correctional Facility, we can begin to understand the social, political, and economic shifts that drove the United States—"the land of the free"—to triple prison construction in just over thirty years, resulting in the largest (yet unnoticed) public works projects in modern history—the prison boom.

GLOSSARY

Penal-industrial complex. Economic, social, and political institutions related to the causes and consequences of the prison boom.

Prison boom. The period beginning in 1970 during which the number of US prison facilities tripled.

Prison building. Constructing or erecting a prison within a municipality.

Prison closings. The process associated with the political economy of closing a prison, emphasizing the role of state and federal agencies involved in choosing between or selecting facilities or municipalities for closing.

Prison impact. The economic, political, and social benefits/costs for a host community as a result of prison placement.

Prison-industrial complex. A set of bureaucratic, political, and economic interests that encourage increased spending on imprisonment, regardless of the actual need.

Prison placement. The process associated with the political economy of prison building within a municipality, with particular attention to the role of civic leaders and the local political elite in securing the facility.

Prison proliferation. The widespread construction of prison facilities throughout the United States, especially in nonmetropolitan or rural communities.

Prison siting. The process associated with the political economy of prison building, emphasizing the role of state and federal agencies involved in choosing between or selecting municipalities for prison building.

Prison town. A nonmetropolitan municipality that has secured and constructed a prison from federal, state, or private operators.

ONE

Introduction: The Causes and Consequences of the Prison Boom

From its greatest cultural export, blues music, to the production of staple crops like cotton, life in the Mississippi Delta is defined by race and racism, perhaps more than anywhere else in the United States. While Forrest City, Arkansas, is hailed as the birthplace of rhythm and blues singer the Reverend Al Green, it was named to honor a more nefarious association. "Forrest's Town" was named after Confederate general Nathan Bedford Forrest. Credited with founding the town in 1870, Forrest is best known for starting the most infamous domestic terrorist organization in US history, the Ku Klux Klan. This legacy of racism is still palpable in Forrest City, with the Confederate flag prominently displayed on cars, in the county museum, and at the county fair.

Like many Delta communities, Forrest City faced a shifting economic and social landscape after the fall of Jim Crow. In the late 1980s, its white leadership—the top political brass, including the mayor, the director of the chamber of commerce, the state representative, and a county judge—began meeting to discuss the possibility of bringing a prison to the "Jewel of the Delta." At a distance, many activists would characterize these meetings as the stuff of smoke-filled back rooms, with good ol' boys hatching a white supremacist conspiracy to subjugate African Americans in a neoplantation prison-industrial complex. But there is a complication. If acquiring a prison involves such sinister schemes, why do so many rural communities that push for and receive prisons contain disproportionate numbers of black and Hispanic residents? In Forrest City, black leaders, too, agreed that the arrival of a prison might stop the town's economic slide. This complicates how we normally think about the process of becoming a prison town.

The prison town—a nonmetropolitan municipality that has secured and constructed a prison for a federal, state, or private operator—is a strategic

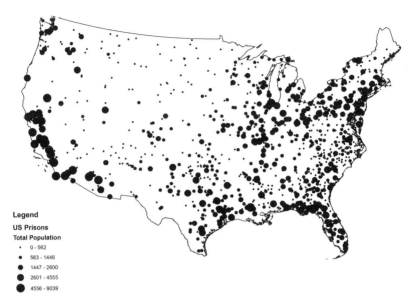

Legend

US Prisons

Total Population

· 0 - 562

• 563 - 1446

● 1447 - 2600

● 2601 - 4555

● 4556 - 9039

Map 1.1. US prison proliferation, 1811–2010

site to investigate the intersection of race, spatial disadvantage, and the expansion of the criminal justice system. Forty years ago, there were 511 prison facilities in the United States. Since then we have embarked on an unparalleled expansion, constructing 1,152 new facilities. This dramatic growth in prison building is known as the prison boom (Garland 2001; Western 2006). Many scholars believe the prison boom to be the logical consequence of the annual imprisonment of more than two million Americans. However, this line of thinking cannot explain why some states build more prisons than others. For example, Illinois, Georgia, and Ohio have roughly 50,000 inmates each in state prisons, but the states house their prisoners in different numbers of facilities (from Illinois's fifty-five to Georgia's eighty-two).

Prior to the boom, prison building was not as salient for rural locales because of the relative availability of other large-scale economic development opportunities like factories, mills, or even military bases. In fact, most towns protested the placement of LULUs (Locally Undesirable Land Uses) like prisons for fear of being associated with a stigmatized institution. Starting in the 1970s, this trend shifted in regard to correctional facilities, with some rural towns lobbying to win a prison. Despite the varied motivations that produced this shift, one thing is clear—few scholars have actually examined the impetus for the "demand" for prisons in rural towns or the subsequent impact of these facilities. The journalism and sparse academic work on this topic frame prison building as a zero-sum game with rural white communities benefiting from the mass imprisonment of poor, urban, black, and Latino communities.

The dominant narrative on prison building also suggests that they are bad for communities—not only the urban communities from which most prisons are believed to draw their populations but also the communities where prisons are built. Moreover, because prisoners are stigmatized and prisons are not aesthetically attractive, many argue that communities should voice NIMBY (Not in My Backyard) and oppose placement. I reveal that prison building is often the best of the last options for town leaders hoping to manage the spoiled identity accompanying the rise of the rural ghetto. By investigating the process of how a town pursued and secured a prison I trace elite decision making, revealing the multiple, and often conflicting, factors in prison placement.

Prison building is often portrayed as a dichotomous decision for communities. On one hand, prisons present the potential for economic development. On the other, prisons are believed to stigmatize rural places. By describing the process that culminated in the placement of the Forrest City Federal Correctional Facility (FCFCF), we can begin to understand the multiple social, political, and economic shifts that drove the United States to triple prison construction in just over thirty years. Forrest City's campaign to win a prison helps explain how rural communities get from NIMBY (Not in My Backyard) to PIMBY (Please in My Backyard). This study also complicates the iconic imagery of rural southern communities (for example, quaint/gentle and backward/violent) by unearthing the complex networks and nuanced negotiations undertaken by local elites in acquiring a federal prison. Not only do I chronicle the political process of prison placement, but I also use local perceptions to show the good, bad, and ugly sides of prison impact.

Thinking about the Prison Boom

The term "prison proliferation" refers to the widespread construction of prison facilities throughout the United States. To date, we have constructed 1,663 prisons, employing on average 231 individuals with annual profits exceeding $40 billion, at a cost of over $20,000 annually to house each inmate. There are many ways we can think about the causes and consequences of prison proliferation. The sociology of punishment seeks to explain how punishment affects society (Garland 2001). A segment of this research agenda describes a prison-industrial complex (PIC). The PIC perspective is central to discourse on prison building. Eric Schlosser (1998) defines the PIC as "a set of bureaucratic, political, and economic interests that encourage increased spending on imprisonment, regardless of the actual need" (54). His work has influenced a number of writers who refer to the PIC as an institutional dynamic in which vested economic interests actively promote prison construction and a punitive system of criminal justice. This theory can be summarized by the following empirical claims:[1] (1) politicians exploit crime legislation to secure votes; (2) private companies seek profits by serving or operating prisons; and (3) rural town leaders use prisons for economic development. From the PIC perspective, the growth of prisons in rural communities suggests that prisons are solely a strategy for economic development.[2]

Because white towns are believed to derive economic benefit from the imprisonment of black men through prison job creation, this exploitation has a racial dimension:

> The ultimate policy irony at the heart of America's passion for prisons can be summarized by what I call "correctional Keynesianism"; the prison construction boom fed by the rising "market" of Black offenders is a job and tax-base creator for predominantly White communities that are generally far removed from urban minority concentrations. Those communities, often recently hollowed out by the de-industrializing family farm-destroying gales of the "free market" system, have become part of a prison-industrial lobby that presses for harsher sentences and tougher laws, seeking to protect their economic base even as crime rates continue to fall. (Street 2002, 36)

Street's commentary demonstrates how prison towns are believed to reify racial and economic stratification by punishing and incarcerating poor black and brown urban dwellers. Many scholars and journalists view the PIC's extension of the "peculiar institution" of racism as an oppressive catalyst generating jobs, capital investments, political power, and community pride in white rural prison towns (Schlosser 1998; King, Mauer, and Huling 2003). At the same time, the destructive apparatus of the PIC drives concentrated disadvantage in the hyperghetto by depriving communities of young black men in their prime years of employment and familial responsibility (Braman 2001; Clear 2001; Smith and Hattery 2008). Others claim the PIC reshapes the labor pool along racial lines, cordoning off blacks from the mainstream labor market (Smith and Hattery 2009).

Scholars assert that the ghetto "underclass" or "surplus population" (Darity 1983) was ripe for mass imprisonment. A journalist finds "most of America's huge prison population is Black or brown, and many of America's prisons are located in very White rural areas" (Tilove 2002). In some in-stances, blacks comprise nearly 80 percent of a state's prison population, while whites make up 90 percent of corrections officers (Wacquant 2001). In this view, the growth of the penal population redistributes economic resources, as the black underclass creates jobs for poor whites.

Other critics have found more overtly sinister goals in the PIC. These scholars and activists believe the prison boom intentionally produces racial and economic inequality for exploitation by private corporations,[3] citing as evidence the growth of private prisons from 7 to roughly 12 percent of total prisons.[4] However, because states operate most US prisons (roughly 83 percent[5]), this extreme position does not hold; in fact, state-level charac-teristics are important predictors of prison placement. Furthermore, because prisons are primarily constructed by state legislatures, each state acts as a sorting mechanism for prison building. If we take the PIC account to be generally correct, two conclusions follow. First, the prison town is a space that exacerbates racial and economic inequality, driving the expansion of the criminal justice system by "demanding" increased prison construction. Second, the archetypical prison town is a space dominated by unemployed and impoverished whites. While the local context is important, larger social and political forces based on regional and state variations help to shape the context of punishment.

Even before beginning this study of Forrest City, I had identified evi-dence that challenged these bedrock assumptions of the prison-industrial complex.[6] Prison placement does not result in disadvantage in rural com-munities as much as it is caused by racial and economic exploitation in rural communities (Eason 2010). Moreover, prison towns are diverse. They vary by size, region, socioeconomic status (SES), and racial composition (Eason 2010). Many prisons are built in micropolitan towns with popula-tions ranging from 10,000 to 50,000. During the height of the prison boom, most prisons were built in southern towns with higher percentages of blacks and Latinos, and lower unemployment, than the average small town (Eason 2010). In fact, the average rural southern town was twelve times more likely to receive a prison than a midwestern or northeastern town. The characteris-tics of prison towns also vary across periods of the prison boom. This is not surprising, given the demographic shifts in rural communities over the past forty years. In addition, roughly a third of all corrections officers nationally are black or Latino (Ward 2006).

These findings complicate the PIC perspective in several ways. First, the role of disadvantage is paradoxical. In contrast to the PIC theory's central argument that rural prison placement is a windfall for towns and causes

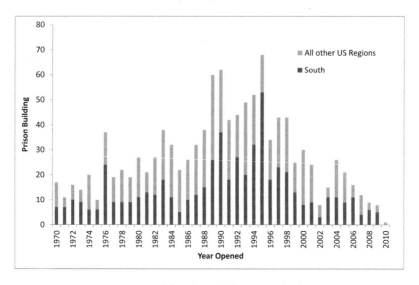

Figure 1.1. Prison boom: US versus the South

racial and economic inequality, my findings suggest that prisons are sited where rural disadvantage is already concentrated. Like urban disadvantage (Wilson 1987; Sampson and Wilson 1994; Wacquant 2001), concentrated rural disadvantage is marked by high poverty, residential segregation, and stigma. Studies show that rural blacks, like urban blacks, live in the most residentially segregated US census blocks (Aiken 1990; Lichter et al. 2007a; Wahl and Gunkel 2007; Cromartie and Beale 1980). Related studies suggest that black and Latino housing patterns are linked to concentrated poverty (Lichter et al. 2008). Therefore, we can think of racial and economic disadvantage in rural communities as fundamental to explaining the prison boom. Prison proliferation moreover benefits blacks and Latinos by providing employment as corrections officers. In a seminal piece, Everett Hughes (1962) describes the relationship between "Good People and Dirty Work" that explains why people believe that any job is a good job. The prevalence of prison building in the South suggests that southern culture may be germane in contextualizing the local "demand" for prisons (Cobb 1992; Reed 1994). Therefore, multiple factors (for example, region, rurality, race, and inequality) need to be accounted for in prison placement.

To account for the multiple, conflicting motives in prison building, the dominant narrative of the PIC needs to be reconsidered. The penal-industrial complex can be differentiated from the prison-industrial complex by its positive focus on punishment. In contrast, the PIC perspective casts prison building as a normative function of overt racism and deterministic capitalism. I improve on the penal-industrial complex as a theoretical anchor in explaining prison proliferation by expanding beyond the singular focus on jobs. This reframing allows us to understand the bureaucratic function of punishment and its role in the prison boom. I redefine the penal-industrial complex as the economic, social, and political institutions related to the causes and consequences of the prison boom.

Finding Forrest City: Fieldwork across Rural Neighborhood Ecology

Along the 130 miles between Memphis, Tennessee, and Little Rock, Arkansas, the horizon is perfectly flat, as if scraped by a giant bricklayer. You will find swamps, a Super 8 Motel, an adult store, a billboard hawking guns and ammo, and Forrest City, Arkansas. Its front door is the intersection of the second-largest commercial truck trafficking route in the country, Interstate 40, and the north–south corridor of Arkansas Highway 1 / Washington Avenue. Driving along the interstate on a warm summer night, we watched the sun nuzzle into the rice paddies growing up from the marshy land.

I relocated my African American family, including my wife and two small children, to the Yazoo Mississippi Delta to understand the decision making of local white elites about economic development. Given the stigma of prison, I wanted to learn firsthand why town leaders would lobby for placement. I chose Forrest City for this case study, in part, because it fit the economic and demographic profile of a disadvantaged rural southern community struggling to attract new economic development (Taub 2004). In many ways, it is also the prototypical prison town. The 2000 census showed that 36 percent of the roughly 14,000 residents were white, with 61 percent African American. The median family income was about half the national average of $50,000, and the poverty rate nearly triple, at about 33 percent.

The vestiges of the two-tier owner/worker Jim Crow system are omnipresent in the town's social structure and physical layout. Poverty is mainly concentrated in the lower town, west of Arkansas Highway 1 / Washington Avenue, while nestled in the hills east of Washington Avenue, off winding, almost secretive roads, many white elite families live in lavish single-family homes on large lots with immaculate lawns and well-sculpted gardens. Some of these families once ran cotton farms and still wield power statewide. Despite their physical proximity, these residents are socially distant. Most blacks growing up in the bottoms have never visited these homes; in fact, many did not think of them as part of Forrest City.

Exploring prison placement requires a multimethod research design and an eclectic data collection style that always connects to some form of observation. To investigate Forrest City, I used an ethnographic case-study method (Yin 2003) that included interviews, archival research, participant observation, mapping, and statistical analysis. Ethnography is an artistic and risky scientific method. It often involves relocating to an unfamiliar community. In this case, our identity as northerners marked us as outsiders. Extensive fieldwork is a test of discipline and perseverance not for the weak of heart. When well executed, however, it not only elicits interesting stories but also helps the social scientist construct theoretical frameworks. To describe the site and our experiences, I use what Duneier labels the Howard Becker principle: "most social processes have a structure that comes close to insuring that a certain set of situations will arise over time. These situations practically require people to do or say certain things because there are other things going on that require them to do that, things that are more influential than the social condition of a fieldworker being present" (Duneier and Carter 1999, 338). Being both participant and observer allows access to the community, but also provides the social distance to notice aspects of rural southern life that natives take for granted. The tension between access and distance aids in understanding, rather than merely describing, observed behaviors. As many ethnographers say, talk is cheap. Without understanding the relationships and the role of the informant in the community, interview data are hollow. Patterns emerged as I transcribed recorded interviews, coded, and wrote memos based on those codes from my notes as a participant/observer. I usually analyzed as I collected, which influenced further data collection. For example, ghetto elements in Forrest City were not immediately apparent, but routine review of my field notes exposed subtle cues of racial and spatial stigma.

In 2006, I spent four months conducting interviews and going through records at the local community college. After that, I moved to a neighboring community with my wife and children (summer 2007 through winter 2008). The qualitative data gathered during these periods consists of formal/informal interviews and observations. After establishing Mr. Stephens as a key informant, I built a network of informants using snowball sampling for interviews. Oisín Tansey (2007) finds that in creating a narrative history of a specific event, researchers should interview specific actors or segments of a community. I used this rationale in formal interviews with current or past Forrest City decision makers. Other informal interviews and observations arose in frequenting churches, bars, barbershops, restaurants, and stores; talking with hotel staff, neighbors, office staff, small business owners, civic organization members, recreational facility staff, police, and City Hall employees. In constructing the social history of Forrest City, I also conducted archival research using print and electronic media (primarily newspaper articles from the *Forrest City Times-Herald*), nonprofit, and government records. I used numerous local, state, and federal government agencies as sources for quantitative analysis and descriptive statistics.

In addition, by making the cross-country move to the Delta, finding a place to live, placing my six-year-old son in elementary school, and engaging in other daily activities like grocery shopping, we began to gain an understanding of the people and place. I had no sooner understood the impediments to economic development embedded in places like Forrest City when codes and common themes emerged from the field and led me to see the broader structures and processes shaping the town's concentrated disadvantage. After a deeper investigation using historical and secondary data, I uncovered classic ghettoization processes like white flight, increased public housing, and de-industrialization, resulting in the social isolation of poor African Americans. After triangulating and further interrogating both the data and the research site, I was able to link ghetto structures and formation to a history of racist education and economic policies and practices. I used these pieces to engage with the literature, creating a micro-macro theoretical link. While the rural ghetto was not the central focus of the initial investigation, it emerged as the best way to make sense of the dynamic social, political, and economic context facing rural decision makers.

Although conducting qualitative research can be an isolating process, I am forever indebted to the people of Forrest City for opening their hearts and homes and community to my family—no one perhaps more than André Stephens. Stephens, the executive director of the Saint Francis County Community Development Corporation (SFCCDC), is a key player in local development, as evidenced by the recent construction of a multi-million-dollar senior housing center (*Forrest City Times-Herald* 2011). Mr. Stephens has lived in Forrest City for nearly two decades, yet some residents still consider him a Yankee. He has joked about this with me claiming, "Me and you are considered just Yankees. That's better than being a damn Yankee"! He immediately welcomed me because of his respect for the colleague who brokered our connection.[7] He adopted my family as fictive kin (Anderson 1978; Stack 1974) and provided office space and other support for my study through the SFCCDC. Because it serves indigent clients, working in the Saint Francis County Community Development Corporation provided initial access and, eventually, entrée into other spheres of life that would have been impossible otherwise. Mr. Stephens introduced me to numerous informants, including the few remaining white elite families who still owned most of the land in town, despite the recent emergence of black political power in the mayor's office and city council positions. Mr. Stephens's social position as an outsider and professional position as a local developer afforded him access to decision makers on both sides of the town's long-standing racial divide. He was strongly interested in illuminating the economic plight of rural black communities in hopes of better positioning his life's work.

Through Mr. Stephens and the SFCCDC, I made several contacts that would prove crucial to the study. I first met Charles Freeman when he interned at the SFCCDC. He had just completed his first year at North Carolina Agricultural and Technical State University, where he studied finance and computer science. He had been the starting tight end for the Forrest City High School football team and was recruited to play at North Carolina A&T. His surname is significant both locally and historically to blacks. During slavery, blacks did not have surnames because they were property. Shortly after the Emancipation Proclamation, many took a popular US president's surname, like Lincoln, Washington, or Jefferson; others took their master's surname. Other more militant blacks took the surname Freeman or Freedman to announce their liberation. As a Forrest City native, Charles Freeman is critical yet very proud of his hometown. His family is well respected and well known. His father and uncles recently sold the convenience store they operated, which housed a gas station and laundromat.

Charles and I played basketball many times at the newly constructed Forrest City recreation center. He is left-handed with a hoop game reminiscent of the late, great Hank Gathers. He is brown-skinned, six feet two, and burly but not fat. No real hops (jumping ability) to speak of, but he has a quick drop-step spin in either direction out of the post. His feet are nimble as he runs down the quick, small guards. I have enjoyed sharing meals and hanging out at "Club" Wal-Mart with him. He served as local guide and confidant to help me make sense of local customs. He is also an excellent example of how young adult men should navigate rural southern culture—I often modeled my behavior after him. This decision was strategic: he is not only one of a few young adults I encountered in the area with strong aspirations toward upward mobility but, more importantly, he commands and gives respect. Charles looks other people in the eye and says "Yes, ma'am" or "No, sir." Whether the person is black, white, young, or old, Charles shows he is interested and genuinely cares by asking after family members. He has the beautiful manners of a proper southerner.

Shortly after arriving in Forrest City, Charles and I embarked on a transect. Ethnographers use transects as data-gathering tools to ascertain how informants make sense of space and place. I used these driving tours as opportunities to understand what institutions and neighborhoods were important to key informants. Gaining the lay of the land taught me the spatial fissures along wealth, race, and disadvantage within Forrest City. During the initial ride, Charles was quite open in his opinion of Forrest City. As I drove, he pointed out recent infrastructure improvements including paved sidewalks in "old" downtown and other traditionally underserved neighborhoods, the newly constructed recreation center, and the modern air-conditioned additions to the grade schools. The recreation center and school improvements gave Charles a great sense of pride and satisfaction. They signaled a marked change from past policies that did not invest in youth. These improvements were the crowning accomplishments of the first black mayor, Larry Bryant.

The school improvements took years to accomplish because Arkansas school budget increases were tied to local communities imposing a millage—an additional tax for specific school projects. After years of complicated political battles, the millage was passed in Forrest City, making infrastructure improvements at the schools possible. A major part of the uneven academic performance of Forrest City schools can be linked to poor funding. While Arkansas is ranked educationally below most states, the eastern portion that is part of the Mississippi River Delta performs the worst. Forrest City is no exception.

During this drive, I also took note of the modern, planned industrial spaces closer to key highway nodes like Interstate 40, Arkansas Highway 1, and the newly constructed Dale Bumpers Road, which all lead to the prison. The bypass from Arkansas Highway 1 and Interstate 40 that leads directly to the prison is named for former Arkansas governor and United States senator Dale Bumpers, to acknowledge his role in securing the federal correctional facility. Lichter and Fuguitt (1980) demonstrate the competitive advantages to businesses of being located near an interstate, and the more modern industrial areas in Forrest City follow this logic. Just north of Interstate 40, corporate branches include a distribution center for Pepsi, a Sanyo television manufacturing plant, and a Boar's Head meat processing plant. Arkansas Highway 1 separates the industrial park from a motel campus that includes national chains like Holiday Inn, Best Western, Days Inn, and Hampton Inn. Just south of Interstate 40 along either side of Highway 1, a series of strip malls is anchored by a new, large Wal-Mart.

In many respects, de-industrialization and globalization have restructured the physical geography of towns like Forrest City. Shops and restaurants line both sides of Washington Avenue. Fast food restaurants like McDonald's, Burger King, KFC, and Sonic dominate this streetscape near

Figure 1.2. Forrest City central commercial district, Arkansas Highway 1, Washington Avenue

the highway. The occasional Winn Dixie Chicken or Bonanza Steakhouse nestles between them. Although some residents walk to these centrally located strip malls, most drive. A car culture prevails over rural southern communities. The newer, larger Wal-Mart on the west side of the highway is not simply a store in this town. Open twenty-four hours a day, it transforms into what Charles calls "Club Wal-Mart" for many young adults on Friday and Saturday evenings. This newer store is directly across Highway 1 from the superseded, now vacant Wal-Mart on the east side. The area has a high volume of commercial activity, people, and cars, and Charles called it the center of town. There are few other local entertainment options, and young adult activities often involve travel to Memphis or Little Rock. Hanging out at Wal-Mart is a low-stress, low-investment option for socializing. Wal-Mart is not the only global corporate space lining Washington Street in Forrest City. The multitude of commercial establishments along Interstate 40 and Arkansas Highway 1 appealed to interstate travelers and local residents alike.

Even in the agricultural sections of Forrest City, there are facilities one would expect to find in urban neighborhoods, like a roller-skating rink, a bowling alley, and a movie theater. In fact, Forrest City has a country club equipped with a golf course, tennis courts, and a swimming pool. While Forrest City possessed most of the businesses and facilities that one would find in a larger community, quantity, quality, and size varied: Forrest City had fewer of them, and they were usually lower quality and smaller. For example, the movie theater had a limited selection of first-run movies. Some younger informants complained that the owners/operators would not bring "controversial" or "urban" films, and the hours of operation were limited mainly to the weekends. These limits also contribute to "push" factors for young, upwardly mobile residents to relocate to Memphis or Little Rock for entertainment.

While newer commercial and retail developments were clustered near the interstate and the new Wal-Mart, public and financial services could be found in the traditional center of town on either side of Arkansas Highway 1 near Broadway Avenue. They include city hall, the police and fire departments, the chamber of commerce, a recently constructed courthouse, the Saint Francis County Museum, several banks, realtors, and insurance companies. While there are plenty of storefronts, few businesses operate in this area; they either died or moved to the main highway by the smaller Wal-Mart, leaving the county square a virtual ghost town. The faded, chipped, white outline of lettering for the Don José Mexican restaurant haunts an abandoned structure on Washington Street. Space has been redefined in communities like Forrest City, with the shift of commercial activity away from traditional downtowns, sometimes called "Wal-Martification." Here, the central business district shifted from proximity to town government agencies to the Wal-Mart near the interstate highway. While macroforces like globalization exert pressure, decision makers in communities like Forrest City ultimately determine what businesses are developed locally. Local community leaders have agency, even without many development options.

South along Arkansas Highway 1 between the old and new centers of town are several banks, the civic center, a grocery store, a drug store, and some hair salons, most notably, the House of Fashion, owned and operated by Terri Stephens, wife of André Stephens. Farther down are churches, including First Baptist and other red brick and gray buildings that are or once were of great significance. In between the churches and some commercial buildings, a red brick, two-story apartment building had roughly twenty units. Signs of neglect spoke volumes—paint peeling off white window trim, some windows wide open and missing screens, others with broken screens dangling, the front entrance door slumped off the hinges. Disrepair like this is associated with disorder in urban settings (St. Jean 2007). While enlightening, these initial signs could not fully prepare me for what I would learn about rural communities during my study of Forrest City.

Modeling Prison Placement

It is useful to separate the building of a prison and its impact on a community into several distinct stages. Throughout this book, I will distinguish between prison siting, prison placement, prison building, and prison impact. Siting refers to the role of a government entity—usually the state or federal government—in selecting a site on which to build a prison. Placement draws our attention to the process by which local civic and political leaders attempt to secure such a facility—that is, how they convince the state to site a prison in their town. Building refers to the construction process itself, while impact points to the social, economic, and political costs and benefits as a result of the arrival of a prison.

While there are certainly local nuances to any type of "demand," there are also broader, seemingly universal, forces that predict a bid for prison placement (or, for that matter, any other LULU). Prisons represent different things to different people. Some see suffering and stigma, while others, especially communities that have seen better days, envision economic development opportunities and jobs. These conflicting views manifest a dynamic tension at the community level. So how do prisons or any other LULUs find communities willing to receive them? Understanding the placement of LULUs requires one to account for multiple levels of stigma, including the region, the town, and even within the community itself. Understanding prison placement in the United States requires a unique lens sensitive to rural disadvantage. Rural disadvantage is more persistent and entrenched than urban poverty; locals' hopes for prison impact make no sense without this context. Yet rural poverty remains concealed and off the beaten path, as scholarly work on stratification in rural areas lags behind urban areas in both breadth and depth.

Understanding prison placement requires adopting the perspective of the type of community most likely to receive one. Given that prisons are more likely to be built in impoverished rural communities with sizeable poor black or Latino populations, any explanation of prison "demand" must take this type of community structure into account. In the NIMBY to PIMBY model below, I suggest that race leaders/middlemen and white elites form a growth coalition (Logan and Molotch 1987) in response to the rise of the rural ghetto. Despite an otherwise racially contentious political climate, the growth coalition allows the key players in the city to come together across racial lines and secure a prison. Ultimately, the decision to pursue a prison reveals how some rural areas make decisions to manage stigma and social inequality. I argue that the counterintuitive notions of PIMBY for prisons is

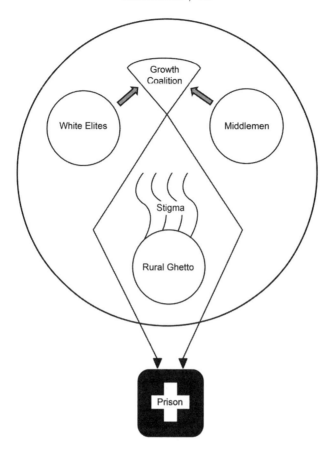

Figure 1.3. NIMBY to PIMBY: modeling prison placement

based on a town's efforts to manage spoiled identity (Goffman 1963; Rivera 2008). This model of prison placement captures the dynamic tension facing rural communities with limited economic opportunities. We cannot truly judge someone else's living arrangements until we visit their backyard. *Big House on the Prairie* offers a glimpse into the backyard of the rural South.

The case of Forrest City demonstrates the complexity of context and institutions in the matching process of economic development. Classic growth machine models cannot account for undesirable land uses, as they frame any economic development as PIMBY. The environmental justice approach to LULUs, in contrast, positions communities of color solely as victims of undesirable land use. But, as the case of Forrest City will show, the path from NIMBY to PIMBY is not necessarily predictable, with twists and turns along racial lines. Understanding how communities come to demand a LULU—the process of placement—requires an understanding of the role of stigma in those same communities. Stigmatized places are more likely to "demand" stigmatized institutions, particularly if the stigma of the community is equal to or greater than the stigma associated with the institution in question.

Rural towns most likely to receive a prison suffer the quadruple stigma of rurality, race, region, and poverty. Despite the negative stigma associated with prisons, locals shape positive meaning from prison placement. White elites and black race leaders/middlemen use similar frames in discussing prison placement as a positive response to the bourgeoning rural ghetto. However, positive views of prison impact are differentiated along community roles and race, with White elites viewing the prison most positively. Specific actors or sets of actors are crucial to understand prison building.

As a result, I propose the following model of prison placement. A functioning growth coalition that can properly signal prison demand to state/federal authorities requires that white elites must be joined (or at least not opposed) by middlemen. Philip Selznick (1949) posits co-optation as "the process of absorbing new elements into the leadership or policy-determining structure of an organization as a means of averting threats to its stability or existence" (13). In formal co-optation, "there is a need to establish the legitimacy of authority" to the "relevant public," whereas informal co-optation produces "the need of adjustment to the pressure of specific centers of power within the community" (Selznick 1949, 259). In the case of Forrest City, race leaders were both formally and informally co-opted into the growth coalition. In race leaders' support for prison construction in exchange for minority set-aside contracts, we see informal co-optation. Then-local NAACP chapter president Larry Bryant's decision not to oppose the project at the 1990 community meeting serves as an example of formal co-optation. Together, these instances clearly point to race leaders' willing participation in both types of co-optation. This case study should not be oversimplified as one of black race leaders being duped by the white elite or becoming victims of oppressive neoliberal forces.

Although this model is based on Forrest City, a prototypical prison town, slight adjustments can be made to understand the process of prison placement depending on the region, state, and local racial composition of towns that have or will pursue prisons. For instance, given the racial composition of prison towns in the Texas panhandle, middlemen will most likely be Latino, not black. Surely local cultural and state procedural mechanisms may differ, but the process of placement should not differ wildly from Forrest City.

Outline of the Book

This book answers two broad questions. First, what is the source of prison "demand" that spurred the prison boom? Second, how do prisons impact rural towns? Chapters 2 through 5 address the question of prison "demand." Chapters 6 through 8 address prison impact. I begin by reframing the Please in My Backyard (PIMBY) question in chapter 2 by asking, "Have you seen my backyard?" This chapter explores the potential motivations behind prison placement in rural communities by focusing on the role of stigma in defining a town's identity. In underscoring events that affected Forrest City's reputation, including a rape trial and a manufacturing worker's strike, we can see how stigma builds in rural communities prior to prison placement.

In comparing life in Forrest City to residing in the Chicago Housing Authority developments, a resident states, "it's the same, only quieter." I use this quote to advance the notion of a rural ghetto in chapter 3, suggesting that processes like white flight, de-industrialization, and the expansion of public housing created a new form of inequality in communities like Forrest City. Borrowing from urban sociology, I detail how the rural ghetto has emerged as a post–Jim Crow form of subjugation instrumental to the prison boom. Through ethnographic and historical data, we came to understand firsthand how the Delta is deeply defined by systems of racial oppression. Before this respondent compared drug abuse, drug selling, and crime in her Forrest City neighborhood to Chicago, I did not make the experiential link between these communities. From here, I show how elements of concentrated disadvantage like murder rates and residential segregation provide a basis for considering how the ghetto concept applies to certain rural communities. More importantly, I suggest that just as there are urban ghettos, rural spaces of concentrated disadvantage should be understood as rural ghettos that have similar functions in rural ecology.

In chapter 4, I show how local decision makers construct narratives of how the FCFCF will improve the town's reputation. In order to build support for placement, the prison, an otherwise stigmatized institution, is reframed as a savior, a stabilizer, or a way to advance Forrest City. These narratives are used in the campaign to effectively reframe NIMBY (Not in My Backyard) to PIMBY (Please in My Backyard) regarding placement. Residents show a willingness to accept a stigmatized institution based on characteristics of the community and the institution. I suggest that when a town becomes more stigmatized than an institution like a prison or hazardous-waste facility, the town is more willing to accept these institutions to save their reputation.

In chapter 5, I highlight the prison placement process using the case of the FCFCF. I build a theory of prison placement, suggesting that a community's willingness to accept a stigmatized institution depends on characteristics of both the community and the institution. Surprisingly, despite the negative stigma associated with prisons, rural community leaders produce a groundswell of support by framing the prison as a way to save the community from continued economic decline. While having a rural ghetto could be a sufficient impetus for securing a prison, the case of Forrest City suggests at least two other necessary conditions. First, local white elites must want the prison and exercise social capital to acquire the facility. Second, local black/Latino leadership must also support (or at least not oppose) the decision. These interlocking interests form the basis for a growth coalition between white elites and race leaders (Logan and Molotch 1987). While I am not suggesting that these otherwise contentious groups are sharing power, my case study suggests that race leaders are co-opted for their public support.

Chapter 6 uses local perceptions of prison impact to present the numerous challenges and opportunities prison building provides. While the FCFCF is overwhelmingly viewed positively by residents in Forrest City and Wynne, this chapter also describes a disjuncture in local opinion: while local leaders portray the prison as a windfall, some residents have a more mixed reaction. Perceptions of prison impact are nuanced and differ with an individual's position in the local social structure. To date, the few studies measuring prison impact focus on positive economic growth from prison placement. By understanding local rural perceptions of the prison's impact, I call for a theoretical reorientation to measure prison impact.

Chapter 7 delves further into investigating the impact of the FCFCF. I use descriptive statistics to detail impacts of the FCFCF in Forrest City and a neighboring town, further demonstrating the pros and cons of prison impact. Simultaneously, the chapter establishes that the rise of the rural ghetto presents obstacles to rebuilding Forrest City's reputation, despite the presence of the FCFCF. On the eve of opening, a resident compared the living conditions in the federal prison to those of fellow residents and concluded that conditions for prisoners are better than many Forrest City residents. This provides a signal that, despite the perceived improvements from prison building, the town continues to struggle. I maintain that despite the presence of the FCFCF, Forrest City's reputation has suffered.

I conclude the book in chapter 8 by discussing the theoretical and policy implications of prison proliferation. Given the current fiscal crisis facing many states, policy makers must ask two equally important questions. First, can states afford to build more new prisons while still maintaining old ones? Second, given their political backing by unions and local legislators, can state governments afford to close prisons? I discuss these critical questions by first demonstrating how prisons slow economic decline in disadvantaged communities across different periods of the prison boom. I also show that prisons distort rural demography by increasing total population counts, male/female ratios, and measures of racial segregation and poverty. I suggest these difficult policy questions can be best answered by analyzing the results unearthed by the proposed model for the specific state.

This study also has implications for prison abolitionists and other criminal justice activists and provides a bridge to potential new allies in the fight against prison expansion. Prison activists generally work in underserved, disadvantaged urban neighborhoods that routinely experience prisoner reentry, but not the disadvantaged rural communities where prisons are primarily located, which also experience high levels of prisoner reentry. The positive benefits of prison building for rural towns of color complicates the campaign to end mass imprisonment and prison proliferation. Lastly, I discuss the future of social scientific research on prison towns and disadvantage. The discursive connection between rural and urban microlevel community functions of stigma and disadvantage suggest that we reestablish a rural/urban continuum. We must return to rural communities as a central site for investigating systems of race, punishment, and disadvantage. Finally, a methodological appendix describes the methods used in this project.

PART ONE

Prison Placement

TWO

Have You Seen My Backyard? Rural Ecology, Disrepute, and Prison Placement

Prisons have not always been the most viable development option for rural locales. Until the 1970s, a depressed town might have reasonably hoped for other kinds of large-scale economic development opportunities, like factories, mills, or a military base. Following de-industrialization and the retrenchment of the military-industrial complex at the end of the Cold War, factories moved to Asia and Latin America as military bases closed. In response, small towns changed their tune regarding prisons. From a market perspective, many towns might have considered a prison a perfect substitute for a canning factory. In reality, most protested the placement of prisons as LULUs (Locally Undesirable Land Uses); neither residents, nor citizen groups, nor politicians appreciated their towns being associated with stigmatized institutions (Blankenship and Yanarella 2004; Combessie 2002; Goffman 1961; King, Mauer, and Huling 2003). This trend began to shift around the mid-1970s when some rural towns began lobbying to "win" a prison. While the central question of this book deals with the cause of the shift from NIMBY (Not in My Backyard) to PIMBY (Please in My Backyard), Forrest City's story suggests that the NIMBY question needs to be reframed.

If presented with the question of NIMBY, a Forrest City local might turn it around and ask, "Have you seen my backyard?" I heard this response many times as residents and civic leaders patiently explained what life was like prior to building the prison. To find out why rural civic leaders/residents want a prison, one must ask how they feel about their town. This ethnographic approach allows us to unpack the often-conflicting motivations underlying prison demand in rural communities. To this end, this chapter will show how traumatic events can stigmatize an entire town—in terms of the residents' collective memory, as well as large, lasting effects limiting future development opportunities from outside investors.

Forrest City's civic leaders and residents described their town in ways that resonate with sociological ideas about stigma and spoiled identity (Goffman 1961; Rivera 2008). For example, residents in Forrest City might say "bless their heart" in describing owners of struggling businesses in the old central business district downtown near City Hall. Many scholars find that rural communities of color face limited development opportunities and seek LULUs primarily because they are stigmatized (Blankenship and Yanarella 2004; Carlson 1992; Martin 1992). While there are necessary and sufficient conditions for prison placement, the role of stigma in prison "demand" can be segmented along two dimensions: local leaders must recognize that their town is stigmatized, and they must also begin to reshape local policy to account for constrained development opportunities. LULU "demand" can also be understood as a willingness to accept a stigmatized development (Mohai and Saha 2006). To demonstrate this, I will first consider how national economic trends through the 1990s impacted the rural South. Next, I describe how a series of inauspicious episodes in that period stigmatized Forrest City prior to prison building, further constricting scarce economic development opportunities. Then, I will explain how a prison starts to look like a good idea, considering these circumstances. Lastly, I describe how a legacy of stigma traceable to Jim Crow–era neighborhood politics continues to enshroud the town. In doing so, I demonstrate how the timing, direction, quantity, and quality of stigma across neighborhoods and places can help us understand prison building.

A Shifting Economic Base

While structures, collective memory, and shared meanings of communities change over time, all communities have functions. Many argue that the economy is the most important factor in defining local space. When cotton was king, Forrest City served as a distribution and sales center. In the modern global economy, international markets determine crop prices, and metropolitan areas serve as distribution centers. Despite its location on Interstate 40, Forrest City has not functioned as a major industrial or commercial center in quite some time. Like so many rustbelt cities of the North, Forrest City's local economy has suffered from de-industrialization during the information age of the last thirty years. Many farms in the region were traditionally family owned, but since the 1960s, large corporate farms have pushed out local Delta farmers. The mechanization of farming facilitated a move from an agrarian to an industrial economy. Lacking the ability to mechanize rapidly, facing the loss of many young adults to urban areas, and other shifts in the market, many small Delta farmers were unable to compete in national and international markets—Saint Francis County was not immune to these trends.

Although the town fathers didn't understand it at the time, by the mid-1980s Forrest City was swiftly approaching a perilous precipice. Despite de-industrialization and a continued dependence on the local agrarian economy, Forrest City was once a center of light industry, ranging from textiles, rubber, and canneries, to the most significant development, Sanyo television. The addition of Sanyo in the early 1980s offered a renewed sense of economic stability for Forrest City elite. But even with the brief economic expansion from the addition of Sanyo, changes in education and housing policy set by elites had cast the die for Forrest City's future.

The population of Forrest City swelled by the 1980s in comparison to surrounding communities as it became one of the largest employment centers in the region. However, these were often branch plants (Taub 2004), light industrial facilities that take advantage of local tax breaks in rural, primarily southern, communities. When the tax breaks expire, the corporations leave without making any significant investments in the communities or the properties they abandon. While rural communities may gain a short-term employment boost, this type of corporate welfare ultimately leaves towns with the bill for infrastructure improvements to roads and sewers and environmental cleanup. Branch plants are a way for corporations to use rural southern communities as rest stops en route to the Global South. This trend had taken hold in Forrest City as well. Given these shifts in the global economy, the economy of Forrest City could be summarized in a word—struggling—prior to building the federal correctional facility.

Further complicating the economic woes of Forrest City was arguably the most critical stretch in damaging the town's reputation—this period was described by one informant as the worst luck any community could suffer in such a short time. Over roughly an eighteen-month period between 1984 and 1985, Forrest City endured a series of events that would bring national media attention and forever alter the collective memory of its citizenry. The surreal sequence of violence surrounding the arrest and trial of Wayne Dumond (about which more below) were featured on the television news magazine *20/20* and covered extensively in a book manuscript during the same time period that local workers at the Sanyo television manufacturing plant went on strike in an effort to organize a union. The strike made national news and was even included in an academic article on employee/management relations. The intensity of national media converging on small-town happenings exacerbates stigma, making these places infamous in the local and national collective memory. Recent examples include the Jena Six in Jena, Louisiana, and the racially motivated dragging death of James Byrd Jr., a black man, in Jasper, Texas. Such infamous moments often structure the context in which future events are interpreted.

In spring 1985, workers at the Sanyo plant in Forrest City went on strike for the second time in six years. During a demonstration, an informant recounts, plant administrators used an incident that caused minor damage to a Japanese administrator's car to depict the mostly black demonstrators as violent and threatening to the administrator's life. Once again, Forrest City was thrust onto the national stage. The story was carried in the *Arkansas Gazette* and *Business Week*. "Pickets carried signs that read: 'Japs Go Home' and 'Remember Pearl Harbor.' Windows were broken, guns were fired, a car was overturned, and at one point the plant was nearly overrun by strikers" (Byrne 1986). While property was certainly damaged and violence threatened, the Japanese management at Sanyo characterizing the striking workers as violent is consistent with the finding that Japanese automakers avoid siting their US plants in areas with black workers (Cole and Deskins 1988). The reporting was brutal:

> Japanese managers were shocked. Says Sohma (the Sanyo plant manager): "You cannot leave this alone. Union leaders are destructive. I want the union to be strong, but I want it to be intelligently strong to help people instead of stirring up things" . . . The cultural gap is wide. The Piggly Wiggly supermarket may stock bamboo shoots these days, but Forrest City remains a small, isolated town of conservative values in eastern Arkansas. Many of its 13,800 people, half of them white and half black, are uneducated, poor, and apprehensive of change . . . "People here are still trying to get over the 1954 Supreme Court ruling on integration of schools," says one community leader, "yet Sanyo is asking them to accept Japanese ideas and technology." (Byrne 1986)

The historic backdrop of the Sanyo strike helps explain why these local events drew national media attention. From a social movement or social capital perspective, strikes are the definitive tool for workers to voice and work through dissent with an employer. However, this strike was a losing proposition for workers from the start. First, the Japanese corporate model was hailed as the future of business practice during the 1980s. Second, the Ronald Reagan presidency was at best hostile toward, if not repressive of, organized labor. Many scholars agree Reagan was attempting to cripple it (Minchin 2000). Third, Arkansas was a right-to-work state. This confluence of factors created the perfect storm for unions and workers striking against the idealized Japanese corporate cultural model.

Vincent Roscigno and Keith Kimble (1995) find that barriers to unionization in the rural South include foreign competition, automation, and low-profit, low-skilled industries, a combination that results in continued underdevelopment of these communities. Many of the light industrial manufacturing jobs like the Sanyo plant in Forrest City fit this mold. Barriers to unionization in the South were primarily based on the durability of elite white power, maintained through racial hostility and the subordination of blacks (Cornfield and Leners 1989; Roscigno and Kimble 1995). The political structure in Forrest City at this time was founded along racial lines as several city council seats, leading positions at the chamber of commerce, and the mayor's office were all occupied by whites.

The Sanyo strike stigmatized Forrest City in the national media. The strike also caused civic leaders within Forrest City to brand the unions as unruly and detrimental to the social order or the town. Ironically, the town leader quoted above notes how Forrest City is haunted by remnants of Jim Crow in arguing that the workforce resists change. However, the white town leaders failed to mention their own resistance to change.

Like many Delta communities, Forrest City has failed miserably in investing in public education. This failure has long-run economic consequences. An educated citizenry can make for a ready workforce and is attractive to a wide range of companies. Because of their paltry investment in public education, communities like Forrest City are not positioned to choose high-end companies for an economic "take-off" (Taub 2004, 61). Given their high need and limited options, towns like Forrest City often come to see stigmatized LULUs as the best opportunity to attract new development. Before the Sanyo strike, major industrial employers like General Industries had already left to open a plant in the Global South. The strike drove participation in the labor force down, causing unemployment to rise. For most of the 1980s, the unemployment rate in Forrest City hovered in the teens. By 1986, unemployment jumped above 20 percent and remained high, spiking at over 25 percent in 1989.

There are lessons to be learned about Forrest City from other labor disputes in Arkansas. For example, Timothy Minchin (2000) chronicles the strike at the Georgia-Pacific paper plant in Crossett, Arkansas. This case study draws interesting parallels with the 1985 Sanyo Electronics strike in Forrest City for several reasons. The 1,100 workers on strike equaled nearly one-fifth of Crossett's total population, even if all the workers did not live in

Crossett. In Forrest City, the 2,000 workers who went on strike at Sanyo also represented a sizeable proportion of the workforce. When a large proportion of a town's adult population is employed at a single institution, that institution can wield considerable influence over the local government and its view of the magnitude of a labor dispute or plant closing and its decisions regarding taxes and infrastructure. As in Forrest City, the Crossett strike was a public relations nightmare. A union officer in Crossett described the strike as cutting through families and tearing the community apart (Minchin 2000). The Sanyo strike similarly caused strife between family and friends and evoked statewide and national ignominy on the town's already ailing reputation. In both places, the strike divided the towns along racial lines.

I discovered this racial divide about unions through the unsolicited visceral reactions of white elites when they talked about life before the prison. Many of the white elite held an extremely negative view of unions, in general, and specifically, the attempt to unionize Sanyo. When discussing the Sanyo strike, their faces contorted with disgust. Their look of agony was tied not only to discussing the ugly events that unfolded during the strike; they also felt the strike sent a negative signal to current and potential businesses. They felt that the attempt to unionize, and the strike specifically, broadcast to potential industries that Forrest City was comprised of unruly, uneducated blacks, who wanted handouts from the union instead of jobs that required hard work. According to the chamber of commerce, a willing and ready workforce was central to attracting good companies to the "Jewel of the Delta." While corporations during this era either received tax breaks or fled to the Global South, elites in towns like Forrest City demonized unions as the cause of de-industrialization. Meanwhile, annual millage fights persisted, white elites refusing to raise property taxes to fund education.

Unequal Justice Redux: Stigma from a History of Violence

When asked what life was like before the prison came, all informants told me things were bad. They listed record unemployment in Saint Francis County and Forrest City and the workers' strike at the Sanyo plant as instances that sullied the reputation of the town across the state. However, more than a decade prior to breaking ground on the prison facility, Forrest City achieved national infamy with a bizarre story that invoked the strong negative imagery of southern rural communities reminiscent of the book and film *Deliverance*. One quiet spring evening in 1984, the teenaged daughter of locally elected county coroner Walter "Stevie" Stevens was brutally raped at gunpoint. A Forrest City resident, Wayne Dumond, was arrested in 1985 and charged with the crime. While Dumond was awaiting trial, two armed men entered his home and castrated him. The national news program *20/20* reported that Saint Francis County Sheriff Conlee bragged to locals about the act and proudly displayed Dumond's genitalia in a jar on his desk. Sheriff Conlee was notoriously corrupt and eventually imprisoned on charges unrelated to this case.

During my time in Forrest City, informants characterized the Stevenses as one of the "good ol' families" in town. Scholars believe that in small, tight-knit southern communities, according to an unwritten rule, public servants protect the interests and well-being of elites (Davis et al. 1941; Dollard 1937; Tomaskovic-Devey and Roscigno 1997). Given the association between Walter "Stevie" Stevens and Sheriff Conlee, rumors surfaced that they conspired to have Dumond emasculated. Sheriff Conlee's investigation into the attack on Wayne Dumond only furthered rumors about his role in the castration. After claiming that he had questioned between 100 and 150 people (roughly 1 percent of the total population of Forrest City), Sheriff Conlee said that he could not find Dumond's attacker. In concluding his investigation, he found that Dumond's wounds were self-inflicted. In another outlandish turn of events, while he still awaited trial, Mr. Dumond's home was burned to the ground, and his wife and children fled the state in fear for their lives.

In some respects, violence in Forrest City exemplifies and reifies a broader regional history of violence (Butterfield 1995; Lee and Ousey 2005; Woodruff 1993). Given the history of violence, specifically lynching, in this region of Arkansas, it would be easy to assume that the vigilante actions detailed above were racially motivated. However, all actors described, including Wayne Dumond, are white. While these vigilante acts of castration and arson were not, in this case, overtly racist, it is difficult to disentangle this type of violence from the historical context of towns like Forrest City. In fact, some would argue that acts of violence (even if believed to be tacitly supported by the state) preserve the racial hierarchy. The literal castration of a working-class white man, and the burning down of his home, conveys a figurative message to blacks that lynching is still a possibility, given the not-so-distant past where racial violence was the norm.

Although Conlee was later found guilty on corruption charges and Dumond was convicted of rape, this story resurfaced during the 2008 Republican presidential campaign. The Dumond case was used as an attack on Republican nominee hopeful Governor Mike Huckabee. After being paroled through Huckabee's influence, Wayne Dumond moved to neighboring Missouri, where he was subsequently convicted of raping and murdering another young woman. Huckabee's opponents used the story to highlight his gubernatorial administration as negligent and soft on crime.

The Dumond story has also been used to label Forrest City as "filthy." While some residents in surrounding towns use this label literally, others used it figuratively in referring to the corruption of Sheriff Conlee that continues to taint the town's reputation. Additionally, the Dumond saga, including the rape, castration, and arson, are also woven into the violent tapestry still visible in Forrest City today. One could argue that, symbolically, a prison represents a system of social control for corrupt elites like Conlee and working-poor criminals like Dumond. Regardless of how one interprets the Dumond case, its legacy of corruption and violence undoubtedly looms large for such a small community. In isolation, either the Dumond case or the Sanyo strike might have damaged a town's reputation. Their coincidence ensures that this period endures as a dark time in the minds of many residents of Forrest City. Understanding this period can help trace what the town saw in the prison.

Pondering Placement: Considering Sources of Stigma

While this chapter focuses on how stigma narrows economic options for towns like Forrest City, the role of the political elite is central to this discussion. Following perhaps the worst eighteen months any small town could have, the top political brass, including Mayor Danny Ferguson, John Alderson, and other members of the chamber of commerce, began discussing strategies to repair their town's image. Following the Sanyo strike and trial of Wayne Dumond, Forrest City faced record unemployment and a marred public image. Led by Mayor Ferguson and the chamber of commerce, civic leaders would deploy multiple strategies over the next few years to stem this tide. They began talking about attracting a prison as one of these strategies, but this idea would not gain traction for several years.

Despite being a majority black town, blacks were underrepresented for years on nearly every position of power, from the school board to the city council and the state legislature. Even today, blacks do not have a voice in the chamber of commerce's activities. In fact, during my time in the field, there was open hostility between the black mayor Larry Bryant and the white chamber of commerce director David Dunn. In responding to a question about how he sees the chamber working with the mayor's office Dunn confessed, "We don't really speak." When asked about the chamber, Bryant volunteered, "I sign a check every month to the chamber and I don't even get a report of activities." Donald Tomaskovic-Devey and Vincent Roscigno

(1997) argue that racial divisions in rural southern towns may have an instrumental value, finding, only where elites are homogenous relative to some organizational base and traditionally dependent on racial exploitation and vision will they foster a racially divided, impoverished working class, and traditional relations of production. Understanding the group dynamics of the ruling class within Forrest City this way provides broader, more strategic explanations of why racial divisions fester.

Filthy Town: The Enduring Stigma of Race Politics in the Rural South

When I first entered the office of Forrest City mayor Larry Bryant, I could not help but notice the numerous awards and placards adorning the wood-paneled walls. There is barely enough space between to distinguish them. A picture of a small shotgun home is centered in the array of achievements. When I ask Mayor Bryant about the photo, he becomes especially excited—it represents his family's humble beginnings. Thick, grayish-green shag carpet covers the floor on which he looks down as he recalls sharing clothes, meals, and everything else with his numerous siblings, so they could all could get by. He revels in his siblings' professional success before recounting his own journey in life, including his nomination by the National Conference of Black Mayors as Mayor of the Year 1999. His voice, slow and contemplative at first, gathers momentum and barrels out from beneath his thick salt-and-pepper mustache as he boasts that all of his siblings started in Forrest City, graduated from good colleges, and work professionally in fields ranging from medicine to business. He owned several businesses and worked as a news anchor in Memphis before becoming the first black mayor of Forrest City. Despite his casual attire—a pullover sweater—he purveys the confidence and authority of a news anchor. Now in his fifties, he smiles as he compares sharecropping along with his siblings and parents with their current professional success.

In the midst of his elation, his face drops. He turns from viewing his wall of accomplishments with a long, heavy sigh and confesses he feels more appreciated by outsiders than by his hometown. He looks past or through me almost as if he were talking to himself and laments, "You know what they run on me last time out? When I ran for reelection? They said the town was a filthy town, and we need to clean it up. Forrest City might not have everything that I'd like, but it's a long ways from being a filthy town." He felt that white elites labeled Forrest City "filthy" in large part because he was the first black mayor and he would not readily bend to their will. Although Forrest City became a majority black town in the late 1980s, the first black mayor was not elected until 1997. My first meeting with him occurred nine years after he first took office. Like so many other rural southern communities, the ghost of Jim Crow was omnipresent in Forrest City. Whites' reactions to newly elected black officials is so commonplace that it has become a cliché. Like other barrier-breaking black politicians, Larry Bryant experienced white racism during a mayoral reelection. Similar rhetoric was invoked to describe the presidential candidacy of Barack Obama. Although his competition was also African American, Bryant would lose the next mayoral race.

Mayor Bryant readily admits that Forrest City faces numerous substantive challenges. Like many other "high-flyers" (Carr and Kefalas 2009), he returned home to help because the community had seen better days, but the modern politics of race and racism in the Deep South carried out under the guise of color blindness complicate the notion of the "high-flyer." As a proud man, protective of his birthplace, he is outraged that whites labeled the majority-black town *filthy*. He strongly believes that many of the challenges facing Forrest City result from discrimination by white elites in the town and surrounding communities. Because he was very outspoken on racism, many white elites labeled him "the black folks' mayor," claiming that he only served one side of town during his first term in office. Although the annual Saint Francis County "Cotton Picking' Festival" in Forrest City served as a strong reminder, the days of Jim Crow when cotton was king are gone. Mayor Bryant felt that when he spoke out against racist practices in the Forrest City region he was advocating for black people who could not advocate for themselves.

These actions are consistent with those of a race leader (Drake and Cayton 1945; Pattillo 2007). The roles of race leaders, race men, and race heroes are based on the model of black metropolis as a "world within a world" (Drake and Cayton 1945, 397); they shape the moral order and ecology in towns like Forrest City. Because power, land, and wealth in Forrest City are concentrated in white elite hands, blacks, even with political power, still play a secondary role in town decision making. In many ways, blacks like Mayor Bryant are positioned like those leaders in the Chicago ghetto described by St. Clair Drake and Horace Cayton more than six decades ago. "Race Leaders are expected to put up some sort of aggressive fight against the exclusion and subordination of Negroes. They must also stress 'catching up with white folks,' and this involves the less dramatic activity of appeals for discipline within the Black Belt, and pleas for Negroes to take advantage of opportunities to 'advance.' A Race Leader has to fight the Job Ceiling and Black Ghetto and at the same time needle, cajole, and denounce Negroes themselves for inertia, diffidence, and lack of race pride; and the functions sometimes conflict" (1945, 393).

Although social space and political power are partially determined by physical space, we might not expect much diversity across a town of sixteen square miles. However, a few wealthier race leaders like a doctor and defense attorney have moved into the formerly all-white neighborhood in the hills. At the time of our first meeting, the mayor lived in a modest, more racially diverse neighborhood. Unlike housing discrimination faced by race leaders of Chicago in the 1940s, modern race leaders in Forrest City are not bound to a physical space like the black belt. The challenge facing modern race leaders, or what Mary Pattillo (2007) calls middlemen, is slightly different. Forrest City white elites stigmatized the black mayor and citizenry in efforts to maintain power through racial division (Tomaskovic-Devey and Roscigno 1997).

Continued signs of white control and dominance were also omnipresent in other institutions. For example, many African Americans view the Saint Francis County Museum as a bastion of white supremacy—I did not find evidence suggesting otherwise in my visits. These modern-day observations of Forrest City serve as artifacts of Jim Crow. Racist acts, signs, and symbols can stain victims, but may also blemish perpetrators. In the case of Forrest City, surrounding communities like Wynne viewed entrenched racist practices like flying the Confederate flag at government facilities as backward.

Drive-By Racism or Racism to Drive By?

In the majority black town of Forrest City, the Saint Francis County Museum was seen as "a place for white folks." White elites all mentioned the museum as a sanctified cultural institution, whereas blacks by and large understood it as one of a handful of holdovers that preserved and celebrated white supremacy by sanctifying the Confederacy and other institutions that preceded civil rights. A black key informant who introduced me to Forrest City, Charles Freeman, had previously visited the museum. He wasn't his usual gregarious self when talking about these visits—he struggled to express what made him feel unwelcomed. After much hesitation, he reluctantly admitted that the practice of flying the Confederate flag at the museum was highly offensive.

One day, I stumbled on this practice after interviewing the museum director. Harvey Hannah is in his mid-forties, white, balding, corpulent, and wearing glasses with thick dark gray frames. While he is not formally trained as a curator, he possesses the passion of an enthusiast and takes care of everything in the museum from administration to event coordination and planning. With charming southern manners, he talks freely about Forrest City's challenges and virtues. He even shares the local legend of ghosts that occupy the Saint Francis County Museum. He feels that race continues to be a divisive force in city operations. He expressed hopes that Forrest City can one day reconcile past racist acts and celebrate the qualities common to all people in this town. He feels that the Saint Francis County Museum can play an important role in this process.

Mr. Hannah claims the museum has exhibits celebrating black and white accomplishments in Forrest City. He referenced artifacts showcasing the all-black high school under Jim Crow, with pictures of African Americans. There were also some pictures of African American veterans from Forrest City, including some who fought in World War II. According to Mr. Hannah, these exhibits upset some whites because they did not like pictures of blacks in what they believed to be their sacred space. He explained that he selects a different historic flag to fly every day at the museum and acknowledges that blacks are sometimes upset at this and other museum practices. He felt vindicated that blacks and whites were both made uncomfortable by what he considered "quality education" on the history of Forrest City. By quality education, he means the cultural legacy associated with each flag and artifact. Mr. Hannah feels that the museum is strategically placed to carry out the mission of educating the public and fostering a sense of community.

As Mr. Hannah walked me to the front porch after our interview, he picked up a flag. He began unfurling it, and I asked innocently what he would be flying today. As he replied, his Arkansas accent seemed thicker: "Oh, the stars and bars." While Mr. Hannah was extremely helpful in providing access to the museum and freely sharing his opinion of the town, the prison, and other topics, his flying the Confederate flag was very educational to me as a black, northern researcher.

Standing on the front porch of the Saint Francis County Museum with Mr. Hannah as he hoisted the Confederate flag, I felt a sense of shame descend upon me. Just then, a dark-colored SUV drove by with African American passengers pointing, presumably at the Confederate flag. I turned to walk down the stairs and again thanked Mr. Hannah for the interview. Upon reaching the bottom of the stairs, another car drove by. Two cars in this short period felt like rush hour in Forrest City. It made me aware that I could be implicated as an accomplice in Mr. Hannah's act of drive-by racism. Like a drive-by shooting, Hannah's raising of the Confederate flag had the element of surprise. While I was not asked to drive the vehicle, pull the trigger, or light a cross in a front yard, I felt as if I had silently witnessed and knowingly participated in a crime. This feeling of being an unwilling passenger in a drive-by shooting is best understood as racial paranoia: "distrustful conjecture about purposeful race-based maliciousness and the 'benign neglect' of racial indifference" (Jackson 2005, 3).

While I felt complicit in this overtly racist gesture, I first wondered how blacks in communities like Forrest City interpret the presence of the Confederate flag. I recalled that during our transect, Charles repeatedly mentioned the museum's practice of flying the Confederate flag, which was especially problematic to him given that Forrest City is majority African American. He seemed quite puzzled, asking, "Just, I mean, how do you do that!?" To many blacks in Forrest City, whites' cultural celebrations of their heritage of racial domination and exploitation were often cloaked in subtle southern manners. Yet the acts themselves were brazen. While many local blacks in Forrest City expressed resentment, few openly voiced their objections. Flying the Confederate flag at the county fair and the museum was a not just a strange celebration of the past. Whether intentional or not, the flag still tells blacks to stay in their "place." Flying the Confederate flag is a not-so-subtle reminder of Jim Crow.

Southern whites have various ways to rationalize the continued use of the flag. In driving around the Forrest City/Wynne area, the stars and bars is not an uncommon sight. Decorative Confederate flags on front license plates are proudly displayed on pickup trucks or SUVs. On the street lined with the primary, elementary, and secondary schools in Wynne, one resident has draped a thirty-five-foot Confederate flag across the width of her garage wall and proudly leaves the garage door open for all to see. When I broached the subject during interviews with white elites, they brushed it off, claiming that poor whites were the "salt of the earth," as if their lack of education were a reasonable justification for displaying the flag. While this implies that only poor uneducated whites practiced such rituals, white civic leaders offered little explanation for this practice among the broader white citizenry, and I did not press this issue. I doubt the same level of sympathy would be extended to poor blacks.

Feeling implicated and silently complicit in a racist activity also led me to ponder how rural southern blacks navigate a terrain with racial land mines. Hughes (1962, 6) best explains how such complicity is achieved in stating, "we have taken collective unwillingness to know unpleasant facts more or less for granted. That people can and do keep a silence about things whose open discussion would threaten the group's conception of itself. . . . To break such a silence is considered an attack against the groups; a sort of treason, if it be a member of the group who breaks the silence."

Flying the Confederate flag continues to be taken for granted in parts of the rural South. Despite the civil rights movement and the fall of Jim Crow, the legacy of racism lingers like noxious fumes in communities like Forrest City. The conspicuous legacy of Jim Crow–era racism in Forrest City contributes to the ongoing race relations problems that civic leaders suspect hampers the town's economic growth (see chapter 3). Offensive signs, like the Confederate flag, may limit your town's economic development trajectory, to the point that LULUs become attractive. At this point, we can discuss other sources of stigma related to prison placement.

The Prison as a Stigmatized Institution

In explaining how a town becomes stigmatized enough to "demand" a prison, we should first understand that the prison is a stigmatized institution. Within criminology, the prison has traditionally been studied as an institution unto itself (Jacobs 1977; Sykes 1958). Erving Goffman (1961) characterizes the prison as a "total institution" because inmates are isolated from society, regimented, and in contact primarily with other inmates. The goal of the total institution, according to Goffman, is for individuals to conform to institutional culture. This pressure to conform is often less about inmate rehabilitation and more about maintaining the institutional culture. Gresham Sykes details the brutal ways both inmates and guards maintain the social order.

Over time, the purpose, mission, and even architectural design of the penitentiary has changed considerably (Morris and Rothman 1998; Garland 1990). The penitentiary was supposed to rehabilitate the dregs of society. "Although it has discarded corporal punishment and is reasonably habitable, the modern prison mounts a fundamental attack on the inmate's person and sense of moral worth" (Western 2006, xi). Because individuals are removed from society and acculturated into the total institution, prison inmates are stigmatized. The local meaning of prisons became increasingly contested because of the stigma associated with the institution. As prison building became more prevalent, some rural towns protested placement because of the negative cultural connotations associated with their inhabitants (Goffman 1961; Combessie 2002). In fact, some scholars argue that the stigma of prisons permeates the local surroundings, creating tensions between the town and the institution (Combessie 2002). Bruce Western

(2006) further argues, "prisons conceal and deepen social inequality" (168). In sum, the prison is still considered a stigmatized institution and therefore undesirable to most communities. The negative stigma of prisons can place a community in need of economic development at odds with itself.

Revisiting Rural Ecology: Trying to Get to the Top but Still on the Edge

One day, André Stephens asked if I had seen the ritzy side of Forrest City. After months of living in and exploring the town, I answered his question with a bewildered expression. I had seen the poor, the very poor, the modest, and the middle-class portions but was dumbfounded by the suggestion that millionaires lived in very exclusive properties in the hills.

We took a transect to the semiprivate neighborhood known as Edgewood. Many residents in the bottoms of Forrest City are unaware of these homes, given their limited social contacts with the well-to-do occupants. I discovered that this limited knowledge is partially based on access—although the roads are paved nicely, the only two entry points are not very inviting. They are steep, winding, and nearly impossible to find at night if you do not travel them regularly. Many properties have large lots, picturesque gardens, and access to small ponds.

Ascending into the hills, the "filthy town" label seems a complete misnomer. This Forrest City is immaculate, wealthy, and nearly exclusively white. Mr. Stephens pointed out the homes of those he felt "held the purse strings" in town. He noted that many of the remaining white homeowners were elderly and either lived in these neighborhoods or kept a home on a seasonal basis. Racial residential segregation patterns for the 1990 and 2000 census confirmed that many white households were clustered in the hills.

As we drove, Mr. Stephens recounted how difficult it was for the first blacks to move into this neighborhood. Local legend holds that because the buyer was a doctor, the seller assumed he was white. When he learned the buyer was black, he tried to back out of the deal and even considered removing the house from the market. Given the legacy of Jim Crow and the physical space that symbolizes the social hierarchy—wealthy white landowners living in the hills and poor black workers living in the bottoms—the doctor's move was a significant blow against historic racist practices of restrictive covenants. The move up the hill represented the arrival of blacks not only economically but also socially and politically, showing that space, not just race and socioeconomic status, play an important role in group identity and shaping collective memory (Foote 2003; Lobao, Hooks, and Tickamyer

2007). Despite these modest advancements in integration, whites were neither ready nor willing to give up power, as evidenced by their continued concentration in the hills. Despite their shrinking numbers, the elite still control the wealth and therefore much of the political structure. Roscigno and Tomaskovic-Devey (1994) suggest that the concentration of African Americans and traditional white elite dominance spurs interracial polarization and competition in the political sphere. The modern political structure in Forrest City is a testament to this model.

Stigma and the Prison Boom

While the broader argument in this book centers on the rural ghetto as a source of the stigma for prison placement, this chapter demonstrates how stigma operates in rural ecology to produce conditions for prison "demand." It has explored how Forrest City's reputation became sullied through a legacy of segregation and national media attention. By focusing on the context, signs, and symbols of stigma, we can better understand why a town may be in the market for a prison. These signs are latent and inherent, and pertain to how stigma and its operational mechanisms work in limiting potential economic development. In short, why do places like Forrest City have so few economic development options that they are forced to pursue LULUs, like prisons? This chapter has demonstrated how stigma is important to placement and can serve as an impetus for prison building in towns like Forrest City.

In tracing the downward arc of Forrest City's reputation prior to prison placement, one can understand why a key informant claims, "This was the worst eighteen-month stretch that any small town could ever had!" During interviews, I learned that civic leaders in Forrest City continue to internalize the shame of vile behavior that became synonymous with the town: rape, castration, arson, bribery, corruption, and a violent confrontation during a worker's strike. These events live on in infamy in the minds of the town fathers. While the media turns its spotlight on major cities like Chicago or Detroit, accounts tend to focus on certain neighborhoods. For small towns like Forrest City, the limelight can be especially glaring, as it amplifies the blemishes of the entire town.

By weaving seemingly unrelated events together, we can understand the complex structures and cultures in rural communities like Forrest City. From this vantage point, institutions traditionally considered LULUs can represent any number of possibilities. For example, a prison can represent a means of controlling corrupt elites like Conlee and working-poor criminals like Dumond. Traumatic events can stigmatize the entire town both in terms of the residents' collective memory (Foote 2003) and in large and lasting effects limiting future development opportunities. If many rural towns' development opportunities are diminished, the competition for LULUs like prisons will increase. Depending on the level of stigma from a history of violence, LULUs may even offer an upgrade to a town's image.

We have to understand the broader historical context to extrapolate theories explaining why a rural southern town faced with increasing stigma and limited development options demands a prison. The next chapter turns from stigma to land-use patterns to illuminate the varied contexts of rural communities. An understanding of both is necessary to make sense of why civic leaders in Forrest City came to "demand" the Forrest City Federal Correctional Facility.

THREE

"It's Like the City, Only Quieter": Making the Rural Ghetto

For people living in communities of concentrated disadvantage, the day-to-day experiences of social isolation hardly differ between urban and rural spaces. Aretha Brown has lived in both. A native of rural Arkansas, she returned home after more than a decade of living in the "low-end"—a predominantly black, poor neighborhood ensconced between the infamous Ida B. Wells and Robert Taylor housing developments in Chicago. There, she confessed, she was strung out on numerous drugs, including crack, and ran with the prostitutes, pimps, and other players who were part of the street lifestyle. Since her return home, Mrs. Brown "hasn't touched a rock"; however, according to her, what folks were doing for money and drugs in Chicago was nothing compared to what they are doing today in her rural hometown. She currently lives in the bottoms with several of her adult children. An abandoned cotton-processing plant serves as a backdrop to her grandchildren playing in the yard. The rusting silos and metallic barns reflect the area's de-industrialization and decay. Despite Mrs. Brown's efforts to direct them otherwise, her children are entrenched in the local street life, which keeps Mrs. Brown keenly aware of happenings in Forrest City. On a hot spring day, we stood in her front yard beneath the sun. With sweat and glycerin from her Jheri curl beading on her golden brown forehead, she confessed, "It's like the city, only quieter." She lamented the crime and frequent drug-related burglaries in her neighborhood as she pointed out a crackhead staggering past her home.

Like urban ghettos, rural ghettos emerged from macrolevel shifts, including African American migration, de-industrialization, and white flight. Essential elements of modern urban ghettos include residential segregation, concentrated poverty, relative population density, and a high percentage of African Americans (Jargowsky 1997) in social isolation (Wilson 1987).

These communities are more likely to have high crime rates (Sampson and Wilson 1994; Sampson, Raudenbush, and Earls 1997) and often lack the organizational density to marshal resources to defend themselves from the adverse effects of concentrated disadvantage (Small 2009). However, ghetto-ization is not just about structural characteristics related to poverty. Broader, classical definitions of the ghetto also make it an important analytical tool for understanding processes of community change (Clark 1965; Drake and Cayton 1945; Du Bois 1899; Spear 1967). The process of how ghettos are created has been inexorably linked to urban community change (Drake and Cayton 1945; Du Bois 1899; Park, Burgess, and McKenzie 1925; Taub, Taylor, and Dunham 1984).

In 1990, geographer Charles Aiken introduced the idea of the rural ghetto. While his concept focuses on processes resulting in concentrated racial and economic disadvantage, large-scale studies of the rural ghetto did not take hold until 2007, when rural sociologists began mapping concentrations of rural black poverty (Lichter and Johnson 2007; Lichter et al. 2008) and residential racial segregation patterns (Wahl and Gunkel 2007; Lichter et al. 2007a). The notion of the rural ghetto has not penetrated broader sociological discourse on ghettos despite stellar ethnographic work mapping disadvantage rural communities (Duncan 1996; Fitchen 1991; Solomon 2003). Although changes in the economic, physical, and social landscape of rural areas suggest the term applies to them, images of ghettos remain aligned with poor black urban centers.

This blind spot makes it difficult to measure outcomes and processes of ghettoization in rural communities, although the ramifications of disadvantage are likely to be as large and negative as in urban settings. Our understanding is impaired for three reasons. First, data are frequently limited to counties as the unit of analysis; this fact obscures the scale of concentration effects in municipal units. Second, quantitative analysis often ignores the social processes of rural community cultures. Lastly, compared to urban areas, ethnographies of rural areas are sparse. Despite problems associated with cultural analyses of the ghetto (Small, Harding, and Lamont 2010), some argue that ethnography is the best way to investigate infrequently studied disadvantaged communities (Burton 1997). Ethnography is a powerful tool that can unearth social processes and structure related to community change. Given the dearth of US rural ethnography, one goal of this project is to serve as a call for more community-based investigations of rural life.

Admittedly, I came to Forrest City with some preconceived notions, imagining it as an example of a high-poverty community with the kinds of racial and class-based conflicts described in rural southern ethnographies

(Dollard 1937; Duncan and Coles 1999; Falk, Hunt, and Hunt 2004; Stack 1996). While the conditions in the town met many of these expectations, I also discovered certain structures, including concentrated poverty and white flight, more aligned with classic urban sociological definitions of a ghetto. The process of unearthing the rural ghetto led me to investigate historical demographic, crime, and housing trends in Forrest City during the post–civil rights era. These trends provide evidence of ghettoization in Forrest City beginning in 1970. This chapter focuses on the changes in Forrest City's neighborhoods that helped to drive prison placement. By emphasizing the process, structures, and the role of stigma in creating the ghetto neighborhood within Forrest City we can learn why white elites "demand" prisons.

To this end, I reframe classic theories of community structure and process in several ways. First, I go beyond the urban-centered view to explain spatial inequalities in rural areas. For example, while African American migrations to the North are associated with the concentration of disadvantage in urban areas (Katznelson 1976; Tolnay and Beck 1992), researchers now link reverse migration to the South with increased poverty in rural communities (Foulkes and Schafft 2010; Fuguitt, Fulton, and Beale 2001; Falk, Hunt, and Hunt 2004; Hunt, Hunt, and Falk 2008). Second, the rural ghetto exposes a shift from overtly oppressive Jim Crow racism to a subtle, color-blind racism (Bonilla-Silva 2006) emblematic of a new rural southern political economy (Tomaskovic-Devey and Roscigno1997). Third, I argue that spatial inequality, independent of scale, reflects stratification processes across the rural-urban continuum (Sorokin and Zimmerman 1929; Wirth 1928).

The salience of the rural ghetto is not merely academic. While the effects of mass incarceration (Western 2006) and prisoner reentry (Rose and Clear 1998; Petersilia 2003) on urban inequality have been explored, with few exceptions, links between crime, criminal justice, and rural inequality have not. We know that murder is concentrated in high-poverty, nonmetropolitan counties (Lee and Ousey 2001), but we know little about the specific concentration of crime in rural towns and neighborhoods. For example, since 1985, the annual murder rate for Forrest City has been roughly twenty-nine per 100,000, comparable to that of Chicago (Chicago Crime Index 2007). Moreover, between 1990 and 2006, over 1,000 former Arkansas Department of Correction prisoners reentered Forrest City, or an average of sixty-three annually, a significant number in a town of 14,863. Most of these former prisoners return to a few geographically contiguous black neighborhoods. While the concentration effects of prison reentry have been examined in urban areas (Clear, Waring, and Scully 2005), little is known about their impact on rural communities. Understanding neighborhood-level mechanisms could help us remediate them, but rural ghettos remain invisible because they are far flung, arising at otherwise diverse intersections of rural culture and concentrated racial disadvantage. Tracing their emergence may inform ways to prevent or mitigate urgent crime and criminal justice problems.

Robert Sampson (2012) has demonstrated how the ghetto (for example, concentrated disadvantage) can be considered an ideal type of the enduring neighborhood effect. Here, I posit the rural ghetto in similar fashion, as the spatial concentration of racial and economic disadvantage resulting in a stigmatized neighborhood within a town. In other words, I use spatial scales (Lobao, Hooks, and Tickamyer 2007) to emphasize the importance of the neighborhoods (Sampson 2012) in bridging the epistemological divide of past investigations of the rural ghetto. Spatial scales, according to Linda Lobao, Gregory Hooks, and Ann Tickamyer (2007, 3), are "the geographic levels at which social processes work themselves out, are conceptualized, and are studied." Using the appropriate scale, we can make sense of rural ghettos functioning within rural town ecology and "identify how and why spatial context contributes to inequality" (3) outside of the urban context. By understanding the processes that produced the rural ghetto, we can better understand why rural communities "demand" prisons.

Marks of the Rural Ghetto

The use of social and physical space in rural ghettos differs slightly from that in urban ghettos. For instance, "street hustling," also known as the informal or "off-the-books" economy, is associated with high rates of unemployment and is often concentrated in disadvantaged urban neighborhoods (Duneier 2000; Venkatesh 2009). The rural ghetto has no street vendors or hustling. You cannot purchase a copy of *Final Call* or *Mohammed Speaks* during a red light, nor will you be greeted by the squeegee man, sock man, cigarette man, flower man, performance artists, or panhandlers. While these public characters (Jacobs 1961; Duneier and Carter 1999) are endemic to urban ghetto life, in rural communities hustling takes an entirely different form. For example, you can get your car repaired in the driveway of a home in what appears to be a residentially zoned neighborhood.

When I needed an oil change and other minor work on my car, a key informant recommended a mechanic. I was a little surprised to find him on a street lined with single-family homes. I learned that he also earned extra cash as a driver for local organizations on conference trips. This type of unregulated, normalized, commercial activity is akin to street vending, a form of hustling, although it is not performed quite the same way, nor does it have the same substantive value or meaning (Duneier and Carter 1999; Venkatesh 2009). Similarly, in rural areas, the abundance of mobile homes and dilapidated buildings serve as structural reminders of substandard homes and help to mask homelessness (MacTavish and Salamon 2001). While variations in social and physical space between rural and urban ghettos may be wide, outcomes across these spaces of inequality are nearly identical.

This section documents how structures, processes, and outcomes aligned with classic urban sociological literature have emerged in rural space. I begin by describing a vital ghetto characteristic—stigma. Because stigma can be expressed in different ways, documenting the particular ways stigma is manifested in Forrest City is critical. I use racial scripts (Jackson 2005) and cognitive maps (Suttles 1972) to make racial and spatial stigma legible and to clarify the local culture of boundary maintenance against ghetto behavior (Burton, Garret-Peters, and Eason 2011; Sherman 2009).

Social Isolation and Stigma

Bernadette Ransom, a longtime South End resident, celebrates Larry Bryant as the first black mayor of Forrest City. She also recalls a comment he made during his second term in office: "The only thing I didn't like about Mayor Bryant was that he told people not to drink (alcohol) on their front porches so his kid wouldn't see it when they drive by." As Ms. Ransom talked with my wife and me on her front porch, our children played together in her yard within earshot. After reflecting on Mayor Bryant's comments she became visibly angry and began cursing loudly, "I don't give a fuck . . . I don't give a fuck." Just before shouting a third time, she glanced over at the children and almost whispered, "I don't give a care." Like many other residents of the South End, drinking on the front porch was a way to escape the heat inside the house; it had become a norm for Ms. Ransom, as it had for many small town poor/working-class folks who lacked air conditioning. However, to race leaders (Drake and Cayton 1945; Pattillo 2007) like Mayor Bryant, drinking liquor on the front porch violates the politics of respectability (Higginbotham 1993) and can be considered an affront to the moral code of small-town life (Burton, Garret-Peters, and Eason 2011; Sherman 2009).

By cursing with small children nearby, Ms. Ransom is signifying that we are at her house. She is demonstrating how many residents internalize stigma and suffer social isolation (Wilson 1987). By stopping, she also demonstrates that she can treat guests with respect. While acknowledging the norm that cursing is consistent with stigmatized ghetto behavior, her actions can be interpreted as rejecting or undermining the norm by cursing in the first place. In recognizing her behavior is inappropriate, she also manages to mitigate or deflect the stigma associated with it. "The distinction is between realizing a norm and merely supporting it. The issue of stigma does not arise here, but only where there is some expectation on all sides that those in a given category should not only support a particular norm but also realize it" (Goffman 1963, 6). Ms. Ransom cursed because she was frustrated by Mayor Bryant's comments about his child being exposed to alcohol consumption. According to her, "his kids could see me doing much worse if they came inside my house." With that, she is not necessarily commenting on her behavior, but rather pointing out the everyday life of people in her neighborhood—an everyday life that includes being a victim of crime and poverty.

In many ways, Ms. Ransom realizes she is stigmatized and socially isolated because she is poor, black, lives on the wrong side of the tracks, and does not have a heteronormative family structure. By acknowledging, then refuting, the stigma of race and class, she was also attempting to mitigate the shame of stigma. The diversion from her profanity-laced rant in front of small children can be interpreted as a limited acknowledgment of the politics of respectability and the moral order of her town. When she says that she does much worse inside her home, however, she is simultaneously rejecting the standard imposed by race leaders (Drake and Cayton 1945; Pattillo 2007). While Mayor Bryant's critique of public consumption of alcohol may have been well intentioned, many constituents like Ms. Ransom felt stigmatized, and many in Forrest City concluded Mayor Bryant was out of touch with his base. Although Mayor Bryant would reclaim his seat in 2010, this incident may have made the difference in his 2006 reelection bid.

"Take That Back to the South End": Signs and Symbols of Racial and Spatial Stigma

Like Aretha Brown and many other African Americans currently residing in Forrest City, Toni Coleman has spent a good portion of her life in Chicago. She was born and raised on the Near West Side of Chicago. As a young adult, at the height of the crack and homicide epidemic in the mid-1980s, she fled the infamous Henry Horner Homes in search of a quieter, more stable life in Forrest City. Now in her late forties, Mrs. Coleman is the receptionist for the Saint Francis County Community Development Corporation (SFCCDC). The office is usually bustling with staff, including four interns, home for the summer from a variety of HBCUs (Historically Black Colleges and Universities); three white interns from a college in Memphis; three administrative assistants paid through AmeriCorps Vista, a national service program to fight poverty; and two full-time assistants to the assistant and executive directors.

On this warm summer morning, the office is hiring another assistant to help with the administration of a new grant. After only a week of advertising in the *Forrest City Times-Herald*, people are flooding in to pick up applications. Given that Saint Francis County consistently leads Arkansas in unemployment (9.2 percent in 2007), the position is in high demand. Mrs. Coleman occasionally cuts her eyes at the other administrators, and they share a laugh in relation to the numerous applicants. After one especially unkempt group leaves, an otherwise subdued Mrs. Coleman spouts, "Coming in here as if they just woke at midday, wearing wrinkly, mustard-stained T-shirts, a baby on the hip wearing a T-shirt and a diaper! Some with their hair standing straight up on top their heads, needin' a perm, sometimes with a friend in tow looking even worse!" An office mate chimed in, advising, "Maybe you just need to pray for 'em? If they're coming in here looking like that, they must have it pretty rough." Mrs. Coleman rolls her eyes, purses her lips, and turns her head. "Please!" She adds, "They'd better get their wig fixed if they want a job," and concludes. "They'd better take that back to the South End!"

Based on my observations in public and semiprivate spaces, loud talking, arguing, cursing, or other behavior deemed unsavory were often met with the phrase, "take that back to the South End." At first, I did not pay much attention to it because it is so similar to the phrase, "take that back to the ghetto," a euphemism in popular African American speech that "decent" black folks employ to admonish or correct the behavior of "ghetto" or "street" people (Anderson 1978). "Take that back to the South End" can be understood as a racial script—dialectic shorthand based on race, gender, or other aspects of an individual's appearance or attitude. In the case of African Americans and ghettos, they carry stigma. They also inform behavior in racialized situations, allowing one to gauge the sincerity of the other's actions. The use of racial scripts is not a problem in itself, but it reinforces and maintains stereotypes. According to John Jackson (2005, 15), "'racial scripts' dehumanize, much like the processes they ostensibly critique. They turn us all into mere objects of our own social discourses, no less the actors who read and interpret scripts than the inert pages themselves."

I began to notice how "take that back to the South End" was used in everyday speech in Forrest City. Forms of popular street fashion, like sagging long shorts, braided hair (especially on men), or gold teeth/fronts, were all met with disapproving looks or comments like that one, used repeatedly by office staff, recreational facility staff and patrons, and sometimes in public spaces like Wal-Mart. It is worth noting that the phrase was used almost exclusively by African Americans, without regard to gender and age. It was taken for granted and carried a negative intragroup racial stereotype of behavior regarded as setting African Americans back. While the HBCU interns liberally tossed the phrase about in front of me and the white interns, they were more judicious in the company of the middle-aged, female, churchgoing office staff, which made Mrs. Coleman's tirade all the more surprising.

Mayor Larry Bryant boasted that the newly constructed, state-of-the-art Forrest City Recreational Facility was paid for with locally generated tax dollars. "Not one cent," he said, came from state or federal coffers. This public project was the centerpiece of his administration and a symbol of self-determination and pride for Forrest City. The center was a "cosmopolitan canopy" (Anderson 2011) where young, old, black, and white gathered for a variety of activities, including exercise. One of the most popular was pick-up basketball. Disputes over foul calls are as much a part of the game as trash talking. Here, whenever a game ground to a halt over alleged rule violations, one of the older staff members would come into the gym or peek out of the office and yell, "hey, if you're in here to play, then play! Otherwise, take that loud mess back to the South End!" While used frequently, the racial script "take that back to the South End," was not used indiscriminately.

I did not initially connect this script with a neighborhood or place. Ironically, the South End is north of the recreational facility and west of the main thoroughfare, Arkansas Route 1 / Washington Street, where South and End Streets meet, and home to Southside Park. For many African American youth and young adults, Southside Park is the place to be, especially on late summer evenings. Not coincidentally, the Saint Francis County African American interns recalled a time from roughly 1996 to 2000 when gangs ruled the park, and it was the spot *not* to be. During this time, major national gangs like the Crips, Bloods, Vice-lords, and Folks from the West Coast and Chicago were recruiting heavily in Forrest City middle and high schools. Thus the park was both a hangout and party scene and associated with violence and danger. It is also within walking distance of most of Forrest City's poorest residents and public housing.

"Take that back to the ghetto," reflects not only racial, but also spatial stigma. Gerald Suttles (1972, 22) finds that people's mental or cognitive maps are "part of the social control apparatus of urban areas and are of a special importance in regulating spatial movement to avoid conflict between antagonistic groups." Here, I suggest that rural residents use cognitive maps to mitigate the ghetto, but with different goals than urban residents of defended neighborhoods. They are less concerned about avoiding conflict between antagonistic groups and more concerned about maintaining and controlling a group stigmatized as conflicting with, and antagonistic to, the larger community's social order—that is, ghetto inhabitants. While the defended community treats outsiders as enemies, the Forrest City community treats certain residents as *the enemy within*. Their boundary maintenance is an effort to minimize the town's conflicts with this ghetto enemy. The use of racial scripts and cognitive maps in stigmatizing the South End neighborhood suggests concentrated spatial and racial disadvantage in Forrest City.

Mapping the Ghetto

Poverty, segregation, and population density vary over race and space in Forrest City. As a way of exploring how those measures vary, and why, the following section turns to spatial aspects of rural disadvantage and how those patterns mirror aspects of urban ghettos. Ghettoization is a key determinant of why civic leaders sought the Forrest City Federal Correctional Facility.

Concentrated Poverty, Segregation, and Relative Population Density

The spatial concentration of poverty is partially based on population density, but it must be contextualized within the local community structure. Some demographers regard population density as the feature that distinguishes rural from urban areas (Jargowsky 1997), but our understanding of the term itself has changed over the twentieth century with changes in the US Census Bureau's definition of urban areas. Population density can now be used to determine the degree to which a given municipality is urban. For instance, Chicago has roughly nine times the population density of Forrest City. On the one hand, this is a reasonable argument for claiming that theories of ghettoization are not applicable in a place like Forrest City. On the other, Chicago's population density is also twice that of Cleveland, Detroit, Milwaukee, and Saint Louis, five times as great as that of East Saint Louis, and seven times greater than Gary's, and few would object to comparing processes of urban change across these communities.

Forrest City is between three and six times as densely populated as surrounding towns, so it is not rural in the same way that these other places are. Based on population density alone, Forrest City might better be compared to Nashville. Using the same argument, because the population density of Nashville is roughly the same as Forrest City's (a little more than 1,000 persons per square mile), Nashville might be considered rural. Relative population density, then, should be measured as only one aspect, rather than the defining characteristic, of urbanization. Its confluence with concentrated poverty and residential segregation establish the basis for comparing urban and rural ghettos.

According to the 2000 black/white residential dissimilarity index, the most common measure of racial segregation, which ranges from zero (complete integration) to 100 (full separation), Forrest City scored an 83. Dissimilarity scores above 60 are high (Wilkes and Iceland 2004; Massey and Denton 1993; Sims 1999), and Forrest City is considered hypersegregated (see map 3.1). Public housing saturates its rental market. In 2000, HUD-subsidized residents alone made up nearly 8 percent of the population. The 448 HUD units with 1,246 residents constitute 20 percent of the 2,238 units available for rent—not including renters with subsidized housing vouchers. All told, roughly 30 percent of rentals, fifteen times the national average, are HUD or USDA public or subsidized units.

Public housing clusters poor blacks in certain neighborhoods. Although US Census poverty data is suppressed at the block level, the close proximity (within roughly 1/3 square mile) of five public housing developments clearly demonstrates the high concentration of the 28 percent of black residents who live below the poverty line. Between these developments, 315 low-income units (including seventy-two senior and disabled units) suggest that disadvantage is not simply concentrated in Forrest City but in black neighborhoods.

Public Housing Proliferation and a Constrained Rental Market

Rental and home-buying markets provide additional insight into community structure. For example, the number of new homes constructed can indicate how fast the local economy and population are growing. More importantly, we gain an understanding of how a community receives potential residents. According to 2000 census data, roughly 50 percent of homes in Forrest City are owner occupied. Since the 11.3 percent overall vacancy rate is much higher than the national average, and renter occupancy is much greater than that of the average rural community, it would seem that rental units should outpace demand. In other words, rentals should be readily available. This made it all the more surprising that realtors seemed extremely concerned about an outsider calling about rental units.

My wife and I attempted to secure a rental property in Forrest City for nearly four months. Because we are black with middle-class aspirations (graduate students technically live in poverty), we posed problems for realtors in and around Forrest City. They stigmatized us when they read us as

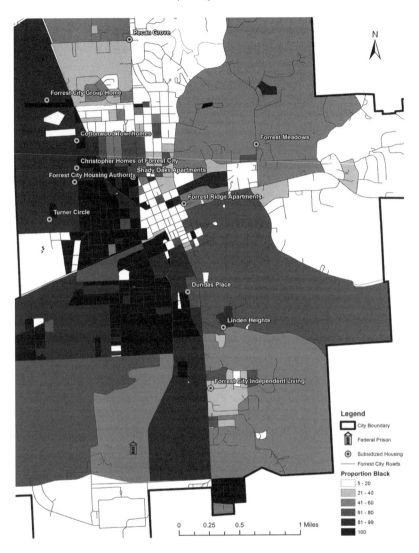

Map 3.1. Forrest City, Arkansas, public housing and black-white residential segregation by US Census block, 2000

black, but if they read us as middle class, they stigmatized Forrest City. I was obviously an outsider; I have a distinctly urban accent, and my voice is undeniably black, masculine, and not southern. Massey and Lundy (2001) explore how discrimination in the housing market can be achieved without in-person contact by evaluating phone calls in this process. Their findings demonstrate that racial discrimination in urban housing markets can be based on the tone of a caller's voice and the use of black English with poor black women experiencing the most discrimination. My professional phone voice is often low, a bass monotone with hints of a drawl, and my family roots in rural Ohio give me a distinctly midwestern accent. My partner, in contrast, is a native southerner who can distinguish and mimic southern accents, making her more racially ambiguous over the phone. While my phone calls were rarely returned, hers were, almost immediately. One owner, who was offering a house in Cherry Valley, twenty miles north of Forrest City, told my partner that it was a large, three-bedroom, two-bathroom home on several acres.

> My partner said, "Oh, but I wanted to rent in Forrest City."
>
> "Oh, you don't want to rent in Forrest City," he replied.
>
> "Why not?" my partner asked.
>
> "There are too many coloreds there."
>
> "Well you may not want to rent to me." She said. "Because I'm African American."
>
> "Oh, I'll rent to you. I have no problem renting to you. You're not like them. But you know how it is when you get too many of them together . . . It's just when you get a lot, it's a problem—that's what comes with it."

This incident speaks to the many forms of racism in Forrest City. In particular, this incident speaks to what Elijah Anderson (2015) calls the *iconic ghetto*—or the "powerful source of stereotype, prejudice, and discrimination" allowing whites to ascribe unknown blacks with the burden of being guilty of being ghetto until proven otherwise. The irony here is that while I was being treated as a dangerous drug dealer or what Anderson refers to as an *iconic negro*, my partner, based on voice alone, was being clearly distinguished as "not like them." Unlike Massey and Lundy (2011), in our case, race and gender seem to matter most for the identifiable black male. Therefore, the *iconic ghetto/negro,* is not just a racial phenomenon, but also gendered. Given the level of concentrated disadvantage and violence within the town the intersectionality of the black male threat may be heightened. However, it is difficult to know whether our experiences with real estate agents were based solely on race, gender, or the intersection of the two.

While this exchange provides only anecdotal evidence of housing discrimination, we approached the question scientifically by calling the dozen or so realtor/rental agencies in the Forrest City/Wynne area and found that this response, while more explicit than most, was typical in that it stigmatized Forrest City by race. It seemed to be a common practice among white

Delta residents, a standard practice of rental agencies. This property-owner succinctly expressed concerns many Delta whites have, but cannot articulate. While it might be tempting to dismiss this particular person as ignorant and racist, another interpretation is to see his comments as a useful illustration of how the rural ghetto is a stigmatized space that affects a town's image.

Tight rental markets present challenges for struggling towns. The constrained rental market delayed my family's efforts to find a place in Forrest City and, eventually, pushed us into the neighboring town of Wynne. We were not alone. After settling in Wynne, we met others who had similar difficulties. Like many aspects of life in Forrest City, dentistry is still segregated; black residents patronize the lone black dentist. During our time in the field, Forrest City added a second black dentist. Although the dentist had relatives nearby, her family settled in Wynne for the "better" schools. Before we left the Forrest City/Wynne area, we talked with a middle-aged, white male medical professional working in Forrest City. He said he rented in Wynne because "the housing in Forrest City was either $50,000 or $500,000." Many believe that at least a third of new residents relocating to the area for employment opportunities live in Wynne. By constraining segments of the housing/rental market, rural ghettos effectively repel nonpoor migrants.

Shortly after relocating my family, André Stephens introduced me to the newly elected mayor of Forrest City. Despite the extreme heat that day, the mayor wore glasses, a blue buttoned-down shirt, a dark sport coat, khaki pants, and brown dress penny loafers. I was dressed in my politics-of-respectability standard Banana Republic uniform, which included short sleeves, khakis, and black slip-ons. In talking with Mayor Gordon McCoy, I shared several things. First, I explained that my family and I had tried very hard to live in Forrest City, but we were pushed to Wynne because of difficulties with the Forrest City rental market. When he asked my opinion of his town, I informed him of the questionable practices of the rental agencies, based on my experiences. I cautioned him that the continued disrespectful treatment of potential renters could discourage future renters from settling in Forrest City. Despite our race-leader regalia, including our business casual dress, educational attainment, marriages, families, and "proper" mode of speaking, he replied, "You should see how some of these folks tear up houses. Renters need to have stricter rules . . . these people will tear your stuff up." He continued this diatribe for several minutes, repeating, "these folks'll tear up your house; I've seen it." By repeating this statement, Mayor Gordon propagated the racial script (Jackson 2005): "these people" is akin to "you people," a script commonly used by whites to disparage minority groups.

During the same period, a discourse emerged that stigmatized the behavior of a so-called underclass. The black middle class, specifically middlemen, have been the chief purveyors of this kind of racial script (Pattillo 2007).

While some may interpret these comments as typical of conservative race leaders, what these comments fail to convey is the vitriol and general disdain McCoy had toward not just poor black people, but black people in general. Many blacks in town referred to him as "the white establishment's replacement for Bryant." In direct contrast to Bryant, he was seen as a "yes man" to the chamber of commerce, seemingly following their every wish/command. Whereas members of the chamber called Bryant a "Jesse Jackson" type who disliked whites because he was openly critical of the town's past racist practices, McCoy was perhaps the town's harshest critic of blacks. His rhetoric completely lacked even the ceremony of linked fate (Dawson 1994). From this perspective, Mayor McCoy might not even technically fall into the category of race leader. Our conversation on the housing market suggested that he was more interested in securing order, or the appearance of order, than in desegregating the town.

In Forrest City, spatial processes reproduced racial segregation by concentrating poverty. The next section zooms out from the constrained rental market to explore how African American migration patterns, shifts in the economy, and changes in US public housing policy have contributed to the rise of the rural ghetto. The intersection of these macroprocesses across Forrest City neighborhoods highlights the mechanisms creating the rural ghetto.

Rise of the Rural Ghetto

In historical terms, the rural ghetto only recently emerged. Blacks in the South lived in deplorable conditions under the caste systems of slavery and Jim Crow. Extreme poverty, social isolation, and racial violence were the norm. However, prior to 1970, anything resembling the modern rural ghetto would be hard to find because, under Jim Crow, blacks were unified spatially through segregation. Therefore, while the black middle class could attempt to make distinctions from other blacks socially, they could not live separate from poor blacks until after Jim Crow. Following the civil rights movement, macroshifts in demography, de-industrialization, and the housing market changed Forrest City. Increased population density, concentrated poverty, and residential segregation seeded and spread this new form of spatial inequality.

Complicating the Call to Home

André Stephens's migration narrative elucidates the processes of commu-nity change in rural ghettos. Although raised in a northern metropolis, his favorite childhood memories involved visits with relatives in the southern countryside, which he tried to replicate by fishing in the city's park district lagoons. He "always felt like a country boy trapped in the city." When we spoke, he described his "call to home" (Stack 1996) and motivations for establishing the Saint Francis County CDC over fifteen years ago as a part of his "calling," or a form of ministry. He has served as an assistant pastor in congregations in Forrest City and Memphis and feels that the Saint Francis County CDC allows him to "do God's work," using his skills as a former home loan officer at a major bank in a northern central city. Like many race leaders/middlemen (Drake and Cayton 1945; Pattillo 2007), he feels that he can best achieve "racial uplift" of the local black population by improving substandard housing and joblessness.

As natives of the same city, we discussed coming of age in violent neigh-borhoods. When his neighborhood began getting "hot" in the late 1970s and early 1980s, his parents relocated to an inner-ring suburb. As he was leaving high school, his parents relocated to the South in another effort to escape rising crime. His family history mirrors other African American migrations. His grandparents were originally from the South and moved North during the great migration; his middle-income parents followed the pattern by fleeing the rising violence in the inner city; as an adult, he and his wife and five children settled in Forrest City as part of the reverse migration.

While Mr. Stephens's "call to home" seems typical (Stack 1996), migra-tion to and from communities like Forrest City is a complex process. As a de-voted husband and father, he believed the move would protect his children from the city's neighborhood violence. Even so, he recalls a balmy night in late spring 2006, when a young black man stood outside, hurling insults and threats to lure Mr. Stephens's oldest son, then a high school junior, out of the house. Mr. Stephens went out to talk to him and noticed he had a pistol behind his back. The young man continued yelling and skulking behind the barrier provided by his car. During a heated exchange, witnessed by neigh-bors, the police were called. The young man fled just before they arrived, using more choice words to express his displeasure over the younger Mr. Stephens's flirtation with his girlfriend. The crowd dispersed. Fearing for his son's life, at 4:00 a.m. Mr. Stephens moved him across the state to complete high school living with his grandmother.

The episode can be oversimplified as a by-product of the southern culture of violence (Butterfield 1995), but it also shows the multifaceted, dynamic processes of modern rural community change. Violence has long played a prominent role in migration (Tolnay and Beck 1992) and northern urban community change (Drake and Cayton 1945; Hirsch 1983; Taub et al. 1984, Watkins and Decker 2007). African American migration narratives are often idealized as struggles for freedom and equality, but the resulting economic, demographic, and cultural shifts are as important as their framing narratives. At the turn of the last century, blacks seeking a "promised land" (Lemann 1991) in the North fled racial violence only to become its victims as they worked to integrate neighborhoods or were pushed across picket lines during the early years of organized labor. A decade into the new century, the reverse migration of African Americans has been attributed to the high cost of living, extremely disadvantaged neighborhoods, and sustained black-on-black violence in shrinking cities such as Chicago and Detroit. From this vantage point, the pull of the northern promised land became, as the poet Langston Hughes describes, "a dream deferred."

Migration Patterns

As Carol Stack (1996, 14) eloquently notes, "we had been led to believe that the great migrations that formed the modern states were one-way, permanent movements. People's footsteps, it seemed, were facing one way, as if they had stopped cold in their tracks somewhere out there in the urban diaspora. We had also assumed that people in the modern world, once torn from their roots, never look back." However, the great migrations display much more complicated patterns than this. Prior to 1970, African American migrants can be traced along three axes (Bacon 1973): rural areas outside of the South, urban areas outside of the South, and urbanizing areas in the South (such as Forrest City). Figure 3.1 illustrates how Forrest City's racial profile changed in part because of these migration trends.

While the first great migration, from approximately 1910 to 1930, has been tied to lynching and other forms of racial violence in the countryside (Tolnay and Beck 1992), the second, lasting from approximately 1931 to 1970, is connected to the mechanization of farming and a cultural shift among African American veterans, who returned to southern communities expecting better opportunities based on their service. Sparse economic opportunities and second-class citizenship pushed many out of communities such as Forrest City to employment in the industrial sector in Chicago, Detroit, and Saint Louis. Those remaining behind continued working on farms owned and operated by wealthy white families even as the economy shifted

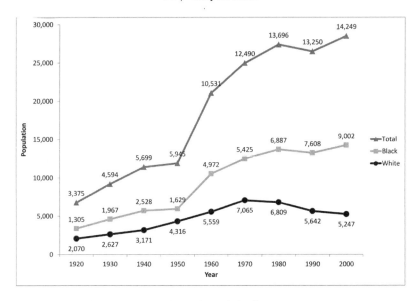

Figure 3.1. Forrest City total population by race, 1920–2000

from agriculture to light industry. Whites accounted for roughly a third of the population increase in Forrest City between 1940 and 1950; the number of blacks decreased by over a third.

However, since 1950, the African American population in Forrest City has increased every decade. By 1960, the total population had more than tripled to just over 10,500, solidifying Forrest City's status as a micropolitan area. Overall, the population nearly quadrupled between 1920 and 1970. While rate of growth, distance from a central city (Beale 1990; Lang and Dhavale 2004), and network connectivity (Neal 2011) matter, increases in population and relative population density are necessary for spatially concentrated disadvantage to emerge in nonmetropolitan communities such as Forrest City.

Shifts in federal and local education policy are also central to population change. Forrest City was near the epicenter of the civil rights struggle. As in other southern communities, many white residents left the desegregated public school system for exclusively white institutions like Forrest City's Robert E. Lee Academy, known as "segregation techs" (Clotfelter 2004), in the decades after *Brown v. Board of Education*. Whites who did not want, or could not afford, to pay migrated to whiter, and increasingly affluent northwestern Arkansas, now home to the conglomerate corporate headquarters of Wal-Mart, Tyson Foods, and J. B. Hunt Transportation Services and Shipping, as well as the flagship campus of the University of Arkansas at Fayetteville. Forrest City's contemporary elites feel the Delta's loss in human and social capital profited others.

Nonetheless, in contrast to other Delta towns, Forrest City's population continued to increase. As middle-income whites left, blacks moved in. Between 1970 and 1990, the number of whites fell from 7,065 to 5,642, while blacks increased from 5,425 to 7,608. This near parity might suggest that black in-migration sparked the classic urban trend known as white flight (Clark 1965; Spear 1967; Hirsch 1983; Squires et al. 1987; Taub 1984; Wilson 1987), but the impetus seems, instead, to have been school desegregation. White flight is a contextual process, subject to change. The more enticing question is why African American migration increased.

The diverse motivations behind the latest African American "call to home" are not well explored. The reverse migration is not just about reclaiming a southern identity that African Americans may or may not possess. Although the average African American migrating South is more educated (Hunt, Hunt, and Falk 2008) and affluent than receiving community residents (Hunt, Hunt, and Falk 2004), the spectrum is broad, and receiving communities are diverse. Metropolitan areas like Atlanta have a burgeoning African American population, but the black population of the rural South also grew significantly between 1970 and 2000 (Frey 2001; Fuguitt, Fulton, and Beale 2001; Robinson 1990). For many impoverished blacks, the push from the urban North and the pull of the rural South resulted from broad structural processes. Like classic urban ghettos, rural ghetto growth is linked to housing policies that shifted the socioeconomic status (SES) and race of migrants. Their emergence complicates the notion of a new, better South.

Making the Ghetto

Now in his early sixties, John Alderson has committed most of his adult life to public service, in a way that's typical for many southern white elites (Cobb 1992). He has served as executive director and chair of the Forrest City Chamber of Commerce and professor at Eastern Arkansas Community College. Because he returned to Forrest City in young adulthood, Carr and Kefalas (2009) would classify him as a "high-flyer"—active in civic affairs, serving both professionally and as a volunteer on service organization boards, including some that target disadvantaged youth. Scholars and local residents view returning young adults as essential to the survival of rural towns.

Alderson's family has long been considered the ruling class in Forrest

City; they once owned and operated a multi-million-dollar farm. I met several former employees, some replaced during the farm's mechanization, others let go when it was sold. They all spoke highly of the family and their charitable activities in town and described Professor Alderson as warm, caring, thoughtful, and very opinionated. His background is in economics and finance, and he is a strong proponent of free-market development strategies. He is especially vocal about how unionization attempts have hurt Arkansas workers. Like many key informants, independent of race, he de-coupled the concentration of public housing and the so-called underclass. Decision makers in Forrest City believe that the poor suffer not from structural constraints but a culture of poverty that does not value education and hard work.

Like many white elites in Delta communities, Professor Alderson is a decision maker on large public works projects, like public housing. While several studies (Aiken 1990; Fitchen 1994; Fitchen 1995; Foulkes and Newbold 2008) have shown that the rural areas most likely to receive public/subsidized housing residents are experiencing economic decline, the question of why they accept or seek public housing is not well theorized. In 2007, Alderson offered the following explanation for the proliferation of public housing in Forrest City: "there's a whole lot of rent subsidy with other apartments . . . as well as houses. And . . . I honestly and truthfully don't think anybody really had a feeling for or anybody had a handle on it. It's just one of those things that just sort of happened. These people needed housing, so we built it."

This statement epitomizes *abstract liberalism*, a form of color-blind racism (Bonilla-Silva 2006, 28). I do not claim that Alderson's statement is racist per se, but given his prominence in Forrest City, his explanation of the concentration of public housing is insufficient. Abstract liberalism allows city officials and town elites to frame these decisions as beyond their control, relieving themselves of responsibility for outcomes associated with concentrated disadvantage. A locale must, after all, demonstrate a willingness to accept subsidized housing to attenuate local residents' opposition (Hirsch 1983). Many local elites are happy to improve housing at the expense of the federal government while simultaneously blaming residents' problems on a "culture of poverty," as if culture were independent of structure.

In Forrest City, subsidized and public housing blossomed after the fall of Jim Crow. In the late 1960s, the USDA began constructing public housing in rural communities. Nationally, 16,000 projects hold roughly 445,000 rural households (George et al. 2008). After the demolition of the infamous high-rise Pruitt-Igoe Housing Development in Saint Louis in the mid-1970s, low-rise construction in rural areas took off. In 1972, the USDA constructed fewer than 4,000 housing units, but in 1976, annual construction more than tripled. The early 1980s were the zenith, with more than 30,000 new units constructed annually. In Forrest City, HUD constructed 90 public housing units. From 1987 to 1993, the USDA constructed 195 units of affordable housing, subsidizing 174 of them. Since 1993, at least 622 units, or 28 percent of all rentals, are public or subsidized housing. This massive expansion of public housing into rural areas reflects a national trend and drove structural changes that attracted the urban poor (Lawson-Clark 2002; Fitchen 1991). We know that public housing in urban areas concentrates poverty (Bursik 1989; Holloway et al. 1998; Quillian 1999), but it may also be integral to spatial concentration of race and poverty in rural communities.

In urban neighborhoods, residential segregation is the central mechanism that concentrates black poverty, especially in public housing (Wilson 1987), weakening a community's ability to respond to crime (Bursik 1989; Sampson 2012) and exacerbating white flight (Xie and McDowall 2010). Hattery and Smith (2007) demonstrate that residential segregation in nonmetropolitan counties concentrates poverty with other deleterious outcomes. My research shows that concentrated disadvantage has not been the historical norm in Forrest City, but rather emerged more recently, concurrent with the arrival of rent subsidies and public housing. The table below illustrates demographic and housing trends in Forrest City. In 1970, half of all residents lived below the poverty line. Since 1980, roughly a third do. Adjusting for inflation cannot fully account for this socioeconomic shift. Note, however, that the proportion of African Americans below the poverty level has increased. Although US Census block data for 2010 and 1980 are not available, the data do reveal that residential segregation increased from 0.63 in 1970 to 0.83, a marker of hypersegregation, in 2000. During that same time period, the percentage of Forrest City poor who were African American doubled from 44 to 88 percent. These trends support the claim that residential segregation concentrates poverty in rural micropolitan communities.

Forrest City also experienced significant shifts in income, homeownership, and occupancy over this time period. Adjusting for the consumer price index, the median household income in 2010 was two-thirds of that in 1970. Between 1970 and 2010, the percentage of vacant housing nearly quadrupled and home ownership decreased. Renter occupancy increased by an approximately equal percentage even though, on average, more rural people own than rent (George et al. 2008). Renters now constitute the majority of occupants in Forrest City. These trends further demonstrate the unequal distribution of public housing in black neighborhoods, as endemic as high

Table 3.1. Housing and demographic trends, Forrest City, Arkansas, 1970–2010

YEAR	Median Household Income		% Population Below Poverty	% Below Poverty Black	Total # of Blacks in Poverty	Total Black Population	% Housing Vacant	% Housing Renter Occupied
	Real $	2010 CPI$						
1970	6,616	37,184	50.0	43.7	2,736	5,425	4	43
1980	10,274	27,188	33.9	77.7	3,636	6,887	4	42
1990	15,283	25,498	40.4	83.3	4,497	7,608	9	44
2000*	23,111	29,265	33.7	88.3	4,396	9,002	11	49
2005–2009*	24,477	24,879	35.6	81.6	4,464	8,970	15	56

US Census 1970, 1980, 1990, 2000 from Geolytics and the National Historical Graphic Information System. American Community Survey (ACS) 2005–2009.
*Adjusting for population in group quarters.

population density, white flight, poor black in-migration, and local practices of colorblind racism. All contribute to the ghettoizing of rural communities.

Spatially concentrated racial and economic disadvantage does not spring up magically, nor does it result merely from the preferences of poor people of color to live with their kind. There are broad structural forces at work on the national and global level, such as deindustrialization and changes in public housing policy, that impact neighborhood changes within Forrest City. These shifts create uncertainty and destabilize the economic environment within which local town governments operate. The shifting southern economy, and the contentious nature of local politics, make Forrest City an interesting case study to understand prison placement. The next section provides a way of thinking about the role of the ghetto in prison placement and prison proliferation in the United States.

Locating the Ghetto in Prison Placement

Forrest City, Arkansas, can tell us something about the spatial concentration of racial and economic disadvantage. Indeed, social isolation in the modern rural ghetto may be usefully juxtaposed with theoretical debates on the boundaries and definition of the urban ghetto (see *City and Community*, Ghetto Symposium 2008; Beveridge 2008; Blokland 2008; Chaddha and Wilson 2008; Gans 2008; Haynes and Hutchinson 2008; Monteiro 2008; Small 2008; Vigil 2008). Pattillo (2007), for example, argues that modern definitions should be extended to include more socioeconomically heterogeneous, predominantly black neighborhoods, including a possible resuscitation of the notion of the "black metropolis" (Drake and Cayton 1945), with multiple types of actors and institutions operating in rural space. Others have argued that the term *ghetto* should be used to make sense of suburban communities (Haynes 2001; Murphy 2007). These broader definitions would allow for new typologies while simultaneously avoiding stereotypes—a necessary move considering the robust context of spatial inequality shaped by multiple levels of state actors involved in the creation and maintenance of disadvantage.

One way that this investigation into rural ghettos differs from prior studies is its focus on the neighborhood as a unit of analysis, thereby emphasizing the role of racism in the social exclusion of African Americans. Spatial segregation produces social isolation in two ways. First, the in-group chooses to cluster and, over time, may be stigmatized by the larger society (Wirth 1928). Second, the larger society may discriminate against a group based on its ethnicity, religion, race, or socioeconomic status (Hirsch 1983; Massey and Denton 1991; Wilson 1987; Wacquant 2002). Distinguishing self-segregation from structural constraints in the creation of modern ghettos is important because of the wide variation in interpreting cultural responses to changing structures. I suggest that ghettoization processes, and cultural responses to it, vary across the rural-urban spectrum depending mainly on differences of spatial scale and historical timing. Concentrated disadvantage does not depend on scale (Lobao, Hooks, and Tickamyer 2007); it arises in neighborhoods in big and small municipalities alike.

In rural community studies, a loose definition of *ghetto* refers to concentrated disadvantage, independent of race (Davidson 1990; Burton, Garrett-Peters, and Eason 2011), effectively de-coupling racial stigma from ghettoization processes. Concentrated disadvantage alone, however, does not fully develop the concept of the rural ghetto. It overlooks local community cultural practices that create and characterize ghettos. Reframing modern rural ghettos as forms of concentrated disadvantage or areas of persistent poverty divorces present-day structures and outcomes from historical racist practices that produced ghettos and stigmatized African American communities. While rural whites living in concentrated poverty on the "wrong side of the tracks" have also been linked to stigma (MacTavish and Salamon 2001; Kusenbach 2009), I find the ghetto firmly anchors community culture and structure to the historical processes of racism that stigmatizes African Americans.

I define the rural ghetto as the concentration of racial and economic disadvantage in a stigmatized neighborhood in a micropolitan town. This definition allows us to examine the macroprocesses reorganizing social and physical space in rural communities; for example, the reverse migration of African Americans, the restructuring of the housing market, and white flight. The emergence of the rural ghetto provides an empirical and theoretical link to Jim Crow and should be understood as a major force reorganizing social and physical space in rural black belt (Allen-Smith, Wimberly, and Morris 2000) communities like Forrest City, as evidenced in increased population density, residential segregation, concentrated poverty, and stigma. In the context of the broader ghetto literature, this case study data reveals similar patterns in other rural southern communities. The argument posits residential segregation as the key mechanism concentrating racial and economic disadvantage through public housing proliferation. The rural ghetto discursively connects rural and urban racial and spatial inequality and elucidates a community context that results in health disparities, high crime rates, and increased prisoner reentry. It ultimately represents the persistence of American apartheid in the post–Jim Crow South.

Forrest City demonstrates that macro-processes depend on micro-decision making (Massey 2007). As Jim Crow collapsed, the rural ghetto emerged under the political control of the landed white elite, as the new social system subjugating blacks (Tomaskovic Devey and Roscigno 1996). Policies enacted by Forrest City elites drove de-industrialization, residential segregation, and public housing proliferation, concentrating blacks in durably disadvantaged neighborhoods lacking resource power and carrying chronic stigma. Adjusting spatial scales (Lobao, Hooks, and Tickamyer 1997) to the neighborhood level (Sampson 2012) helps render stratification processes and ghetto structures legible. The rural ghetto discursively connects rural-urban racial and spatial inequality, ultimately representing the persistence of American apartheid in the post–Jim Crow South.

While defining the ghetto in this new way can inform future studies of rural neighborhoods in many ways, I want to suggest three in particular. First, scholars find that rural black and Hispanic housing patterns are linked to concentrated poverty in counties (Lichter et al. 2008; Lichter and Johnson 2007); others, that concentrated poverty in densely populated geographic areas, like cities, varies by region and race (Massey and Eggers 1990). Yet others find the greatest effects of concentrated economic disadvantage in hypersegregated areas (Sampson and Sharkey 2008). While we can imagine similar patterns in highly disadvantaged rural areas, again, these outcomes have not been fully explored within rural towns. Second, given that we can find traits like concentrated poverty and residential segregation by income across rural communities (Snipp et al. 1993), scholars should devote more attention to variations in racial stigma assigned to disadvantaged communities. If we build on past studies (Snipp et al. 1993) and decouple racial stigma from socioeconomic status by differentiating among poor whites, Latinos, blacks, and Native Americans, we can better clarify how race and poverty intersect in space. This theoretical move will allow us to create new theoretical models for understanding the intersection of poverty, race, and place.

While I argue that the modern "ghetto" is aligned with African Americans because the specific racialized stigma attached to these communities is based in prejudice toward poor blacks, this does not preclude us from considering the spatial concentration of racial and economic disadvantage for Latinos, Native Americans, or whites, all of which result in stigmatized neighborhoods within a town. The key factor in differentiating these communities would be the source of racial stigma. Undoubtedly, severe concentrated poverty is itself a stigma and common among all these groups in rural communities.

A new theoretical model could help us not only understand the processes of creating disadvantage across these rural communities, but also why LULUs are disproportionately sited in these communities. In the next two chapters, I present the perspectives of Forrest City leaders, in their own words, on why they supported prison placement. What their accounts reveal is the centrality of an emerging structural change in rural communities to their decision to pursue and secure a prison. Their words make clear that, more than simply creating jobs, they hoped to manage Forrest City's spoiled reputation from the rise of the rural ghetto.

FOUR

Finding Beauty in the Hideous: Prison Placement as Reputation Management

JIMMY KIMMEL: So where were you imprisoned?

T. I. (EMPHATICALLY): Arkansas. Forrest City, Arkansas. The armpit of America!

—From *Jimmy Kimmel Live* on ABC, September 22, 2010

Early in 2011, Clifford Joseph Harris Jr., a music artist, reality TV/film actor, and music producer also known as T. I., was again sentenced to serve time in the Forrest City Federal Correctional Facility. Like so many of the young African American men sentenced to prison each year, T. I. is a technical parole violator because of drug use. What is extraordinary in this case is that a Google search for "Forrest City, Arkansas" will yield as much information on T. I.'s incarceration as on the town itself. You could reasonably argue that the present-day reputation of Forrest City rests in part on the incarceration of an entertainer convicted of a minor, nonviolent offense. In some respects, T. I.'s repeated incarceration has once again made Forrest City infamous.

Coach Twillie expressed a similar sentiment years before T. I. would come to make Forrest City his home. When I asked him why he supported building a prison in Forrest City, he confessed, "I didn't want my town to end up like Gary." Twillie's unique position afforded him the opportunity to provide perhaps the most insightful perspective on repairing the town's image. As mayor pro tem, Cecil B. Twillie, also known as Coach, bemoaned the need to save Forrest City's reputation from what felt was nearly irreparable damage. Like many key informants holding influential positions in Forrest City, Coach keenly expressed his desire to stay and fight on behalf of the community, as its best days seemed to be slipping by. By no means was Coach alone in his desire to fight for Forrest City; this mounting tide of internal support was prevalent among longtime residents, business owners, and political leaders alike.

In an earlier chapter I reframed the NIMBY (Not in My Backyard) question to ask, "Have you seen my backyard?" Respondents chronicled the depths of the town's despair, listing record unemployment and industrial flight, specifically the worker's strike at the Forrest City Sanyo manufacturing plant, as instances that sullied the town's reputation. While interviewees expressed a shared sense of what damaged the town's reputation, I also found a peculiar omission—the rising tide of crime and violence that resulted from the flourishing local illegal drug trade. Although some interviewees mentioned the infamous case of Wayne Dumond, respondents did not talk about crime and violence in Forrest City in general. Even those who did mention an increase in the drug trade, especially crack, usually left out the accompanying rise in violent crime. But even if my informants failed to mention it, the town had experienced a spike in murders since the mid-1980s that compounded the stigma associated with Forrest City.

For leaders in Forrest City, the town's reputation had become a crisis. This chapter explores how key local decision makers understood their pursuit of the federal correctional facility as a way to improve Forrest City's reputation and reality. Leaders across the racial divide supported prison placement as a mechanism to diffuse stigma primarily associated with the rise of the rural ghetto. Otherwise feuding racial factions within Forrest City's political elite used similar Neighborhood Narrative Frames (NNFs) as a strategy of managing spoiled identity and justifying prison placement (Small 2002). Frame analysis or collective action frames are powerful explanations that can drive social change (Benford and Snow 2000; Goffman 1974). While environmental justice scholars have used action frames to understand NIMBY practices (for example, Čapek 1993), I use the concept to show how black race leaders/middlemen and white elite in Forrest City mitigated NIMBY attitudes by positioning the prison as a rallying symbol signaling the economic recovery of the town. In Forrest City, NIMBY became PIMBY.

From a purely economic view, prisons are a "trash" good (Coursey, Hovis, and Schulze 1987). In other words, the symbolic and use value of prisons for most communities is negative. This chapter examines the relationship between stigmatized communities and LULU demand: one community's trash is another community's treasure. But economics are not everything. I begin by explaining the good, the bad, and the ugly sides of prisons to flesh out a new way of considering their value to rural communities. I then discuss how frame analysis applies to the case at hand. After establishing the problematic nature of prisons, I then ask why rural leaders still want them—which is another way of getting at the culture of economic development in places like Forrest City. I build on Wherry's (2012) approach to the role of culture in economic decisions by demonstrating how white elites and black middlemen framed Forrest City as a place more stigmatized than a prison. Race leaders and white elites alike framed the prison as a means of saving Forrest City from its troubled past and potentially destructive future. They also framed the prison as a growth machine, or as a way to advance the town. Ultimately, these frames illustrate that prison "demand" is based on managing a spoiled town identity that resulted from the emergence of the rural ghetto. This is more than a story about "jobs"; it's a story about the prominent role of local culture in what otherwise appears to be a purely economic decision.

Prisons: A Good, the Bad, and the Ugly

In explaining how a town becomes stigmatized enough to "demand" a prison, we should first understand what prisons are for. While the purpose of prisons has been debated by social scientists for centuries (Morris and Rotham 1998; Robinson 1972; Foucault 1975), most scholars agree that prisons serve as a means of social control, especially for undesirable or surplus populations (Darity 1983; Rusche and Kirchheimer 1939; Wacquant 2001). In fact, for centuries the prison has been theorized as a form of despotism (Bentham 1791; Foucault 1975; Beaumont and Tocqueville 1833).

Garland (1990), however, asserts that punishment cannot be reduced to a single motive. Punishment is not just a reaction to crime nor is just about maintaining control. There are multiple logics of punishment operating through institutions and cultural responses to crime. For example, Western (2006) argues that political and economic forces, not crime, drove mass incarceration. Punishment in this instance is about politicians getting more votes and exploiting the plight of poor, uneducated, and minority populations to do so. Likewise, there cannot be a single cause driving prison proliferation. Many scholars (Gilmore 2007; Schlosser 1998; Street 2002) argue that the prison boom is a by-product of mass incarceration. The link between incarceration and prison proliferation cannot be oversimplified. Prison building is not simply a function of incarceration; there are political, economic, and social forces driving the prison boom.

Different state political regimes deploy disparate penal logics, as evidenced by divergent prison building practices across states with equal number of prisoners. For example, Virginia and North Carolina annually incarcerate 34,000 and 37,000 prisoners respectively. Yet Virginia has fifty-four prisons while North Carolina uses seventy-nine facilities to house its prisoners. Prison building varies both across states and also within regions. For instance, Florida has 121 prison facilities for more than 100,000 inmates incarcerated annually. This is a vastly different prison-to-prisoner ratio than Louisiana, which has only sixteen prisons to house over 41,000 prisoners annually. If prison proliferation were simply a function of mass incarceration, Louisiana would need to build over thirty more prisons to keep pace with Florida. Thinking about punishment this way allows us to more fully explore the impact of prisons on society as well as cultural explanations for prison proliferation. Given that the majority of prisons during the boom were built in rural areas, this approach also allows us to examine the multiple intersections of punishment and inequality in prison towns.

But even as the number of prisons has skyrocketed, prisons remain stigmatized institutions. The prison is understood as a self-contained institution with its own culture (Clemmer 1940; Goffman 1963; Jacobs 1977; Sykes 1958). Philippe Combessie (2002) asserts that prison stigma permeates its local surroundings, creating tensions with the institution. Prisons may be tucked away in hard-to-find places for security reasons, but they are also ugly. Their primarily purpose of security conflicts with any potential aesthetic value; their hideous appearance is as good a reason as any why most prisons are built on the outskirts of town. Groups ranging from prison activists to urban planners have objected to prison siting. In the 1990s, even the relatively conservative National Organization of Minority Architects urged its members to refuse to participate in any designs related to prison construction because they believe prisons are stigmatized houses of racial exploitation.

Prisons are considered stigmatized institutions, and therefore undesirable to most people and communities. Like incinerators, paper mills, nuclear power plants, and waste facilities, they are considered Locally Undesirable Land Uses (LULUs), and they are disproportionately sited in poor/minority communities (Davidson and Anderton 2000; Mohai and Saha 2006). And yet, the prison has arguably become a more popular form of development in rural America than cotton processing plants, incinerators, landfills, power plants, or asylums. Towns that have paper mills are, at best, known for their horrific smell, and at worst, associated with horrific tragedies, like dismemberment. Case in point: a Forrest City resident recalled the awful death of a worker in a cotton processing plant near her home. The worker fell into a bin as he monitored the cotton being transferred and was crushed and suffocated under the weight of the raw material. And yet, some communities have to take LULUs. To make sense of how any community attracts a LULU, it's helpful to consider how communities value place.

One way to approach this problem is by thinking of landscapes on a scale of sacred places to profane places (Foote 2003; Wherry 2011). When communities sanctify a place, they typically do so from a sense of pride; when they obliterate a place, it is usually done out of a sense of shame. Sites deemed profane, and therefore shameful, might be associated with senseless violence, murder, or a painful tragedy. Once stigmatized, these locations are vandalized, ridiculed, branded, and sometimes obliterated. When a place is obliterated, the memories associated with an event or events that occurred at that site are denied or forgotten. Sometimes a site is sanitized before being put to a completely different use. That is to say, sites once considered profane can become sacred by being sanitized. LULUs can have transformative properties, offering some sites a form of sanitization. Likewise, profane sites can be a good place to put a LULU. These institutions can also shape a community's collective memory and identity—in Forrest City, the prison did just that. The leaders used it to galvanize divergent interests and groups across the political economy.

At some point in the past, it would have been obvious to argue that most communities view prisons as profane spaces, because of their association with violence. But today, we have prison museums with exhibits of prison contraband, capital punishment, and inmate art. In Arizona, the Yuma High School mascot is a criminal. This harkens back to the founding days of the high school in the prison. Other places have always welcomed prisons: in the 1880s, Walla Walla, Washington, chose to site a prison over Washington State University. Places like these show pride in prisons, recasting them as sanctified institutions. Today, places continue to demonstrate a wide range of attitude toward prison siting, including, sometimes, pride. Rural communities place pride and honor in work. No matter how terrible the job may be, there is more pride in working a job under poor conditions and pay than not working at all. While some segments of the population still consider them profane, prisons may represent opportunity for struggling communities.

Whatever its valences, the penal institution has become part of our landscape, particularly rural landscapes. And in fact prisons have been part of the rural landscape for quite some time. As the almshouses and prisons of the city gave rise in the mid-nineteenth century to the new form of penal institution called the penitentiary, the location of the penitentiary was moved to the countryside. Along the way, the purpose, mission, and even architectural design of the penitentiary has morphed considerably (Morris and Rothman 1998; Garland 1990). In the early history of this move, rural towns protested penal placement because of the negative cultural connotations associated with penitentiary inhabitants (Goffman 1963; Combessie 2002). While the debate over whether or not prisons bring economic growth remains, most scholars agree that rural communities believe that prisons are engines of economic growth (Gilmore 2007; Schlosser 1998). The negative stigma of prisons, with their undesirable populations, may place a community in need of economic development at odds with itself. Given the proliferation of prisons in rural communities, Lawrence and Travis (2004, 5) argues that we've seen the "development of a prison construction advocacy position." A LULU like a prison can help recast the image of stigmatized towns.

Reputation Management Strategies

Goffman (1959) suggests that individual stigmatized actors develop three types of responses to mitigate stigma and to gain acceptance by others. First, stigmatized individuals cease contact with nonstigmatized actors. Second, they confess to being stigmatized. A third strategy involves "covering" stigma or trying to "pass." Lauren Rivera (2008) applies this framework to nation-states, arguing that states can isolate themselves from the international community, apologize/acknowledge past wrongs, or use strategic self-presentation to "cover" or "pass" as unstigmatized. More specifically, neighborhoods suffering from high poverty and racial residential segregation may also use an acknowledgment strategy for managing stigma, but these strategies are constrained by the racial narratives and the practices these narratives facilitate in specific, storied places (Wherry 2012). These frameworks can be used to understand how rural towns manage their reputations. For municipalities, sovereignty is difficult, given the proximity of other towns, geographic constraints, and egress via state and federal highways. A stigmatized town therefore has limited options for isolation. Not unlike urban neighborhoods (Wherry 2012), strategic self-presentation and public acknowledgment are, however, strategies readily available and widely used within small towns, including Forrest City.

These strategies were deployed through the use of specific narratives. As Mario Small (2002, 22) has developed the concept, neighborhood narrative frames are "the continuously shifting but nonetheless concrete sets of categories through which the neighborhood's houses, streets, parks, population, location, families, murals, history, heritage, and institutions are made sense of and understood." Individuals do not simply see the world as it is—they see the world as it *should be* and will mobilize others to reconcile the gap between these divergent points. For black and white leaders in Forrest City, the town's poor reputation represented a significant gap between the world as it was and the world as they thought it *should be*. Narrative frames help explain why groups undertake action—especially collective action to mobilize around specific causes or shared values. In the case of Forrest City, the town's marred image was a violation of values across racial lines causing them to mobilize in efforts to stave off decline. Therefore, stigma can serve as a catalyst for unity and action by being a common enemy among divided leaders.

The narratives in Forrest City emerged from the discourse of the town's leaders as they explained why they supported prison placement. And yet prisons present a moral dilemma because they are undoubtedly stigmatized, a cause of racial and economic exploitation, and serve as a reminder of human suffering. Furthermore, if one considers the sense of linked fate (Dawson 1994) that black elected officials in rural towns may feel to the disproportionate number African Americans incarcerated, one might have expected more local opposition from race leaders. For these reasons, it is difficult to comprehend why any town would site such a facility. Nevertheless, both black and white leaders in Forrest City unanimously supported the bid for the prison. Before turning to how Forrest City's leaders imagined the Federal Correctional Facility as the town's savior, we must explore in more detail the narratives associated with prisons themselves.

The Prison as Redeemer: Saving Forrest City

For Professor Alderson and other white elites, securing a federal prison was one possibility on a long list of strategies to save their town. Elites used state and federal connections not only to secure the prison but also to vet the type of facility that would be most beneficial to Forrest City. They considered a private prison, but decided that it would not generate enough high-paying jobs. Led by then-mayor Danny Ferguson, they also engaged the state legislature on the possibility of building a prison. These conversations eventually led to the siting of the federal prison. At the same time, other members of the city's top brass also pursued light industry to try and slow the corrosive effects of de-industrialization and globalization. These strategies emerged amid the backdrop of record-high unemployment in Forrest City during the 1980s. Following the most recent Sanyo strike, unemployment was over 30 percent. The strike and record unemployment had a ripple effect. Other industries, like the canning company, downsized or left during the 1980s as well.

In 1984, in response to the ignominy of the Dumond and Sanyo fiascos, Professor Alderson led the chamber of commerce in conducting an image inventory of Forrest City to save the town's reputation. The Memphis-based firm of Walker and Associates conducted surveys of Forrest City residents, business leaders, and other stakeholders around the state, including public officials, to gauge Forrest City's reputation. According to the image assessment, the challenges to town's economic recovery ranged from poor race relations to uneven service at local establishments and a need to expand the town's economic base. While the survey was not based on scientific sampling techniques, the report provided numerous insights on Forrest City at that time. While Walker and Associates were careful in pointing to Forrest City's assets—such as the high supply of low-skilled labor, strategic interstate location, planned industrial park, transportation system, and the increased production of factories to pre-recession levels—they also pointed to the challenges facing the community, including the need to expand the employment base, ameliorate racial tensions between black and white citizens/politicians, and reconcile labor and management.

In terms of leadership, the report's rather scathing finding was:

Leadership is the most serious obstacle confronting Forrest City/ St. Francis County. The problem is neither the quantity nor the quality of local leaders. There are many leaders of many groups and interests. These individuals are for the most part intelligent, experienced, and motivated. They appear unable, however, to put the community's interests above their own. They appear short term in their perspective. And, they appear unwilling or unskilled in the art of compromise and negotiation. The differences among polarized interests are many and for the most part well defined. They include traditional divisions among blacks and whites; and between affiliation; and retail merchant interest by neighborhood and racial ownership. And finally, they include issue-related divisions, such as the sale of the hospital, which are temporal in nature but serve to exacerbate the more permanent divisions of the other two categories. (Excerpts from the Community Economic Assessment of Forrest City / Saint Francis County by Walker and Associates, 1984, p. 23)

During our interview, Professor Alderson read me sections of the inventory. He used an authoritative tone as he cited the various causes of Forrest City's economic malaise. He explained that he wanted to use the image inventory as a tool of evidence-based policy making. When I asked him what life was like before the prison came, he tried to avoid directly answering the question. Instead, he (literally and figuratively) threw reports my way.

J. E.: So, not just economically but I am trying to get a sense of what you felt life was like before the prison got here. Right, you talked about the industrial base.

JOHN ALDERSON: [he interjects] Tough! Tough! Tough! . . . Lack of jobs, lack of opportunities. Uh . . . Sanyo dropping the number of people they had employed.
General Industries closing. Uh . . . a couple of other things closing . . .

Professor Alderson provided the most sobering insight into the need to re-
deem the town's image. Speaking from his current position as a professor in
Business and Economic Development at Eastern Arkansas Community College, he said, "whenever you . . . [long pause] . . . whenever you have a situation where you feel you need to have a campaign to make people feel good
about their community . . . it's probably evident that people don't feel good
about their community . . ." If things are bad enough that you need an image
inventory, in other words, your town may be in the market for a LULU.

After the image inventory, Alderson and the chamber of commerce spon-
sored a campaign to make the citizens of Forrest City feel better about their
town. The campaign included buttons with the slogan, "Forrest City is great.
You'll love it!," seminars on customer service provided by the chamber of
commerce to local businesses, and mystery shoppers to surprise waitresses
or retail clerks with special premiums, including bold print stickers reading
"GREAT JOB!" for outstanding customer service. This strategy achieved at
best short-lived, modest success, as servers either knew or quickly learned
the chamber members promoting this program. Furthermore, the "Great
Job!" stickers did not do much to help advance or secure low-wage, low-skill
employment. While campaigns like the "GREAT JOB!" sticker from mystery
shoppers would come and go, the white elite never made any real effort to
improve systematic problems like race relations.

As a life-long resident and a descendent of a prominent farming family,
John Alderson believed securing the prison was central to reviving Forrest
City's image. Professor Alderson has a complex, strong personality. While
he occasionally makes off-color, politically incorrect comments that could
be considered racist on their face, characterizing him as a racist would over-
simplify his role—many people in town, both black and white, view him as
a pragmatist. It would also be a mistake to interpret his role solely through
the lens of the "southern gentleman" providing leadership on the old plantation, despite his family's wealth and position (Cobb 1994). Professor Alderson's passion for the people of Forrest City extends far beyond his role as
a member of the southern white landed elite, and even beyond his personal
biases.

His commitment to Forrest City is evident in the hustle and bustle of
his office. While his office walls display numerous civic awards and plaques
of recognition, more impressive is the number of people he interacts with

daily. Beyond his official positions, Professor Alderson works with disadvantaged youths and outreach in the community through multiple civic organizations. Between these activities and his community college students, the hubbub threatened to overwhelm his offices at EACC (Eastern Arkansas Community College). I had to request to close the door during our interview because of the commotion. He had a hard time keeping eye contact, as he kept pulling reports from piles or off the shelves in his otherwise neat and orderly office. He brought this same level enthusiasm to the campaign to win a prison.

During the 1990s, the two most powerful local political actors (the mayor and director of the chamber of commerce) agreed that the town was stigmatized, business was suffering, and securing a prison was a solution to the problems they faced. More than mere personal opinions, these attitudes are vital in understanding how these officials represented the white elite in Forrest City. Ironically, the campaign to bring the prison represented a rare moment of solidarity in the racially divided political landscape of Forrest City. In stark contrast to the findings of the image assessment, where racial division and leadership served as impediment to the town's progress, black and white Forrest City politicos managed to set aside their differences (whether petty or practical) in pursuing something that represented the greater good for Forrest City. Cecil Twillie would be a key broker across this racial divide.

Coach has a lanky six foot three or six foot four frame. His shoulders and neck hunch slightly, so he only looks about six two. Although I never inquired, I imagined this slight hunch is from playing golf everyday, now that he is a "retired" high school principal. If one had to characterize a man based solely on his handshake, Coach is stern, but extremely thoughtful and caring. His hands were large and soft, yet firm like a third-baseman's glove. He is always very positive and affirming. When a distressing topic emerges, he keeps things in perspective, often replying, "that's rat poop . . . just keep steppin' right on over it!" While this can come off as a put-down, it's his way of saying not to sweat the small stuff and keep moving forward. He believes that there's nothing that can't be overcome with proper preparation. He is married, has three daughters, and is active in his Baptist church, serving as a deacon, trustee, and Bible study teacher.

Coach always seems to have a glimmer in his eye, as if he knows something that you don't, and he's itching tell you, but only if you ask very nicely. He has a medium-brown complexion with a mustache; sometimes he has a close-cut beard. While Coach is in his early seventies, he barely looks a day over fifty. Only a few grays adorn his facial hair, and he is quite spry, both physically and mentally. In addition to playing golf, Coach's days are filled with meetings as the mayor pro tem and a town council representative of Forrest City. He is very active in nearly all matters of electoral politics, including school board elections and the operation of recreational facilities. Although he grew up in neighboring Caldwell, he has lived in Forrest City for nearly five decades. Coach has dedicated his life to public service, and he is a testament to perseverance in the remnants of a racially oppressive plantation system.

Based on my observations and our interview, Coach is a prototypical race leader/middleman (Drake and Cayton 1945; Pattillo 2007) in Forrest City. In addition to being one of the first black members of the Forrest City country club, Coach led the fight to integrate the school administration and school board. He was the first black head coach after desegregation of the public schools. Moreover, he was the last Forrest City High School football coach to win the Arkansas state championship about thirty years ago—this is why he maintains the affectionate title "Coach." Those were better days for the town.

When I asked interviewees what life was like just before the prison came, nearly all my interviewees gave curt answers like "bad," "awful," or "not very good." When pressed further, most of them offered colorful descriptions of what was wrong with the town. Coach was no different. In expressing why he is so deeply involved in improving Forrest City, Coach draws a comparison to Gary, a city that has also seen better days. Coach Twillie's quip about trying to keep his town from ending up like Gary should be understood as framing the prison as saving Forrest City, because Gary is so obviously an icon of urban decline. Coach is not much on hyperbole; if he adamantly claimed that Forrest City was turning into Gary, one can assume that this is a reasonable claim. Hearing Coach compare his beloved Forrest City to Gary was one of my first indications that Forrest City's downward economic trajectory had become associated with a bourgeoning ghetto.

Donald Threm, a reporter for the *Forrest City Times-Herald* from 1980 to 1991 (currently a faculty member at MidSouth Community College in Memphis), echoed these struggles as he encouraged the town to pursue the prison facility. In a January 1990 op-ed he argued: "if the people of Forrest City could vote on what kind of an employer they would like to see located here, they would probably not cast many ballots in favor of a federal prison facility. But it's not like we have businesses and industries beating down our doors to locate here. Cities all over the country are rolling out the red carpet for potential employers, and it's highly competitive. Forrest City should actively pursue the proposed federal corrections facility. It would be senseless to let such and opportunity slip away."

Threm's call to action on the prison came amid a string of retail and manufacturing closings in Forrest City. One of these closings included Revco. According to the *Forrest City Times-Herald*, on January 11, 1991, Revco was one of the largest drugstore chains, with a national workforce of almost 27,000 employees. Revco was one of the first sizable corporations to file for bankruptcy by incurring debts in a leveraged buyout. As part of the company's economic restructuring, Revco planned to close or sell nearly 40 percent of its stores, including several in eastern Arkansas, and including Forrest City. This is another example of companies like Revco economically restructuring to compete in the increasingly global marketplace, leaving towns like Forrest City in the lurch.

The Prison as Stabilizer: Fixing Forrest City

The Forrest City Correctional Facility sits about four miles due south of the intersection of Interstate 40 and Highway 1. You can take the highway bypass to access the main road, or you can get there by a winding pathway of smaller streets off of the main drag, Washington Street. Either route will eventually lead you to Dale Bumpers Road—the namesake of this road was elected governor in Arkansas in 1972. After a short stint as governor, he was elected to the US Senate, representing Arkansas from 1974 to 1998. In 1994, along with Mayor Danny Ferguson, the Honorable Judge Gazzola Vaccarro Jr., and Governor Jim Guy Tucker, Senator Bumpers broke ground on the minimum security Forrest City Federal Correctional Facility.

During his tenure as mayor, from 1988 to 1996, Danny Ferguson earned the respect of blacks and whites alike. Although he was the last white mayor of Forrest City, the Ferguson era represented an improvement from past mayoral administrations that had more openly contentious relationships with the growing black majority in town. As blacks gained more power on the city council, winning four of the eight seats and effectively splitting power along racial lines, Mayor Ferguson became increasingly strategic and more willing to working with race leaders. One informant claimed that Mayor Ferguson never had to break a tie with his vote along racial lines. According to this source, the key to Mayor Ferguson's successful political legacy during this period was working with Coach Twillie. Coach would convene with black council members to minimize disagreement by airing problems and working out solutions prior to the official council meetings. "If Danny didn't have the OK from Cecil, he would not call for a vote," the informant added. He was quick to point out how this was just good politics. He continued, "if you listened to people and their concerns before a decision is made then people are bought into the process and less likely to have a problem with the outcome of the process." Despite continued racial turmoil (primarily caused by the actions and statements of white elites responding to losing their stranglehold on power), Danny Ferguson maintained a civil political culture within the city council. Mayor Ferguson's legacy also includes attracting Yale Hoist Industries and keeping much of the industrial base intact in the face of increasing globalization.

Steve Lindsey is fifty-two, a longtime businesses owner, a member of the chamber of commerce, and chair of the local Lion's Club. He was born and raised five miles north of Forrest City. Over 130 years ago, his family helped settle Forrest City. As a descendant of a founding family, like John Alderson, Steve Lindsey also has a special role and obligation in town (Cobb 1994). He has owned and operated three different businesses, including a bowling alley, a western auto parts store, and the Farm Bureau Insurance agency, a position he has occupied for the past nineteen years. Despite going through a recent divorce, he is known in Forrest City as a good family man, having raised children, worked hard as an entrepreneur, and regularly attended services at the First United Methodist church. In explaining what life was like before the prison, he states:

> Oh, we were struggling financially, uh because at the time, farming has been the mainstay in our community and of course, the farmers have been struggling the past few years with the prices being depressed and the production costs going up so high. And we do have some factory in Forrest City and in our area. But none of it has been real stable. We've lost a few, but we've had a fairly good business recruiter [Danny Ferguson] that works with the chamber of commerce who is no longer there but he did a good job in getting a few folks in to take their place. He was the district [state] representative and worked for the chamber at the same time . . . Danny's worn a lot hats in this town and all of them, he was successful in all of them. But it was struggling, it was day to day you never knew which of the factories was next to go out. Danny was fairly instrumental in working with uh . . . one of the state senators to get things lined up to get the federal prison in here.

Increasing competition among companies and communities across the global industrial marketplace pits communities and companies against each other. Companies seek the lowest rents, driving down the cost to enter and exit communities as locales try to hold onto the jobs those companies offer (Logan and Molotch 1987). For many communities, the quantity of jobs outweighs the quality. That is to say, the number of jobs retained or attracted in a given period has symbolic value for the community—the number of jobs represents the relative economic health of a community. If a town is attracting a number of jobs (independent of the quality), that signals economic well-being, and suggests that other companies will relocate to the community, bringing even more jobs. But to keep the existing businesses and attract new ones, local political leaders must contend with managing their town's public image across a sea of economic uncertainty. This "any job is better than no job" approach has been the dominant mantra in southern rural towns and has led to uneven development (Bullard 2000; Falk and Lyson 1988; Lyson and Falk 1993).

Mayor Danny Ferguson, the Honorable Saint Francis County Judge Gazzola Vaccarro Jr., Saint Francis County Chamber of Commerce board president Buddy Billingsley, and then-director Perry Webb were part of a "great team" that made a series of moves (some public, many private) to keep the town afloat. Their moves included making several trips to Japan in an attempt to save the Sanyo factory; in that, they were successful. Despite this impressive achievement, the 1995 groundbreaking for the Forrest City Federal Correctional Facility stands as the cornerstone of Mayor Ferguson's legacy of business development. In an op-ed published in the *Forrest City Times-Herald* on January 11, 1991, Mayor Ferguson built the case for prison placement. He positioned the prison among a constellation of development challenges for Forrest City:

> Unfortunately, the bad news stands out like the big industries going out and some cutting business, but it is also important to look at the positive side of that like the Sukup expansion and Reltoc which is the oldest industry in Forrest City. I honestly think we're past the bottoming out part and we've started an upswing. I wouldn't be here if I didn't feel good about Forrest City . . . I can assure you there is no doubt that other parts of the state are observing Forrest City, and their confidence in Forrest City is better than in previous years. Things in the 90s have done a complete turnaround for the area. Although the county's unemployment rate remains in the double digits regularly, community leaders say that figure is now positive for the area. It shows people are coming here now and looking for work.

Despite the positive tone of these public statements, Mayor Ferguson is keenly aware of the town's reputation, especially among other political stakeholders and policy makers across the state. He also understood the economic challenges facing communities like Forrest City.

At that time retaining and expanding Sukup, the world's largest family-owned grain bin and dryer manufacturer, was vital to Forrest City's indus-trial base. The company provided hundreds of jobs to citizens of Forrest City. In the face of stiff competition from manufacturing rival DMC, operating out of nearby West Memphis, the Sukup facility eventually reduced its op erations and would be used primarily for distribution. Although another grain dryer and bin manufacturer, GSI, would eventually purchase DMC and close all of the North American warehouses years later, Sukup could not manage two facilities, and it eventually merged its plant in Forrest City with another facility in Jonesboro (about an hour and twenty minutes north). By 2002, Yale Hoist, like Sukup, would also be closed by its parent company, saving the company $7.25 million and eliminating roughly two hundred jobs in Forrest City.

While Mayor Ferguson claimed that the proposed prison would be a stabilizing force and source for optimism in Forrest City, his statement also demonstrates a heightened level of insecurity about the town's status. The prison offered not only a source of internal stability, but also a strategy for remaining in good standing with other policy makers and business lead-ers across the state. Mayor Ferguson understood that the town's continued economic recovery was based on saving face by improving the confidence of political and business leaders outside of Forrest City. Leaders in Forrest City hoped these relationships would help build the impression among their network that the town was conducive for business.

Town leaders expressed the need to stabilize the local political economy in other ways. Steve Lindsey also believed prison placement could provide stability by slowing the population loss of young adults, or what Carr and Kefalas (2009) refer to as *Hollowing out the Middle*:

> I've grown and changed with this town I feel like I've had my finger on the pulse of it because I knew so many people. And I am proud of Forrest City. I'm proud of everything it's done. . . . We've had a lot folks that have tried to gather around and pull in the same direction to benefit the town and this is just one of many pieces to the puzzle. But it's a big one if you ask me this prison has been a big piece to help stabilize our economy and help us keep from being so dependent on the factories as being the only place that our young folks can go to work. I mean they have an opportunity to go out there and work under a federal wage and federal retirement program that's really good. And it's one thing that we needed to help keep our young folks here in town. Uh . . . getting off the subject we were talking about it in Sunday school the other day about the age of church members—that's First United Methodist—that uh over half of them were sixty or older. And we practically have none in the twenty, thirty,

year age range. I got to thinking in our Sunday school class alone none of our children live in Forrest City. Everybody has moved, and its simply because there has been nothing there for them. This isn't, this may not be everybody's cake [the prison] they might want to be a teacher, a lawyer, a doctor, a pharmacist or something, uh but there are some things that might fit into that mold out there that they could come back to Forrest City and do and make a decent wage and maybe make the community better, contribute to the community.

This reflection about his congregation and the lack of young adults touches a broader problem of population loss or "brain drain" in rural America (Carr and Kefalas 2009). Population loss in rural communities has been an ongoing social problem for decades. For Steve Lindsey, the prison represented a chance to slow this trend by attracting young people or providing employment opportunities for those that had left to return. The stability of the prison also signaled a break from factories as the core of Forrest City's industrial base. An invigorated economic base could signal more than a recovery—it could also lead to economic advancement.

The Prison as Growth Machine: Advancing Forrest City

Some members of the town's black community still consider André Stephens an outsider, despite his more than twenty-five years of residency in Forrest City. Given the nature of his organization, the Saint Francis County CDC, he probably operates within and across the black-white political divide in Forrest City more than any other member of the managerial or political elite. He deals with white bankers and foundation officials to fund the much-needed work he has done within the black community, ranging from job training, computer literacy, building affordable housing, and preparing resident to become homeowners. When asked why he supported the prison coming to town, Mr. Stephens exclaimed, "a prison beats the hell out of a paper mill. You get don't get noxious fumes, polluted groundwater, or any other environmental effects. In fact, a prison is like its own little self-sustained city." This was a common view among respondents. Besides, many black residents felt that the prison building was inevitable. If whites would surely benefit, why shouldn't blacks benefit as well? And while race leaders acknowledged that blacks are disproportionately incarcerated, they felt impotent in doing anything about a problem that plagued not only their town but also the greater black community.

Mr. Stephens, moreover, explained that he and his wife, Terri, held strategic views about the prison coming to town. Like other race leaders/middlemen, they welcomed the prison as a potential business opportunity. Terri opened a beauty salon on Washington Street, Arkansas Highway 1, in hopes of capturing high-end clients working at the prison or possibly visitors to the prison. As the prison was officially opened, Terri and André launched the salon. André boasts that since the opening of the prison, their business has never had a week that didn't turn a profit. While this speaks to the impact of the prison, it also demonstrates the power of framing the prison as an income generator or growth machine. The Stephenses were not the only people in Forrest City to have such foresight and optimism regarding the FCFCF.

Members of the city council benefited immensely from the prison, none more than black city council members like Walter Peacock and Coach Twillie. Peacock already owned a plumbing business prior to plans for the prison; Twillie would start a waste removal company once he learned about plans for the prison. While these race leaders definitely expressed a linked fate (Dawson 1994) with more disadvantage blacks, they saw the prison as a way to deliver jobs to their brethren. Given that the prison was a federal project, Twillie and Peacock collaborated with influential black families in town (who declined to be mentioned here) to acquire minority set-aside no-bid contracts for large portions of the plumbing and waste removal of the FCFCF.

But not all race leaders wholeheartedly embraced the prison. In the midst of our interview, Mayor Bryant seems to drift as he recalls the January 10, 1990, public meeting to discuss the possibility of building a prison in Forrest City. In those days, Larry Bryant was a city council member who was also president of the local NAACP. His current feelings about that meeting are visible in the contours of his face as he struggles to reconcile what the prison meant then versus now. Mayor Bryant recalls, "looking for what it means to get a prison here. [They] thought that it would be a *bonanza* and all these people would live here, and, purchase goods here. . . . They [the Chamber of Commerce] had the utopia, probably thought they would all live here. . . . We had a big meeting at the courthouse to get this prison here. And, very few people spoke against it and it was probably 300, 400 folk there." To be precise, only five of the several hundred people present raised their hands to disapprove of prison building in Forrest City during a vote. To provide even more perspective on the opposition, there were only three dissenting opinions among the nearly two-dozen residents that voiced their opinions during the public meeting.

Bryant understood that his future as a politician could rest on the decision. He recounts how he tried to balance his tacit support at the time against the chamber of commerce–led economic development initiative for prison placement. He understood that tepid approval from a race leader, as the head of the local NAACP and a young up-and-coming political figure, could be interpreted as complicity. He also understood any objections he raised to the facility would be perceived as antagonistic to the white elite, and might position him as an impediment to progress at a time when the town was in economic free fall. He was strategic not only in what he said but when he said it. Bryant wanted to appear like his heart was with the black community, but his head was on the right side of history. He spoke around the same time now-deceased longtime community activist, education reformer, and leader at Christ the Episcopal Church Ralph Nesbitt spoke during the meeting.

As a race leader, Nesbitt objected to the prison because of the disproportionate rate of incarceration of African Americans. Bryant told me that he agreed with Nesbitt, in principal. This presented a moral dilemma for Bryant. He could not speak against prison placement because of the community's desperate need for jobs, nor could he support an endeavor that would bring harm to the black community writ large. Unlike Nesbitt, who did not have political aspirations, Bryant had already run for mayor several times against the incumbent Danny Ferguson. Key informants recall Bryant having a deliberately measured, but direct speech during the meeting.

> The promise of economic benefits, however, was questioned by one speaker who expressed concern over the proposal. Another resident asked whether minorities would be hired. "Why should we trust them [officials]?" asked Larry Bryant, president of the NAACP. Bryant had earlier voiced his approval of the measure, saying he believes the prison would stabilize the economy. (Weiss 1990)

Bryant challenged the concerns about the prison, suggesting that, "residents should investigate the proposal before condemning it. Are we going to put our heads in the sand and be negative about everything that comes down the tracks?" (Weiss 1990). History seems to favor his decision to let this one roll by—he did not appear to be against the prison during the public meeting. However, he was privately never sold on the lure of the prison because of his moral quandary about the disproportionate rate of incarceration for African Americans. In the long run, his stance on the prison did not hurt him with the electorate and provided some measure of good will among his political colleagues.

The *Forrest City Times-Herald* article the day following the meeting describing it as "an old time *revival*" with applause and laughter, as an encouraging, and "heartening" event at which residents expressed enthusiasm for the prison (Weiss 1990). In fact, the prison was portrayed so optimistically that construction was projected to be completed in two years, providing 250 jobs overall. At that time, 70 percent of the jobs were projected to be captured by people who did/would live in Forrest City, at an average salary of more than $24,000. Given the median household income of Forrest City in 1990 was just over $15,000, the appeal of the facility remains appreciable.

Even if Forrest City didn't recoup the majority of the benefits, once it was built, the facility was heralded as nothing less than an economic windfall. For example, even if most employees who worked at the prison lived elsewhere, the belief was that if people earned money at the prison, then they would spend some in Forrest City. Accordingly, benefits would come from housing nonviolent, white-collar offenders—making the prison a truly cost-free bonanza. Don Threm's op-ed following the meeting provides choice insight into economic advocacy position of many civic leaders in the Forrest City:

> Spending helps area business and also benefits the city and county through sales taxes. A *minimum to medium security facility would generate nothing but good fortune* for Forrest City. Since the proposed facility is *geared toward white-collar criminals*, people of the city and county would have *nothing to fear from the inmates*. There will be no violent offenders housed here. It's unlikely that an inmate in such a facility would try a jail break. And if one did, he wouldn't pose a threat to anyone. After all, what would he do, *break into a house and unbalance a checkbook*? If, on the other hand, a private firm wanted to build a prison a *medium to maximum-security prison here*, there would be justifiable arguments against it. *Who would actively seek a facility that would house rapists and murderers*?

People in Forrest City wanted to believe the prison was a panacea. This belief was held so deeply that advocates argued tooth and nail with conscientious objections about the moral dilemma posed by prison placement. Threm claimed that naysayers opposed the prison for reasons that had nothing to do with the situation at hand. "There are not justifiable arguments against a federal prison in the Forrest City area," he wrote. "The fact is that the federal government needs beds for 24,000 prisoners. It will eventually contract for some facilities to alleviate the backlog. A prison can be located in Forrest City, or it can be located somewhere else."

During the public hearing on the prison, Scott Carroll, the president of the Forrest City Merchants Association, encouraged the crowd to "seize the opportunity" (Weiss 1990). Additionally, the director of Crosspoint Ministries, Fred Quails, argued, "I think we'd be very foolish if we let it [the prison] go up here to Wynne, and we drive through and smile at it, and come back here and wonder where the hell are we going to get some money?" In addition to its PIMBY (Please in My Backyard) character, the opinion expressed here is interesting for two reasons. First, there is a distinct irony in members of the faith community cursing in excitement in the name of chasing dollars—for a prison, no less. Second, the mention of Wynne speaks to the strong desire to make Forrest City the sole winner from the prison.

There was a sense of solidarity among citizens of Forrest City in this meeting that seemed to cross all divides—race, age, sex, and so on. This sense of solidarity over the prison did not extend to the southeastern Arkansas region, state, or the Mississippi Delta. Although this meeting lives on as a moment of pride and solidarity among citizens of Forrest City, it also featured occasional stinging reminders of the town's troubled past. Longtime resident Dr. Dale Morris, an optometrist and former president of the chamber of commerce, for instance, declared during the meeting, "I just wished *20/20* could be here tonight, they would see a completely different side of Forrest City" (Weiss 1990). This comment received much fanfare by the crowd, which was just as eager as Morris to put the Dumond incident behind Forrest City.

Rethinking Prison Placement

Within the environmental justice literature, LULUs are framed as goods that communities do not want but are nevertheless sometimes willing to accept (Bullard 2000; Davidson and Anderton 2000; Mohai and Saha 2006). This chapter demonstrates that local leaders shape positive meaning around prison placement, despite the negative stigma associated with the institution. I suggest that frame analysis can be used in making sense of prison placement. This is a shift away from regarding prisons as institutions whose impact can primarily be understood through either positive or negative economic impact. Instead of asking whether a community wins or loses with a prison, we should focus on who wins, and what is at stake. Leaders' NNFs positioned the prison as redeemer, fixer, and growth machine. Each frame represents a different cognitive strategy to illicit solidarity among residents of Forrest City for prison placement.

Leaders in Forrest City understood that deep divisions across race, class, labor, and management would have to be minimized to have a successful campaign for a prison. The January 1990 public hearing for the prison was a key turning point in shifting public opinion from NIBMY to PIMBY. The sense of attending a traditional revival during that meeting showed the economic hopes that community leaders attached to the prison. The wish for the presence of 20/20 shows the persistent concern about the town's image. Local elites in Forrest City not only used these frames to mitigate NIMBY, but also to produce action and drive a PIMBY campaign. This campaign would sanitize the past wrongs and infamy associated with Forrest City. Framing the prison as a redeemer taps into the need to sanctify Forrest City's image or eliminate the collective memory of shameful events. Framing the prison as a stabilizer, or a fixer, allows residents to believe there are larger forces shaping the political economy of Forrest City, and that only small adjustments are needed to right the ship. The prison-as-stabilizer frame is a path to solidarity in prison placement. Likewise, framing the prison as a growth machine points the town toward a bright and promising horizon, with the prison as the bridge toward that future.

For many rural communities, prisons represent an instantiation of punishment and source of stigma. For others—particularly those who have seen better days—prisons represent economic development. The potential for growth, coupled with the historic view of prisons as stigmatized institutions, creates tension at the community level. How, then, do prisons or any other LULUs find communities willing to receive them? A satisfying theory of LULU placement must account for the augmentation of stigma at multiple levels.

Given that states have built over 80 percent of all prisons in the United States, states are arguably the most important actors in understanding prison siting.[1] However, host community preferences are also important in understanding the causal mechanism of prison placement. Community leaders reveal preferences based on a willingness to accept an institution and their capacity to marshal resources to secure a facility, placing the negative symbolic status of prisons and other LULUs in tension with possible positive economic benefits. But in stigmatized communities of color with few options for economic development, the need for the stable employment base promised by large public works projects may very well outweigh the institutional stigma of a prison.

The traditional understanding of LULUs points to class-based strategies of stigma management in explaining how communities develop NIMBY strategies. From this perspective, more affluent communities with presumably greater capacity for collective efficacy may be able to resist LULUs; poorer communities with less agency might simply take whatever is forced upon them. The process of prison building, however, depends on a bundle of decisions. This process is multilayered, involving local town officials, state representatives, and depending on the circumstances, county or federal officials. The results of this process stem from community "demand," or at least a willingness to accept.

Social scientists have produced numerous examples of how communities respond to exogenous shocks and how these circumstances affect their willingness to accept or "demand" certain goods, services, or even people. Jonathan Rieder (1987), for example, eloquently chronicles a Jewish and Italian neighborhood's response to school desegregation through busing black and Latino/a children, showing how residents of Canarsie, Brooklyn, experienced desegregation as a time of intense and chaotic change. Like those in Canarsie, those in Forrest City experienced the mid-1980s as a time of danger and dispossession. From the outside, actions of those in Canarsie simply appeared to be racist, but allowing residents in these communities a voice in the story reveals the nuances of a complicated situation. In Forrest City, civic leaders needed to tackle pressing issues, like the annual property tax millage for schools, that seemed to only exacerbated the town's points of conflict: blacks against white, wealthy versus poor, and labor versus management. White elites and black race leaders were galvanized in support of the prison to protect their common interests across racial boundaries. The use of common frames across these otherwise tense and contested boundaries is evidence of solidarity for prison placement.

While in the last chapter I traced how the presence of a rural ghetto may serve as the impetus for locating a new prison, in most cases, at least two other conditions are necessary for a prison to actually get built. First, while elites within a town must desire a LULU to commit to using their political capital in securing a prison, and second, black/Latino leadership must be in support, or at least not oppose the decision. These interlocking interests form the basis for a growth coalition. The next chapter explores how the dynamic process of prison placement occurs, in the words of Forrest City's own.

FIVE

How Not in My Backyard Became Please in My Backyard: Toward a Model of Prison Placement

In many respects, the modern signage you see in and on the way to Forrest City tells the origins of the town's correctional facility. A sign along Washington Avenue / Arkansas Highway 1 touts the town's status as an ACE, or Arkansas Community of Excellence. The ACE program prioritized persistently poor areas for targeted developmental programming and public works projects. The ACE program's roots can be traced to the work of the Lower Mississippi Delta Commission. Because Arkansas is consistently ranked as one of the poorest states, local political representatives need to be well connected to leverage capital in assuring their communities are first in line for assistance. Communities that are part of programs like ACE are better able to make those connections.

The name of the highway bypass leading to the Forrest City Federal Correctional Facility—Dale Bumpers Road—also provides a clue as to the prison's origins. As one might expect, the road is named after the former US senator and Arkansas governor because of his prominent role in securing the facility. On May 31, 1994, the groundbreaking for the FCFCF included Senator Bumpers, Saint Francis County Judge Gazzola Vaccaro Jr., Forrest City mayor Danny Ferguson, and then-governor Jim Guy Tucker. Many key informants identified the close relationship between Mayor Danny Ferguson and Senator Bumpers as vital in securing the federal facility. Prior to assuming the helm as mayor, Danny Ferguson served as a state representative and chamber of commerce director for Forrest City. He developed a close relationship with then-Governor Bumpers during this period. Senator Bumpers had tight connections to former Arkansas governor and then-president Bill Clinton to boot.

Despite local white elites' ties to a sitting US president, connections alone were not enough to secure the awarding of a federal correctional facility to Forrest City. Before reaching agreement to pursue the prison in January 1990, some white elites had expressed grave concerns over the likely success of prison building. A week earlier, the *Forrest City Times-Herald* quoted Perry Webb, the director of the chamber of commerce, as saying that "the main prerequisite that must be met by Forrest City is community support. Without it, the federal government would look elsewhere."

In Forrest City, savvy political maneuvering by white elites was just as important as networks to actually getting a prison built. Local actors wield clout within their municipality as well as with state and federal actors to influence the process. In the case of Forrest City, white elites leveraged political capital with federal and state officials and formed a growth coalition with race leaders to secure the FCFCF. This is a delicate political process, riddled with pitfalls of self-aggrandizing legislators, NIMBY land mines, and backroom deals to leverage legislator's support. Contrary to accounts that portray prison placement decisions as a natural by-product of mass imprisonment (Davis 2003; Huling 2001 King, Mauer, and Huling 2003; Schlosser 1998; Street 2002), the story of Forrest City's correctional facility demonstrates how the process of prison building is treacherous and complex. Reading, interpreting, and acting on the informal and formal signs of the prison siting process requires substantial skill from local operatives.

Rethinking Prison Building

It is helpful, at this point, to distinguish more clearly between prison *placement* and prison *siting*. While both involve the political economy of prison building, prison placement refers to local efforts to acquire a prison—the pull factor—whereas prison siting refers to how state and federal agencies select a municipality in which to build a prison—the push factor. Local NIMBY opposition can manifest in regard to either. To overcome obstacles at multiple levels, town leaders must be incredibly savvy, resourceful, and politically astute.

Michele Hoyman and Micah Weinberg (2006) furnish a short background on the formal process of prison placement. The Bureau of Prisons (BOP) issues a request for proposal (RFP). Communities respond to the RFP, usually including videos and letters of support from political and civic leaders advocating for their community to win the facility. If the BOP responds in favor of the community proposal, then the community must annex or purchase land, in addition to having a site plan and impact report approved at a community meeting before the process is finalized. One reason that the BOP requires statements of community interest is that NIMBY is the default position of most communities; prisons are, after all, stigmatized institutions. Politicians fear a political backlash from target communities and generally assume that areas currently without a prison lack "demand." Because of this, local leaders hoping to secure a prison must demonstrate that their communities back their bid for placement.

From the dominant perspective on prison building, placement—or more specifically, the transition from NIMBY to PIMBY—only appears in passing as a by-product of a racist criminal justice system (Davis 2003; Schlosser 1998; Street 2002). Scholars also typically characterize community support of prison placement as false consciousness or simplistically based on a "demand" for jobs (Davis 2003; Gilmore 2007; Hooks et al. 2004; King, Mauer, and Huling 2003; Schlosser 1998; Street 2002).

Distinguishing between prison placement and prison siting draws attention to a critical, and little understood, aspect of prison building: how prisons go from NIMBY to PIMBY. The previous chapter deals with why local leaders *want* (or "demand") prison placement. This chapter unravels the dynamic process of how rural communities get from NIMBY to PIMBY by using the unique perspectives provided by two of the four local officials intimately involved in pursuing and securing the FCFCF. I then extrapolate from these first-person narratives to build a new theoretical model of prison placement.

Key Members of a Great Team

The FCFCF bypass might rightly be named after Buddy Billingsley and Perry Webb instead of Dale Bumpers. Despite their persona as rather unassuming southern gentlemen, Billingsley and Webb have made vital contributions to Forrest City's economic survival. As president of the board of the Saint Francis County Chamber of Commerce, Billingsley pushed to hire Webb as director. After his arrival, Webb worked with Billingsley in assembling and maintaining both the local Arkansas and the federal coalition for prison building. The FCFCF was undoubtedly Webb's crowning achievement during his tenure as director, but he also helped to retain and recruit a number of businesses for Forrest City, including Sanyo and Sukup. Perry additionally guided Forrest City Grocery, a locally owned business, through the expansion of their warehouse facility in the industrial park. The new facility brought dozens of jobs and expanded the size of the operation from 40,000 square feet to 250,000 square feet. Perry also recruited over 200 jobs by landing Wilson Foods (a subsidiary of Dixie Foods). Webb's success in the job reflected well on Billingsley, who had taken a chance on hiring the thirty-two-year-old Arkansas State University graduate. Although Webb had cut his teeth in economic development at the Waller Ridge Chamber of Commerce, he was considered green in the chamber game at the time Billingsley hired him. But what Webb lacked in experience, he more than made up for in determination. As a lifelong resident of Arkansas, his passion and tenacity for improving his birthplace is evident in everything he does. Since leaving Forrest City in 1993, Webb has brought his enthusiasm to Springdale, which has become one of the fastest-growing small cities in the United States during Perry's tenure as director of the chamber of commerce. His humility keeps him keen to the ways that individual interests furnish opportunities for cutting deals and spurring local economic development.

His copilot, Buddy Billingsley, was equally sharp, but even more perspicuous. Locals describe Billingsley as a "straight shooter." A self-proclaimed air force brat, born in nearby Palestine, Arkansas, Billingsley is a graduate of Forrest City High School. A local patriarch, he has lived nearly all of his adult life in Forrest City. He is well liked and respected among the elite. When asked about his commitment to Forrest City, Billingsley reveals that his two sons work with him and he has two grandchildren living in town. In short, his family roots run deep in this community. Aside from the year he spent as president of the chamber of commerce, Billingsley has spent most of his professional career as a certified financial planner and principal investor at the local Capital Financial Service group. When I spoke with Buddy, he was reluctantly preparing for retirement; one of his sons has taken over the insurance side of the business and the work in securities. On the prospect of retirement, Buddy divulges, "it's kinda frightening when you find out that well it's time to turn it over to somebody else and, you've been active for so long it's kinda hard to wind down you know. . . . And I think they're ready for me to move on . . . the hard part is gonna be what am I going to do? I've got to be active." At age sixty-eight, Buddy remains active, and his passion for Forrest City has remained as intense as the days he worked to secure the prison.

Following in the tradition of classic case studies of elites (Dahl 1961; Davis et al. 1941; Dollard 1937; Dumhoff 1967; Hunter 1993; Lynd and Lynd 1929; Mills 1968), I have used my conversations with Webb and Billingsley to provide a peek into the backroom of rural southern political economy. I asked both men, in separate interviews, to tell me how the FCFCF came to be located in Forrest City. Below, I have spliced together their interconnected tales. Their combined accounts provide invaluable insight into the prison-building process. These members of Forrest City's elite describe the key elements of assembling a winning team, lay out the obstacles in siting and placement, and explain the prison-siting and placement processes.

The Hired Gun

P. W.: I got a phone call in July of that year [1989] and I was in another little town 80 miles away as a chamber guy and a friend of mine lived in Forrest City and he called me and he said, hey, we just had an opening in our chamber down here would you be interested in a job? And my reaction was, "you gotta by kidding, have you lost your mind?" I knew three things. I knew Sanyo strike. I knew Wayne Dumond. And I knew Coolidge Conlee. That was the three things I knew about Forrest City [chuckles] and the economy was in the tank and unemployment through the roof.

. . . But they had actually put together a consortium of financial institutions and business people that pooled their money and put it behind trying to get somebody to come in and take the chamber and do something dramatic with economic development. I had been very successful in the little town I was at previously. Buddy Billingsley was the search committee chairman, and they were looking for somebody that was going to come in and try and make a difference. It didn't bother them if the person they hired had a short tenure and was trying to chase a career, they were OK with that. And that's exactly what I was doing. We were very honest with each other about that so I came in and I'm trying to make a . . . had an opportunity presented to me . . . we're trying to run with it and see if it could actually transpire.

I think one of the magic pieces of being that hired gun is that you have to understand what the community will tolerate and what's acceptable in the community so you have to really engage them and really understand that, and the worst thing I could have done was cram something down their throat that they don't want and have it backfire. And that's just not good business. I don't do that today either but it's just not good practice to do that.

The Winning Team

B. B.: We had a great team and that was one of the big, big pluses in this. We had the chamber of commerce, myself as president. We had Perry Webb as executive director. We had Danny Ferguson as our mayor, and we had Gazzola Vaccarro as county judge. And in my opinion that's one of the key factors in being successful and that's having everyone on the same team. We might disagree in certain situations but when it came to telling the public we had all of us unanimous in our approach. But the organization was in place and everybody knows everybody. A lot of times when you're dealing with politicians especially you have ego problems. Well everybody put their ego aside for the benefit of the goal we were trying to accomplish. And I tell him [Perry Webb] that everything he is he owes to me.

P. W.: I never heard a real, what I would consider a real, leader in Forrest City . . . I never heard a real leader in that community ever go to, go in a prejudice direction and do anything that wasn't best for everybody. I mean that was the common denominator. Now we had different levels of buy-in. Some people would support you because they knew they couldn't not support you. . . . Nobody ever, especially [real leaders] . . . I've been in two or three meetings today that could be construed as three or four guys in a room trying to make behind the door decisions because that's just the way the world works sometimes.

Obstacles to Placement and Siting

P. W.: I expected there to be a groundswell of opposition that had no demographic attached to it. I just thought federal prisons are . . . prisons in general are not something that you want in your backyard, and we expected there to be a large amount of opposition because of that argument. We didn't see that at all. I mean the opposition was not about that, it was about demographic unfairness of prisons in general . . . the status being African Americans incarcerated at a higher rate than the general society.

B. B.: The only opposition that we had really came from people that did not want the prison built close to their, let's say, farm land or their homes. And that was surely understandable. So they weren't opposed to the prison coming, they were opposed to it being close to them. [Their backyard, their immediate backyard] but they were fine with it coming into town . . . that was the primary opposition we had locally.

P. W.: The only people that had a problem with prisons being built, or just being bad for our community, were our elected officials on a federal level. The first congressional representative at the time was Bill Alexander. Bill Alexander when I first talked to him about this, he looked me right in the eye and said, "I'm not about to support a prison!" He said, "they built a state prison in Calico Rock," which is a little town in north central Arkansas, it was in his district, "two years ago and I lost 40 percent of the vote in that county and I didn't have anything to do with that." And so he saw it as a political liability and and he said, point blank, "I'm not about to support a prison, forget it, it's not going to happen."

It was a political liability to him because it was a backyard argument. People did not want a state prison in that community he was referring to and so when it came time for the ballot box they voted against incumbents. That's what he saw and so it was going to be a political liability for him because people would not support it. His assumption was that people would not support it.

Then we went through a process of about two years where the federal Bureau of Prisons says point blank we don't want to do anything with contracted prisons that's not in our deal. We run our own prisons. They told us there's no demand for prisons in Arkansas. The only one [technically] in the state was in Texarkana. So they had one on the east side of the state just in Memphis; they had one in Texarkana [the west side]. The population of inmates from Arkansas is not substantial enough to justify a facility here. There were all the reasons in the world why it wouldn't work had it not been for the lower Mississippi River Delta Commission continuing to push that [agenda].

Now one of the things that I didn't mention earlier is the model that these guys had come to us with using the commission was to place three prisons. . . . They wanted to do it in a triumphant thing and they wanted us, Yazoo City, Mississippi, and I don't think they never nailed down a town in Louisiana, but they were trying put a facility in Arkansas, one in Mississippi, and one in Louisiana. The one in Yazoo City got built as well as the one in Forrest City.

Well this group we were working with had met with the governor, Edwin Edwards, at the time, in Louisiana, and one of his aides, as I understand it, made it pretty clear that this could happen if y'all are willing to make it happen. In other words, you know, you are going to have to buy it. Money is going to have to change hands in order to make this happen and I think that it has been proven that that was his method of operating the state [chuckling], so, so to make a long story short it didn't get any traction with them so they dropped the Louisiana piece.

B. B.: There was some concern about let's say states fighting among themselves . . . fighting among themselves for who's going to get what and we had to make it clear to these different states and especially Mississippi that look we're on your side, and finally Senator Bumpers understood that. We met with Senator Bumpers numerous times and he led, he was our leader in Washington to get this deal accomplished.

Clinton was president and we actually at one time had to meet with Webb Hubble the attorney general . . . he actually had to resign later. . . . At that time, not much different than it is today the politics. Anything that one could find on another. You had Kenneth Starr after Clinton, you had everybody after Webb Hubble because he was a friend of Clinton's from Arkansas [chuckles] . . . We worked through Senator Bumpers and his office on that. It was real interesting. I remember that one trip to Washington that Perry and Danny and myself made and our goal was to get the attorney general to sign off on the prison itself. We met with Senator Bumpers and we came with a no answer. However, by the time we got back to Forrest City the announcement had been made that the attorney general Webb Hubble had signed off on it so that's how influential senator Bumpers was.

Prison Siting

p. w.: I started to work for the chamber of commerce there December 1, 1989, which is a Friday, and that was my first day on the job. On Saturday I left and went to New York to a trade show and I got home about a week later. And then, the next Monday, my second full week on the job, my assistant came in and said, "Bill Clinton is on the phone" . . . [dramatic pause] . . . And I'm immediately thinking that OK which one of my friends has set her up you know . . . so I answered the phone and low and behold it was Bill Clinton. Of course, he was governor of Arkansas at the time. I remember that was Monday, December 11, and he said, "Perry I've got two guys sitting here in my office that I want to send over to see you. Are you going to be there in the morning?" And I said, "Yes sir." "Well they want to come to talk to you about a federal prison." And I said, "OK" [chuckling].

And so the next morning these two gentlemen showed up. They were from a private enterprise. They were not part of the federal government, they were private developers trying to pursue a concept of building privately owned, contracted beds. One worked for an investment firm, and the other one was a prison consultant. Mike Phillips worked for the Llama group. The Llama group was a finance company that was an investment group that was owned by Alice Walton. The Llama's corporate office was in the McIlroy Bank building in Fayetteville. He was the finance guy and he was working with a gentleman named John Key from Memphis, he was a consultant and he had a prison background. I know he had worked for some construction companies that specialized in prison construction and had done some of that kind of stuff so he had a consulting group that he was working with and he and Mike got together and started talking about the concept [of prison beds] and that's how got to know them.

I've met Alice on several occasions, and it's never come up as a point of conversation or anything so I'm sure she did not know what Mike was even working on. She probably didn't even know it was going on, to be honest with you. Matter of fact I know she didn't know because I've met her since and up here right in the middle of them right now in Springdale.

So they had teamed up and they had some money behind them and they were trying to float this idea of building prison beds. The reason they came to Forrest City after talking to Bill Clinton was at that time he was chairman of the Lower Mississippi River Delta Commission, chartered to study the problems of the Delta to figure out how we could address them. Governors of the states [in the lower Mississippi Delta] served on the commission. President Bush, through the war on crime, had already dedicated funds to build several thousand beds of new prison cells.

The idea floated by these gentlemen was that the Lower Mississippi River Delta Commission should support money that the federal government had already allocated. They were trying to get the money already programmed and focus it in the Delta. They were trying to do it in a way that the Bureau of Prisons had never explored before which was through private contractors. Some states' prisons had been built this way, but there weren't federal prison facilities that were built that way. So they came in and talked to us. Obviously, we saw opportunity and great things ahead, but at the same time we saw a lot of political issues with doing that [prison building] and quite frankly didn't know anything about what we were looking at so we really had to start doing our research.

Bill Alexander was our congressman and Dale Bumpers and David Pryor were our senators at the time. Dale Bumpers was very important in the process because he was on the Senate Appropriations committee and was the key to it, quite frankly. And he took the same, in a very less direct way, but he took the same position that Alexander did. He would laugh about it and chuckle and he'd say, "now boys I'm just not sure I wanna get out in front of this you know? Man I'm telling you these voters are fickle now and if I get out in front of a prison it might hurt me." And so he was conscious of the political ramifications of supporting a prison and did not come around, quite frankly, until about, and I don't know exactly when it was, I know it was in the summer, so it was probably in the summer of '91, maybe it had to be the summer of '91.

The key to the whole thing from our standpoint was Congressman Jamie Whitten from Mississippi. And Congressman Whitten is not the congressman for Yazoo City, he's over in another part of Mississippi, but Jamie Whitten had been in the house for like forty-eight years and he was chairman of the house appropriations committee and he controlled the purse strings and was extremely influential, and the Mississippi delegation had been working him and a former congressman from Yazoo City named Webb Franklin. You remember Webb Franklin? . . . Webb Franklin was working for the Yazoo City delegation after he left Congress. And so he was working with Jamie Whitten and we were in the Saint Francis County Courthouse. Senator Bumpers was over there visiting with people and doing something in the courthouse that day and we set up a meeting with him and I got off the phone that morning and I was told that Jamie Whitten was going to support this. And he was going to be behind it and he was going to support the Bureau of Prisons building in Yazoo City and Forrest City.

And so I go to Bumpers that afternoon, and I think Buddy was in the room with me, we were in the law library outside the courtroom in the courthouse. And I just told Bumpers point blank would you support this if Jamie Whitten supports it? And he said well you're not going to get Jamie to support it. But what if he does? And he laughed and he said "If Jamie Whitten supports this, I'll support it." Now I already knew Jamie was going to support it. And I said well I think that may be happening. He said, "really!" And I says, "well I was told this morning that Congressman Whitten is going to support it." And he went, "well if he does then, I'll get behind it." In other words, he wasn't going to get in front of it unless he knew it was going to happen. And Jamie Whitten got in front of it and he knew it would happen.

So that's when his support changed and he agreed to get behind it. Then, quite honestly, the only question then was the Bureau of Prisons going to do it themselves, or were they going to use contractors. And we got the call out of the blue, we actually got it from the press, a Friday afternoon, I don't even remember when it was, June of 1992 I guess, got a call out of the blue one day from the media in Little Rock. The mayor got a call. And Danny Ferguson and said we just got a report that Bureau of Prisons is announcing Forrest City and others are getting federal prisons, there were three or four across the country they announced that day. And that was the first we heard that we were actually going to get it. So it was it big story on that Friday afternoon I remember that.

Prison Placement: Building the Growth Coalition

P. W.: So the year 1990 we were doing things like talking to our congressmen and senators and going to DC and visiting with them and trying to have them set up meetings with the Bureau of Prisons with us. And do some things like that and just letting the process play out. I think it was in mid-January of '90, a month or so into it, that we saw enough benefit where we thought we ought to explore and be open about it. So we had a public meeting up in the courtroom of our county courthouse and it was just jam- packed with people. And I mean it was a diverse group. And I mean it was across the board and it paralleled the community pretty well.

And that was the first chance to listen to a presentation about a project and give input and see what, tell us what you think. Just trying to find out what is the barometer of the community as far as politically is this something that could be supported and even be accomplished. And so we had the meeting and it was an overwhelming level of support.

Then there were some people there that quite frankly were either neutral when we didn't expect them to be, or were supportive . . . I can remember one person specifically, Larry Bryant as mayor, and Larry was head of the NAACP at the time there, and was a good guy . . . And he stood up and to paraphrase his comments, "I'm opposed to incarceration but we got to do something for the economy of the area," and I think what he said was, "I'm not going to oppose this. I really can't support it, but I'm not going to oppose this." I mean he just basically said I'm going to remain neutral in the process. I mean so when that happened when Larry said that that night, that's when I thought this might just actually be doable, this might actually catch some momentum here and this might accomplish something. Up until that point I really didn't know if it would or not. I knew if Larry came out and his leadership and the influence he had in the community if he'd a bowed up and just said this is not good this does not need to happen we'd probably not accomplished it in my opinion. And I don't think he support it but he saw the economics of it I think. . . . He had told me that.

And Larry was in a unique situation where he was talking to us and saying some things to us that he probably couldn't say publicly. And I was a little shocked when that happened, I thought the predominant, most of the people in the room that night were white and from the business community, was there very strongly and so you would expect the crowd to be skewed into the support [direction], or do something for the economy. You would expect that but we went out of our way to make sure that there was a cross section represented and Larry did us a favor by being there. And again I'm glad to hear him say that he supported it. I recall him being kind of neutral, but overall being supportive, but that public meeting he was kind of neutral. But to the point, nobody spoke up and said you cannot do this. This is the worst thing possible you could do to our community. Nobody ever said that.

B. B.: What we did, one thing we did here was . . . we visit with all of the groups in the community; the Kiwanis, the Lions Club, the Rotary Club, presented our program. We had letters supporting our project from every civic organization in town. We had support of the County Quorum Court. We had support of the city council. We had unanimous support you know from all of the elected officials.

Prison Placement: Securing the Land

P. W.: I left in October or so and they were four or five months into construction. While I was there we went through the environmental review process. We had to find the location. You know, they announce their coming, we didn't even have a site. I mean it was that, I mean we didn't have a site finalized. We had some preliminary sites we had looked at but we did not have a site finalized.

B. B.: You know, we had to negotiate, that was another negotiating process to get that land and play games so that somebody didn't hold us up. We had like three or four sites that we had selected rather than to select one site in the beginning. We knew where we wanted to be but we didn't let anybody know that because we knew that they'd run the price up . . . definitely not any of our residential housing areas it was away from that in all situations . . . they were not in any residential area they were outside of town like farmland but as close as possible to utilities so we could have the water and have everything accessible without additional costs . . . to minimize the costs. . . . Right, we talked to all of the local landowners individually. And I recall one conversation where this guy was trying to hold us up and started raising hell with me and Perry and [little snicker] when he finished his rant I looked at him and said, "we sure thank you, we didn't want your damn land anyway." . . . Actually he was not our first pick anyway.

P. W. Gazzola Vaccarro was the county judge at the time and he played less of a role than Danny and I did [regarding the land]. Quite frankly I felt that I carried the lead of the role of all three of us. But one of our city council men there in Forrest City was a farmer, one of the old guard on our city council, and I went to him and just a casual conversation and I said, "can you find, where would you look if you need to find 1,200 acres of land?" And he went, "to buy?" And I said, "yeah." And he went, "holy smokes I don't know. Let me think about that." And he came back and he said, "what's this for?" And of course he knew we were talking about a federal prison and he had put two and two together. I said, "well if this thing comes together I'm going to need about 1,200 acres to look at in order to get 800 acres contiguous." And he said, "let me think about that."

So he came back and he said, "I tell you who you need to talk to," and he had a map. He showed me who I should start talking to and we offered a pretty premium price on the land, and it's ironic how that all came about. Governor Clinton, as this process has started, I went over and met with him and his staff in Little Rock after we were three or four months into the process and as he's leaving the meeting he says, "well I'm not sure what we can do to help you, but if you get them to do it, we'll buy the land," is what he said. And that conversation was just very off the cuff but he said, "we'll put up a million dollars to buy the land, the state of Arkansas will."

So the state bought the land for the city. I bought the land from fourteen landowners. And simple math, I needed to buy 800 acres of land. I needed 800 acres minimum. Clinton had promised us a million bucks. So I divided 800 into a million that's $1,250 bucks an acre. So, what we did was went out and said would you be willing to sell your land for $1,250 an acre, and every one of 'em, with the exception of one, every one of 'em said, "yea!" Because it was going for about 700 bucks an acre at the time, or 750. And so we offered a very high premium price because of that. So we offered it to them and then when they said that they would sell then what we did is we asked for an option. A free look option for two years. And so they gave us basically for nothing, an option to buy their land for $1,250 an acre. So that's how we put it together.

We just started in the center and it was the largest tract. It was a landowner that had 80 acres I think and we just started working out from there trying to connect pieces . . . and we came up with 800 acres. It really was not hard to do because the price was significantly higher than the market rate. Keep in mind from the time we got the promise from Bill Clinton and we followed up on that and we got it done. By the time the environmental reviews were finished and the final decision to build has been done, Bill Clinton has now been elected president.

And so I've got a new governor and we get the word that it's a done deal and we get the site and we need to close on this land, Bill Clinton is already president. And Jim Guy Tucker is now the governor of Arkansas. And his staff went, "well how was he going to get a million dollars to you?" And I said, "I don't know, but he was." And so it was another drawn-out process because we had to go back and figure out under a new governor how to do it again. And I don't know what Clinton's plan was, we never got that far along with Clinton's plan.

The abstract and title company that handled it was there by the courthouse. I had an attorney there that drafted an option to purchase the land for me. He drafted just out of a textbook option and we took to the landowners

and then that closing company closed it all. And I can tell you it closed probably . . . on that property in spring of '93? It was all in one single land purchase
to the Forrest City Economic Development Corporation.

Toward a Model of Prison Placement

The existing literature on prison building focuses almost exclusively on siting or impact (Hooks et al. 2004; Hooks, Mosher, Rotolo, and Lobao 2010;
King, Mauer, and Huling 2003). With the exception of *Golden Gulag: Prison,
Surplus, Crisis, and Opposition in Globalizing California*, the processes of prison
siting and placement as reported are oversimplified as an incidental product
of racism in the criminal justice system (Davis 2003; Schlosser 1998; Street
2002). In this text, Ruth Wilson Gilmore (2007), provides a theoretical understanding of prison siting in a study encompassing state and local levels
of community impact by arguing that the prison boom in California came
about due to a relative surplus in financial capital, political capital, and rural
land. Gilmore offers a Keynesian approach in probing the political forces
driving prison expansion. She finds the surplus population of chronically
unemployed is used as grist for the mill in prison expansion. Using a textual
analysis, she meticulously traces how the political economy of Corcoran,
California, waxed and waned before and after prison building. In the process, rich history of the town's development is unearthed along with the
potential for a model of prison placement. Like Forrest City, Corcoran was
majority minority, rife with scandals involving chiefs of police, and beleaguered by unemployment, poverty, and dwindling farm/industrial economies. She also notes that, "Contrary to contemporary folklore, the towns
where prisons were sited, while deeply divided by class, are not all Anglo
communities (104)."

Nevertheless, there are several shortcomings of this approach. First, despite her rich data, Gilmore's analysis is guided by the existing normative
literature that overwhelmingly finds prison building as detrimental to communities. Instead of focusing on what causes prison placement and how
prison building impacts communities, her analysis is compromised by
focusing on the world as it should be—free of prisons. This angle is based
on an idealized world where prisons are only bad. As such, any benefits
gained by Corcoran from prison building are bookended by real (or potential) detriments. Granted, this work is done in the vein of scholar activism,
so a strong normative bend is expected. Still, this slant comes at a price, and
that price is an incomplete view of the prison building process.

Second, because Gilmore's primary unit of analysis is the state, her analysis centers on prison siting. Despite having detailed historical data as a backdrop for a locally contested NIMBY versus PIMBY battle, her treatment of the placement process portrays local officials as conduits of surplus labor and land succumbing to neoliberal policies and shifts in global economic market against the better intentions of local activists that oppose prison building. Like her, I initial found this a valorous approach. How triumphant it would be to bring down the so-called PIC! However, local decision makers' preferences are key determinants of prison placement. Preferences are just as important in explaining placement as contextual factors that shape decisions. Unlike Gilmore, my model introduces an intervention emphasizing the role of local political actors in prison building.

Third, Gilmore's analysis is centered on California. Although California currently employs the most correction officers, with roughly 11 percent of the 450,000 nationally, and was only recently clearly outnumbering Texas in total number of prisoners, it is not in the top five prison building states over the boom. This is somewhat surprising given that Gilmore claims California is the largest prison system in history. Furthermore, California garners the lion's share of attention of research on mass imprisonment and the prison boom. While much of the attention on California is well deserved, a number of scholars (Barker 2009; Gottschalk 2014; Lynch 2010; Lynch 2011; Schoenfeld 2011) urge us to examine punishment at the state level to comprehend (and dismantle) the multiple regimes responsible for mass imprisonment. For example, Oklahoma has gone virtually unnoticed in the discourse on mass imprisonment and the prison boom despite building more prisons in its history than California. This demonstrates the disjuncture in conventional wisdom between imprisonment patterns and prison building.

Mass imprisonment, however, is not the sole cause of prison proliferation. If mass imprisonment is the "supply" side of the penal-industrial complex, prison proliferation represents the "demand." While prison "demand" is undoubtedly linked to economic development, I have also demonstrated its link to stigma management. As a prototypical prison town with a burgeoning rural ghetto, Forrest City can teach us a great deal about prison placement. By combining a national analysis of all prison towns coupled with an ethnographic case study of a prison town that built during the height of the prison boom, I improve on Gilmore by teasing out the differences between siting, placement, and impact along with the multiple intersections for success/failure in each process. Here I suggest a framework from this case study illustrating several other factors leading to, as well as impeding, prison placement. These factors include:

1. Prison demand is based on local and nonlocal preferences. Without local demand, state and federal officials fear that there will be resistance against the prison leading to higher cost negotiations.
2. Neighborhood Narrative Frames of salvation or advancement justify prison demand. This suggests that if there are NNFs of pollution and chaos, prison placement is less likely.
3. Symbolic distance in the discourse of siting attenuates the contagion fears from the geographic proximity of a LULU, thereby reducing sentiments of NIMBY.
4. Structural (not individual) racism exacerbates economic deprivation and stigma concerns fueling demand. These concerns are used to rationalize the prisons as a stigma management strategy.

Understanding prison placement this way requires that we think about the process from the perspective of communities most likely to build. Lessons gleaned from the case of Forrest City can also be used to rethink, challenge, and extend current development theories to build a model of prison placement. To this end, in working toward a model of prison placement I borrow from a variety of literatures on economic development and environmental justice. Beyond the presence of a rural ghetto, the bid to secure a prison depends on support from local whites and the cooperation—or at least acquiescence—of local black/Latino leadership. In the introductory chapter I proposed a model in which these interlocking interests form the basis for a growth coalition between white elites and race leaders (Logan and Molotch 1987) to manage stigma. While I am not suggesting that these otherwise contentious groups are sharing power, my case study suggests that race leaders are co-opted for their public support. For NIMBY to become PIMBY, race leaders must join (or at least fail to oppose) the growth coalition of white elites pursuing a prison. The four points below are *factors* that affect the development of the model or how it plays out.

1. Prison Demand Is Based on Local and Nonlocal Preferences. Without Local Demand, State and Federal Officials Fear That There Will Be Resistance against the Prison Leading to Higher Cost Negotiations.

Forrest City's signage publicly celebrates Congressman Bill Alexander and Senator Dale Bumpers as the champions of the FCFCF. The first-person narratives of Perry Webb and Buddy Billingsley illustrate how these federal representatives became unwilling heroes. Further evidence from the *Forrest*

City Times-Herald demonstrates how a groundswell of local demand pushed key political figures into supporting siting. In an article titled, "Area Legislative Delegation Delivers Support to Prison," state legislators representing Saint Francis County supported a resolution directed toward Bill Alexander and Dale Bumpers. According to this article from the summer of 1990, Senator Clarence Bell, Senator Ken Ingram, Representative Pat Flanagin, and Representative Bob McGinnis all endorsed the following:

> WHEREAS, the Forrest City area is one of the areas selected as a possible site for establishment of the facility in the area; and
>
> WHEREAS, as a result of the closing of various industrial facilities in the Forrest City area in recent years, Forrest City currently has the highest unemployment rate in the state; and
>
> WHEREAS, the construction and operation of the proposed federal prison facility would provide 300 temporary construction jobs and 250 permanent jobs in the Forrest City area; and
>
> WHEREAS, the Lower Mississippi Delta Development Commission, which is studying ways to improve the economy of the delta area, apparently has or will endorse and support the establishment of the federal prison facility in the Forrest City area; and
>
> WHEREAS, the establishment of the federal prison facility in the Forrest City area would not only provide employment opportunities in the area, it would stimulate business and promote the overall economy of the Forrest City area.
>
> NOW THEREFORE, BE IT RESOLVED, That the undersigned members of the Arkansas General Assembly hereby recommend and express their full support for the construction and operation of the proposed federal prison facility in the area of Forrest City.

Had the federal legislators already been on board with the project, this resolution might have been perfunctory. But, of course, they weren't. At the time, Bill Alexander was facing a reelection bid from Mike Gibson, an attorney from Osceola, who supported the prison. Alexander undoubtedly felt pressure from below to sign on to the resolution, despite the apprehension he expressed to Perry Webb over prison building at that time. Gibson widely advertised his support for the prison, telling the *Forrest City Times-Herald*, "It's good for the people, I'm for it. No waffling . . . this appears to be a tremendous economic opportunity. . . . It's obvious the people of Forrest City are united and want this facility and the badly needed jobs that come with it. I'm glad to be working with the citizens of Forrest City—not against them—to help bring those badly needed jobs." Although this statement about "not wanting to inject politics" into it is patently ridiculous given that he was campaigning, it is worthy of mentioning here to illustrate how vital public works projects can be during elections cycles. Just as Congressman Alexander initially stood against the prison because of his fear that it might cost him votes, Gibson raising the issue of supporting prison building during the campaign forced Alexander to reevaluate his position.

The timing of Gibson's support could not have been more ideal for the local operatives seeking to leverage support—he endorsed the prison immediately following the pivotal community meeting at the courthouse. His comments sounded like a direct criticism of Bill Alexander's inaction on the issue of siting. Without the leverage of an opponent's support in an election year, a local groundswell of nongovernmental organization and elected officials, and the sway of Senator Bumpers, Congressman Alexander might not have supported the FCFCF. Absent local congressional support, the BOP most likely would not have sited the facility in Forrest City.

Prisons, unlike most LULUs, require the political support of the local municipality and at least the state government where they are to be erected. This presents multiple levels of potential NIMBY opposition, during both the siting and the placement process. If we are to understand prison proliferation, we must therefore understand the political economy of prison building beyond the local community. In Forrest City's case, Webb and Billingsley spoke of potential opposition at each step in the building process, from the specific location of the prison within the town to the congressional districts in which the facility would be erected. NIMBY-ism in prison building, then, is not just about the immediate location of the facility. NIMBY can be a reaction across social, political, and economic lines, and can be manifested by multiple actors across multiple fields.

In contrast to the belief that prison building decisions are entirely in the hands of state or federal officials, the case of Forrest City shows that local politics matter, even in building a federal facility. Separate and apart from the multiple levels of NIMBY, a lack of excitement and support from local officials for such a large public works project sends the wrong message to state or federal officials/agencies making the siting decisions. Decoupling placement from siting allows us to understand that prison building is not just about push or pull factors, but the multiple ways and levels at which these factors play out. These factors both shape, and are shaped, by the context of reception for the potential facility. Therefore, siting is not inevitable—prison building is ultimately based on local "demand."

2. Neighborhood Narrative Frames of Salvation or Advancement Justify Prison Demand. This Suggests That If There Are NNFs of Pollution and Chaos, Prison Placement Is Less Likely.

The prior chapter provides some evidence of Forrest City's citizens' objections to the FCFCF. While none of these were salient enough for individuals to start a NIMBY campaign, these concerns could theoretically be used to motivate groups and key actors against placement. For example, although not widespread, some residents raised concerns over the proximity of the FCFCF to their homes. This is why the campaign to build support for the prison was carefully crafted and run to assuage fears small and large. To manage the campaign, local elites use neighborhood narrative frames focused on saving, fixing, and advancing Forrest City. These fears ranged from citizens' concerns over the potential for prisoner breakouts to politicians' concerns over voters' support. Led by Perry Webb, the winning team in Forrest City was effective in managing both. Given the fickle nature of US politics, elected officials are sensitive to issues large and small that can cause voters to turn on them. Realistically, recalls are not a danger in Arkansas, but politicians do fear that they will not be returned to office. This is a key lesson from Congressman Bill Alexander's cautious approach to prison siting in Forrest City. To Alexander, support for a prison seemed an obvious way to alienate his constituency. All told, these fears suggest that NIMBY is the default position of communities toward LULUs.

This political reality is supported by the scholarly literature on LULUs. Most of the scholarly attention to LULUs has come from environmental justice scholars and has traditionally focused on examining the multiple ways NIMBY opposition is expressed (or should be) within the political economy of locales (Bullard 2000; Pellow 2000). Given the stigma of prisons, they are characterized as LULUs (Schlosser 1998; King, Mauer, and Huling 2003; Gilmore 2007). Recently, however, a number of scholars have produced studies of how communities come to accept a LULU (Bullard 2000; Davidson and Anderton 2000; McAdam, Boudet, Davis, Orr, Scott, and Levitt 2010; Pellow 2000; Mohai and Saha 2006). Both perspectives view the issue of community mobilization through their reactions to siting decisions (Bullard 2000; Pellow 2000; McAdam, Boudet, Davis, Orr, Scott, and Levitt 2010; McAdam and Boudet 2012). This framing emerged largely in reaction to the growth machine literature (Bullard 2000), which portrayed the urban growth machine as PIMBY for PIMBY's sake. Critics of the growth machine found that key actors within the political economy of municipalities defaulted toward "yes" for any type of economic development, regardless of whether the type of development was dangerous or desirable (Logan and Molotch 1987). The environmental justice literature has traditionally placed poor rural and urban communities in an oppositional default NIMBY position, regardless of the type of development.

While the environmental justice (EJ) literature is indispensable to explaining NIMBY, it is not enough to explain PIMBY. Instead, by bringing together classic elements of the growth machine with the EJ literature a new theoretical model for understanding prison proliferation can be forged. At the core of this model are elites using narratives NNFs of salvation or advancement in justifying prison demand across a sustained Please in My Backyard (PIMBY) campaign.

3. Symbolic Distance in the Discourse of Siting Attenuates the Contagion Fears from the Geographic Proximity of a LULU, Thereby Reducing Sentiments of NIMBY.

Having established that towns do not simply accept prisons, I assert that evidence here indicates that even when towns want prisons, they may want to keep them at arm's lengths. Geography matters. Consider, for example, Buddy Billingsley's assertion that local opposition to the prison was based solely on the potential of residents' being able to see the facility from individual backyards. New prisons are generally built on the edge of town or in unincorporated areas just outside a town's border. The average prison town has an area of 2.13 square miles; on average, prisons are located 2.45 miles from the center of town. From this perspective, prison building cannot be seen merely as a function of structural constraints like geography or economics. Fully understanding prison proliferation requires grappling with the local culture of a prison town to trace how people make sense of prison building. A new model of prison placement needs to account for the role of culture.

4. Structural (Not Individual) Racism Exacerbates Economic Deprivation and Stigma Concerns Fueling Demand. These Concerns Are Used to Rationalize the Prisons as a Stigma Management Strategy.

The role of racism in continued racial disparities in the criminal justice system is undeniable. Recall that Paul Street (2002) suggests the prison boom is a form of "correctional Keynesianism . . . fed by the rising 'market' of Black offenders as a job and tax-base creator for predominantly White communities that are generally far removed from urban minority concentrations" (36). As previously demonstrated, these suppositions are not based in the empirical reality of prison building. Despite data that show that prisons towns have higher percentages of black and Latino residents than typical rural communities, the dominant narrative on prison building remains enshrouded in a cloak of racial paranoia. Racism is, of course, central to the narrative of prison building in the United States, as Robert Chrisman (2013) explains: "All black prisoners, therefore, are political prisoners, for their condition derives from the political inequity of black people in America. A black prisoner's crime may or may not have been a political action against the state, but the state's action against him is always political. This knowledge, intuitively known and sometimes transcribed into political terms, exists within every black prisoner" (3).

Chrisman originally made this claim in 1971, but it still resonates deeply with scholars and activists seeking to end the so-called prison-industrial complex. But what is the role of racism in prison placement in communities like Forrest City? Although racial disadvantage plays a dominant role in prison building, placement is not simply a by-product of local racist practices, nor is prison placement a by-product of the racism inherent in the disproportionate mass imprisonment of people of color. If rural town officials seeking prisons are in fact motivated by conscious or subconscious racism, they are extremely hard-working racists, because the practice seems extraordinarily indirect. Evidence for racism in prison placement is so obscure and tertiary that it is difficult to argue that it is directly present at all. This is not to say that rural white elites and race leaders' desires for prisons are in no way racist. I am suggesting, however, that even if political elites have racist tendencies, their preferences are not the dominant motives driving the extensive work needed to secure a prison facility in a given municipality. Structural racism does not depend on actors' intent, but there is nonetheless a difference between structural and individual racism, and the lack of the latter in prison placement is worth pointing out. Of course racism is the dominant stratifying force within the criminal justice system. The more interesting and complicated questions involve what role race or racism plays in the process.

Earlier chapters have demonstrated how local racist practices in communities like Forrest City produce rural ghettos. Practices resulting in residential segregation and concentrated poverty should be considered primary effects of racism. Although I argue concentrated disadvantage (for example, the rural ghetto) is central to understanding prison proliferation, the racist practices involved in creating the ghetto are not equivalent to those taken in acquiring a prison. There are elements of exploitation along racial lines in prison placement, but they do not follow the dominant racial narrative explaining the prison boom.

Race and racism also play primary roles in establishing the economic conditions that make prison placement an attractive choice. Tomaskovic-Devey and Roscigno (1997) offer the elite-race interaction model to explain how the local political economy of rural towns in the post–Jim Crow South influences uneven development. They argue that in towns like Forrest City, "where elites are homogenous relative to some organizational base and traditionally dependent on racial exploitation and division they will foster a racially divided, impoverished working class, and traditional relations of production" (Tomaskovic-Devey and Roscigno 1997, 571). The primary method of exploitation in this dynamic model is through racial divisions that result in increases in black poverty, decreases in white poverty, and an overall widening of the black/white poverty ratio. Recall from earlier chapters that black poverty has increased in Forrest City as white flight increased and relative levels of white poverty decreased. Moreover, the presence of racial antagonism and division between white elites and race leaders was a major problem assessed in the image survey. Consider Perry Webb's comments from above, "I knew if Larry came out and his leadership and the influence he had in the community if he'd a bowed up and just said this is not good this does not need to happen we'd probably not accomplished it in my opinion." The experience of Forrest City demonstrates that if there is any group that could sway white elites against prison building, it is race leaders. Without their tacit support, the FCFCF would not have been constructed. In the case of the FCFCF, the elite-race interaction model can be extended to the growth machine to understand how actors who may otherwise have a contentious relationship come together for a common purpose. Incorporating a combined approach focusing on sets of actors allows a more nuanced rationale for prison building.

Conclusion

The discussion of how the FCFCF came to be complicates existing models of prison placement. Disentangling prison demand (prison placement) from the willingness to accept prisons (prison siting) in rural communities presents theoretical and practical implications. First, we can further our understanding of rural community structure and function by rethinking neighborhoods in the rural context (Eason 2010; Sampson 2012; Wacquant 2001). Second, we can also build new theories of how communities conduct image management alongside stigmatized institutions (Combessie 2002). Third, we can revisit political theories of community structure and change (Bullard 2000; Mohai and Saha 2005; Tomaskovic-Devey and Roscigno 1997). And last but not least, we need to rethink the category of LULU to understand that one community's trash is another community's treasure. Having traced the causes and process of prison placement, the remainder of the book will now examine how prisons impact local residents, once in place.

PART TWO

Prison Impact

SIX

The Prison in My Backyard: Reconsidering Impact

We had worked hard on the front end [to get the prison] . . . And after it came, we kinda got pushed to the side like everything else. They [white elites] needed us to be unified and that goes back to that unification I was talking about. . . . They want to be unified here and then when something comes, still not be inclusive.

—Larry Bryant

The nascent literature on the prison boom almost always portrays prison building as having negative impacts on both urban communities of color (Drake 2011; Gilmore 2007; Schlosser 1998) and rural communities in general (Besser and Hanson 2004; Gilmore 2007; Hooks et al. 2004; Hooks et al. 2010; Huling 2001; King, Mauer, and Huling 2003; Schlosser 1998). Even case studies of the most obvious positive economic impact from prison—tourism in the guise of family visits—focus on the costs to the traveling families without mentioning the potential benefits to the impoverished rural communities (Christian 2005). In general, we have thought less about where prisons go and the impact of those prisons for the towns they end up in than we have about the prisoners they house. And even those few studies that have attempted to gauge local perceptions of impacts have started from the assumption that the prison is a nuisance for the town where it is sited (Bonds 2012; Campo Nation 2006; Engel 2007; Morell 2012).

The prison building literature, in other words, focuses on why towns don't want prisons and how useless and/or harmful prisons are to the political economy of local towns once built. Thus far this manuscript has focused on exploring why and how prison placement occurs. The second half of this book focuses on prison impact. I define prison impact as the economic, political, and social benefits/costs for a host community resulting from prison placement. This chapter addresses this problem through the perspective of locals—that is, how prison town residents understand and define how a prison impacts their community. Using the voice of locals to interpret prison impact illuminates the multiple ways that positionality, timing, and context of reception influences the perceptions of local residents.

Understanding locals' perceptions of prison impact matters not only because community climate shapes future relationships between the institution and the community, but also because the political economy of most prison towns resembles the elite-race interaction model (Tomaskovic-Devey and Roscigno 1997). As discussed in earlier chapters, the elite-race interaction model explains why underdevelopment is prevalent in communities suffering from racial tension. In the case of Forrest City, I extend the logic from the elite-race interaction model to elucidate how both the context of reception and iterative interactions between the facility and the community shape how locals understand prison impact. I conclude the chapter by discussing what we can learn from Forrest City in moving toward a model of prison impact.

Thinking about Prison Impact in Forrest City

One way to address the impact of a prison is simply by asking cui bono: who benefits? The question of benefit (or harm) depends on what outcomes are being measured, when the measurement occurs, and how the community is defined. Each of these potential measurements is, in turn, defined by how the question is asked. The economic impact of a prison might differ during initial construction, during later stages of building, and after the prison opens. Alternatively, one might attempt to investigate the political, rather than the economic, impact of prisons. Are the deals cut to get the prisons built repaid, and if so how? Do communities push back against politicians after prisons are sited? In this case, did residents in Saint Francis County push back against their officials for building a prison?

Positionality

Ultimately, a local's understanding of prison impact will be shaped by his or her own position—race, class, gender, sexual orientation, social standing, and role in the polity. On the whole, those in Forrest City view the prison positively. Somewhat surprisingly, no one believed the FCFCF impacted the town negatively. I nevertheless found a few residents, like Mayor Bryant, who were disappointed by the lack of development delivered by the prison, particularly given how it was sold as a panacea for the town. The gap between promise and reality may have been more apparent to Mayor Bryant than to most in Forrest City, because of his involvement with the hard work of letter writing, meetings, and lobbying of federal officials and agencies necessary to secure the Forrest City Federal Correctional Facility. Despite the firm support of race leaders for the prison, he understood that support for the prison in the broader African American community was tenuous. To many blacks, the possibility of benefiting from prison building represents a moral and philosophical quagmire of consciously contributing to their own disproportionate mass imprisonment. While Larry Bryant held similar feelings about racial disparities in imprisonment, he understood that maintaining the facade of unanimous African American community support for the prison was important to the prison acquisition campaign. His tacit approval (or lack of opposition) from the unique position he occupied helped pave the way for the arrival of the prison and meant that he had a personal, reputational investment in the promise of the prison. This investment proved strategic in providing evidence to the white elite that he could compromise for the overall benefit of the town.

Forrest City has a history of activism linked to the ongoing racial tensions in the town. Given this history, a lack of unanimity among local elites in "demanding" the prison would have created roadblocks. For instance, the more time/effort Buddy Billingsley, Danny Ferguson, Perry Webb, and Gazzola Vaccaro would have to spend building local support for the prison, the less they would have to negotiate with local landowners and federal agencies. Delays or changes in the negotiation process could have proven catastrophic for their bid to bring a prison to Forrest City. Federal legislators and agencies could have become more difficult to persuade or might have withdrawn their support altogether. And if local landowners held out for higher prices, the city of Forrest City and the Saint Francis Chamber of Commerce might have been offered lower payments, undoubtedly complicating local support for the facility.

While Larry Bryant originally supported construction of the facility, today he is less than thrilled with the prison's actual deliverables. In hindsight, he feels like he was sold a dream by white elites bamboozling blacks into supporting the arrival of the facility. The prison was supposed to bring a windfall of profits to city coffers. Bryant admits that he never placed much faith in the prison, despite white elites billing it as a cure-all. With a heavy heart he declares that the prison only produced marginal economic benefits to the city. During our interview I challenged this assertion, pointing to the recent state-of-the-art recreation center and other infrastructural improvements, including sidewalks. He got up from behind his desk to poke his head out of his office and asked an assistant for budget figures. In an authoritative tone, he told me to just to sit and wait, because he has something to show me. Then, very deliberately, he walked over to me and pointed to the paper he was handed, showing line items of revenues. His voice and body are animated as he declares that the revenues for the recreation center, sidewalks, police, and fire station improvements came from the so-called penny tax, a 1 percent sales tax. According to Mayor Bryant, "the 'penny tax' has nothing to do with revenues from the prison!" He believes that the benefits of the FCFCF have not lived up to the projections, in part because the new bypass circumvents downtown and the other central commercial areas by Highway 1. Despite his strong feelings about what the prison did not deliver, within Forrest City he is clearly in the minority. He was by far the most negative race leader in his assessment of the prison; both race leaders and white leaders like David Dunn disagree with his assessment.

Even after the arrival of the initial minimum-security wing of the FCFCF, racial antagonism continued. Mayor Bryant found this continuity of racial antagonism especially disheartening. In his telling, these tensions were most evident during his failed attempts to intervene in the housing market during the next phase of prison expansion, which included a medium-security wing. Stakeholders in Forrest City all now agree that they had missed opportunities in the realty market during the initial phase of prison construction. Few, however, could clearly articulate why. In an effort to avoid repeating this mistake during the second phase of construction, Mayor Bryant had tried to meet with local bankers, mortgage lenders, and realtors to say, "hey let's put something together and y'all put something together so that we can have something in place prior to construction, the completion of this construction out here so people could live in Forrest City." But despite his repeated attempts to do so, he could never convene a meeting with the relevant parties before construction on the medium-security wing began. Despite the need to capitalize on the additional prison facility, Mayor Bryant believed the continued racial tensions from his election in 1997 played a role in the inability to get local stakeholders to the table before the medium wing opening in 2004. For Mayor Bryant, the prison represents another way that the white elites in Forrest City played exclusionary political games. These exclusionary games, from his perspective, were a continued source of racial tension that hampered economic development overall. Racial tensions can both be exacerbated by the building process and limit the economic impact of a prison.

Understanding Mayor Bryant's opinion on racial tensions also speaks to the context of reception (the social, political, and economic milieu) for prison building. The context of reception can vary along multiple axes and raises important issues of in-group and out-group comparison, boundary maintenance, and the appropriate level of analysis by which to measure prison impact. In the case of the FCFCF, we could measure prison impact across each neighborhood within Forrest City, the towns, the county, surrounding counties, or distance from the facility. Interpretations of prison impact can change based on any of these analytical choices.

Most in Forrest City didn't have the prison on the forefront of their minds. Although residents were conscious of the FCFCF, the prison did not have a meaningful/substantial imprint on their daily lives. My questions about what was it like to have a prison in town usually elicited a moment of reflection from interviewees, who would often begin by talking about the minimal contact or involvement they had with the facility. For all their shopping in local stores, church attendance, and participation in civic organizations, FCFCF corrections officers and administrators went mostly unobserved. For the most part, Forrest City residents have had very little (positive or negative) involvement with the prison.

Overall, when asked if there were any downsides to having a prison, most respondents answered with a terse "no." Some, like Buddy Billingsley, muddled through their answer by acknowledging their position in relation to the prison acquisition process. Like most residents, Billingsley could find no real faults to have come from building the prison. Taking a deep breath and an exaggerated pause, he answered:

> You know . . . I can't think of any honestly but you know . . . I might be, since it's part of my project, I might be a little biased there but in my opinion, I can't think of any. I . . . you know . . . we have a lot people come into the community to visit [the prison] and crime has not been a problem in that regard. *The crime that's here would be here with or without the prison* . . . You know I see people [corrections officers] in their uniforms at Wal-Mart, driving down the street, sometimes in their yards, coming and going to work, knowing that they have good jobs, and that they're contributing the economy of the community. And to me I can't see any downside to it.

One could argue that a resident's outlook on the impact of the prison is purely a function of his or her own relation to it. Nevertheless, Buddy Billingsley's obvious biases do not preclude his assertion that the prison has been good for Forrest City. His acknowledgment of his jaundiced eye may also give him a perspective on the limits of what prison building can cure.

He mentions the local crime problem in passing. Despite actively framing the prison as a cure-all, he concedes that it is not, really. In fact, his cursory discussion of crime highlights what prisons cannot do—solve the community's crime problems.

Timing of Measures

Most prison studies measure impact after the opening of the facility (Hooks et al. 2004; Hooks et al. 2010). Examining impact from the informed perspective of prison towns, however, offers multiple moments from which to consider impact. I learned about the different phases and types of impact through the experiences and opinions of residents of Forrest City. Once a community decides to welcome a prison, the impact may be measured almost immediately. Acquiring the land requires a significant amount of capital expenditures by the state or local municipality. In the prior chapter, Perry Webb detailed how locals struck a deal with state officials to pay for the land they were acquiring from landowners. Payment for the land is the first major jolt to the local economy prisons provide.

Perry Webb admits that he left Forrest City prior to the foundation of the buildings being laid, or, as he put it, when "they were just stirring dirt." He nevertheless offered multiple ways of thinking about the investment that occurred before the prison's gates officially opened. Perry explained that a period of environmental review precedes each phase of building. The environmental review for the first phase of building in Forrest City happened eighteen months before construction began. At this point, the prison had already made a sizable impact on local banking. Perry maintains, "they [BOP] were dropping a pretty sizable amount of change into our local banks . . . there was about five million dollars that came in just to do the environmental review and construction office. That was deposited through the First National Bank of Eastern Arkansas. That local banking account was used to do all the preliminary stuff. None of the salaries [for facility employees] or any of that came out of that but that was for hiring civil engineers and consultants and those types of things. That was all pushed through those accounts. They had a construction office there six months before I left." These dollars flowed into Forrest City outside of the public eye, providing a significant boost to local bank holdings.

Subcontractors also profited during this preconstruction phase. For instance, Perry recalls that a local company out of Little Rock, Cromwell Engineering and Architects, was hired to design the first building. According to

Perry, the contract for design was somewhere around twelve million dollars. According to the BOP, the overall project (building the minimum, medium, and maximum facilities) would cost between 180 to 300 million. Perry contends that the FCFCF was, at that time, the largest project ever awarded to Cromwell. Federal contract awards to engineering and architectural firms frequently cross state boundaries. While this portion of the project did not directly benefit Forrest City, it did benefit the home state.

Although the plan was to build three facilities (minimum, medium, and high security), to date the Bureau of Prisons has only built two of the three in Forrest City, with the first unit costing around $120 million and the second around $40 million. Perry points out that the BOP was preparing contracts and hiring people even before the BOP broke ground. At the same time, he also acknowledges that the jobs really hit after he left for Springdale.

Outside of a select group of race leaders and white elites, most interviewees did not consider the timing or the magnitude of impact in assessing the prison's role. For example, because of the timing of the Hampton Inn's construction, many residents assume that the development was an immediate response to the town being awarded the prison. Although I could never verify that the hotel was built primarily to capture business from the prison, the perception was prevalent—despite the fact that members of the elite vehemently refuted this claim. Whether or not the prison spurred the building of the Hampton Inn is not as important as the larger questions raised by exploring local perceptions around the issue. For instance, do prisons spur other types of development? If so, how much of any new development is due to the presence of the prisons?

Connecting the Prison and the Community

Aside from making peace with the inherent risk of a prison break, nearly all respondents had a favorable opinion of how the prison impacted their town. To find criticism, I had to probe deeper and ask specifics on how many jobs the prison created or how it affected the economy overall. While most people did not find the prison problematic, some believed the prison did not hire enough locals. They believed that, while the prison did bring people to the area, most new residents settled in Wynne or other surrounding communities instead of Forrest City. When pressed, their comments focused on the role of the warden in determining impact, the role of the prisoners in shaping the town's demographics, and reservations not so much about whether the prison provided a positive impact, but the degree to which it did.

Impact Starts at the Top

Based on his experience, Mayor Bryant believes that the warden holds the keys to how a prison will impact a community. That being said, his view is clouded by the carousel of wardens changing almost annually since the prison's opening in 1997. Mayor Bryant divulges:

> We've seen wardens come and we've seen wardens go. It depends on the leadership of the warden how that prison will interact with the city. The past warden, Warden Morrison, prior to Jeter, lived in Forrest City. He's the only warden that has ever lived in Forrest City. He was a member of the chamber board of directors. He was interactive throughout the whole community. When he departed, Warden Jeter came and he lived in Marion, Arkansas (which is forty-five minutes to an hour drive from here) and he did some things in the community but for the most part, he was an outsider. And then the Warden thereafter him Linda ah . . . I can't think of her last name that tells you what I know about that issue. If she walked in the door, you and I might remember her . . . I've seen her about three times. . . . The first warden was black and he just opened it up. I think he lived in Lee County. And then there was a white one, and then Morrison. . . . He worked with everybody, blacks, whites, everybody. He was out there. He worked toward getting the school millage. He was a proactive person rather than reactive. You didn't have to ask him, he could see something and he would want to fix it.

Mayor Bryant felt that Warden Morrison set the tone for prison employees' relationship with the community by example. By living in the community, patronizing local restaurants, and being involved in civic organizations, Morrison provided incentives for his employees to do the same. Of the six or seven wardens that served the FCFCF during Bryant's tenure as mayor, he recalls only one that lived in Forrest City. Bryant drew a stark contrast between Morrison's behavior and that of the other wardens: "When Warden Morrison was here, you had the interaction in the prison even with the personnel. *See it starts at the top,* if the top doesn't interact with the citizens of the city, then you don't have the interaction."

Bryant also stressed the potential contribution of prison labor to the town—a benefit that disappeared with the end of Morrison's tenure:

> With Warden Morrison they worked with the youth organizations. They worked with the chamber of commerce, they had programs, they invited people out, and they were doing things. I don't know if the rules changed warden so on

and so forth. It got a little more difficult to get prisoners [to do projects]. At one time you could do it this way and they changed rules and different things, organizations that had used prisoners to help. The paperwork got to be overbearing and special training and this that and the other. Not a whole lot of organizations use the prisons to my knowledge as we did during the Morrison era.

The connection to the warden made prison labor a benefit to Forrest City. Although the projects were limited in scope and tenure, the mayor could use prisoners for pet projects, like repairing the high school roof. But this type of direct, tangible benefit is based on a community's relationship to the warden. Later administrations would not allow prisoners to participate if they felt the costs (for example, security risks) outweighed the benefits of a program (rehabilitation or skill building).

Despite Bryant's assessment, facility security, not community building, is the warden's key duty. Still, it is safe to say that a warden the town regarded as "progressive" would encourage community engagement by their staff. To local political leaders, Warden Morrison's ability to see a problem and fix it, as he did in supporting an increase in the school millage, is evidence of his progressive approach. For Mayor Bryant, the Warden's public support of the millage was key in helping to push it through the local political process. This effort forever distinguishes Morrison as an "insider" while the other wardens continue as "outsiders." Bryant resumes:

> It starts at the top. If the person at the top doesn't live in the community, doesn't socialize, doesn't go to church in the community, doesn't go eat in the community at the local establishments and so forth. The ones [wardens] that are there for the most part live out of town. They don't eat lunch at the local establishments. The employees don't eat at the local establishments.
>
> When Warden Morrison was here, he came down town and eat over at the little Greasy Spoon right over there, William's, and you could see him two three times a week. You could find him there. You could find the mayor there. You could find the police chief. You could find the postmaster there. Four of the top black leaders in the town.

This comment reveals a vital insight into Bryant's relationship with Warden Morrison. Morrison's tenure coincided with a period during which an informal network of black leaders all held significant political power in town. Access to the warden provided Bryant with an extended network of power and the prestige of rubbing shoulders with a black federal official.

Conversely, Bryant's lack of familiarity with the current warden is evident in his inability to accurately recall her name, and in his claim that he doubts that he could recognize her if she walked through the door. I informed him that I had learned she lived in Wynne. Because he believed that Wynne was a primary rival of Forrest City, he did not take kindly to this news:

> The prison could be a great thing. Hopefully, when we get a new warden, the new warden will live in Forrest City. The new warden will interact with, not only with the mayor but with county government and will interact with the chamber of commerce and we can sell Forrest City to that person as being a good town . . . it makes a difference if the warden lives in the city where the prison is, it influences the workers to live in the city or shop in the city and join organizations within the city so forth and it makes the city better . . .
>
> Conversely, if the warden lives up there in Wynne and shops in Wynne and has those you know allegiances there, you get what I'm saying. . . . But we missed a lot with the loss of Morrison 'cause he worked with everybody, he lived in the community. . . . Not to say he did anything against any other outside communities, he helped them too. I think they worked; they started under him helping with Jimmy Carter's group that builds houses, Habitat for Humanity.

Warden Morrison's tenure at FCFCF left an indelible mark on Mayor Bryant and set a standard that seems difficult for others to meet. However, it is not implausible/unrealistic for local elected officials to expect their federal prison to be represented in town as more than a big property owner. Warden Morrison's tenure, during which time the prison was an institutional actor (Taub, Taylor, and Dunham 1984) influencing social organizations, and participating in the local political life represents a golden era of prison impact for leaders in Forrest City.

The prison undeniably provides a level of stability to Forrest City. At the same time, the constant turnover in the prison's administration has created a fair amount of turbulence for the community. The comings and goings of top personnel means the relations between the institutional and community leadership remains fluid. Larry Bryant best explains the contradiction of simultaneous stability and fluidity in prison impact: "It's been a lot of turnovers since with the personnel out there. For promotional purposes, you want to be upward mobile, and so you have to move. . . . That's part of it. The leadership is not only in the top, all the way through." Mayor Bryant's narrative highlights the salience of the warden in determining the relationship between the prison and its host community. From his perspective, this relationship is the most important determinant of prison impact. His argument that a prison "can be a great thing" follows this logic. Although Mayor Bryant was the only person to offer extended, informed opinions about the role of the warden in determining the prison's impact on the town, his comments nevertheless provide a way to think about the role of the institutional leadership in shaping prison impact.

A "bad" warden can also lead the prison away from having meaningful contact with its neighbors. In fact, a particular warden created an environment that could be described as downright hostile. During my tenure in Forrest City, Warden Sanders regularly held so-called community meetings to identify potential threats to the facility. The undertone of these meetings was to keep the Mexican gangs and cartels out of Forrest City. I labeled these as *so-called* community meetings because these meetings were by invitation only and held at the FCFCF. I attended a meeting (although briefly) and was privy to the tone and substance of these conversations. These meetings were far from anything resembling community building. Coach Twillie revealed that at these so-called community meeting attendees were regularly indoctrinated and informed about the evils of Mexican/Latino gangs. This strategy was under the auspices of keeping the community outside the prison informed about gang culture and how to stay alert to potential signs that they were moving into greater Forrest City. However, a more cynical view of these activities would categorize them as an elaborate ruse to enlist folks in Forrest City as informants for the prison authorities. This fear mongering was loosely based on fact: According to the 2000 census, the FCFCF housed over 1,900 Hispanics. Given its large number of Latino inmates, Warden Sanders apparently feared the community might suffer an invasion of drug and gang-involved cartel members related to inmates. This fear was not, however, based on genuine concern for Forrest City, given Warden Sanders's oppositional view toward the community (see Appendix A, section "Nearly Incarcerated Ethnographer"). Whatever the motivations, these so-called community meetings did little to improve the relations between Forrest City and the FCFCF. In fact, because Mayor Bryant was neither involved nor ever invited to the FCFCF's "community meetings," he interpreted them as a sign of disrespect from Warden Sanders.

The Political Economy of Prisons

Uncovering how people in Forrest City felt about prison building's effect on politics and the local economy proved a challenge. Most interviewees only thought about impact in terms of electoral politics, so they did not see any real relationship between the prison and local elected officials. When I inquired further about another political possibility—additional political representation at the state and federal levels from prisoners being counted in the local population—respondents instead referred to the extra dollars these "excess" residents earned the municipality from the state and county governments.

Informants noted how the additional population from the prison could itself serve as a stimulus to the local economy. State funding for education, roads, and other public goods is based on population size. Because prisoners are counted as residents in the town they occupy while imprisoned, additional monies are allocated to these municipalities. For business owners like Steve Lindsey, the benefits of such a population increase can be measured across multiple levels and outcomes. He asserts:

> It's been a boost . . . of course just the extra population alone has allowed us to keep our local taxes down somewhat because we've been able to include our [prison] population in our rollback money [apportionment of taxes returned to municipalities from state entities for services like roads, schools, etc.]. But you know [the prison] helped . . . I think everybody's benefited to a certain extant . . . city services have been greatly improved. The city has been able to buy new equipment and update other equipment to benefit everybody. The local economy is better. Dollars are spent here that normally wouldn't be. And those dollars turn over [locally] benefiting average people.

Lindsey's initial claim of a benefit depends on what he refers to as "rollback dollars," which in Arkansas refers to the apportioned amount of revenues returned to local governments by the state based on the size of their populations. To be clear, because prisoners are counted in the local population during the census, they increase the town's population count. The higher a town's population count, the more rollback dollars a city receives. Because prisons are more likely to be built in rural communities of color (and prisoners are disproportionately urban minorities) there is an odd exchange where communities of color simultaneously benefit and are exploited through the building of prisons.

Other residents interpreted my questions about "who benefits" more literally, usually in terms of direct employment or business relationships. When asked about who benefited directly from the prison, Perry remembers that Danny Ferguson's wife worked at the prison. He declares, "You know that's pretty direct impact [chuckling] when the Mayor's wife goes out there. She was an accountant by trade and ended working for the accounting side [of the FCFCF] for the Bureau of Prisons." Although it seems unlikely that Mayor Ferguson went through all the hard work of acquiring a prison just for his spouse to get a job, his wife's appointment gives the appearance of nepotism. It seems more likely, however, that Mrs Ferguson was one of the few people in town with the necessary qualifications for the job.

Steve Lindsey, too, provides examples of direct, tangible economic benefits from the decision to locate the prison in Forrest City. Lindsey, who runs an insurance and investment company, noted that the construction of the prison not only increased his business, but also produced trickle-down effects for the town:

> The initial influx of workers had a great impact on our house sales allowing people that wanted to upgrade or get into a bigger/better house an opportunity to sell that house. Because the local housing market had been flat this [the prison] gave them opportunity to change houses by either building new or buying someone else's. In my business, [this movement in the market] gives me an opportunity to insure another house, where I make more money, then I spend more money. So I just think everybody benefited [smiling].

In commenting on how his increased business produced ripple effects through the community, Lindsey was drawing a distinction between direct impact—the increase to his business—and indirect benefits—the increase the town's broader economic health.

In addition to providing examples of direct versus indirect benefits, respondents were adept in apprizing the multitude of gains from the prison. Coach Twillie humbly attests that "it impacted us some . . . when they first started to build that impacted the construction workers in this area with jobs to do contracts . . . like the buildings, the ground work [landscaping], the foundation work." My respondents struggled, however, to name specific individuals or companies who benefited directly from these contracts. Although Coach named Oscar Conyears, an African American contractor from neighboring Brinkley, as the general contractor who secured federal minority set asides, the details he provided were sketchy at best, and came only with cajoling. What Coach's description lacked in detail, however, it made up for in its broader implications. To Coach, the significance of the story was that blacks benefited overall from prison building because Conyears divvied up the subcontract with other African Americans.

Through interviews with other race leaders I came to understand that Walter Peacock, an African American council representative of Forrest City and the owner/operator of Peacock General Contracting, was granted a subcontract under Oscar Conyears during construction of the prison. Peacock told me that his business includes plumbing, electrical, and air conditioning work. Mr. Peacock recalls that the contract to do the dirt work, install storm drains and pour concrete for the foundation of the FCFCF, came to more than $300,000, a pretty sizable contract for him at the time. Prior to the prison, his largest project had been the Memphis Airport, during which he employed twelve to twenty-four workers at any given time. With the prison, he hired a number of additional Forrest City workers (almost exclusively African Americans), and his crews increased sizably along with the weekly payroll. Even though the positions were temporary—as construction work is—they nevertheless provided an economic boost to African American employment in Forrest City.

Of all the groups that I spoke with, shopkeepers were the most aware of the impact of prison patronage on the local economy. Along with his wife, Mr. Nichols owns and operates William's Restaurant in downtown Forrest City across the street from City Hall. His establishment is beloved by many; it's the local "greasy spoon." In addition to breakfast, lunch, and dinner most days, he serves a special handmade jelly roll once a week. A former biker and resident of Milwaukee, Nichols informed me that he catered several events at the FCFCF when it first opened. He estimates that 20 to 30 percent of his current customers work at the prison.

Another way that prisons impact local economies is through the purchase of food and other supplies. Because the BOP has contracts with major food distributors like Aramark, the FCFCF purchases surprisingly little locally. Respondents told me local business owner David Cohn of Forrest City Grocery kept one or two small contracts with the FCFCF, but the bulk of the facility's supplies came from national food distributors. The prison does seem to purchase more of its nonfood items from local suppliers. When the FCFCF first opened, local shops supplied everything from paper products to car and truck batteries. Forrest City business owners did not openly resent national suppliers, assuming that any business built up the local economy, even if it didn't.

Despite indications in the scholarly literature suggesting that prisons reduce employment and future investment (Besser and Hanson 2004; Gilmore 2007; Hooks et al. 2004; Hooks et al. 2010; Huling 2001; King, Mauer, and Huling 2003), in Forrest City, even the most critical observers of the FCFCF believed that it created new jobs and spurred future development. On the rare occasion that negative views of prison building surfaced, savvier members of the polity complicated and challenged these assertions. Consider Coach's assessment:

There's a lot of people that you know who work at prison right now. . . . Got about six or seven people I go to church with working at the prison. Sure do. Both male and female, that's settled down in pretty good paying jobs for this area. [The prison] gave some people who are already employed an opportunity to deal with hard time employment because they have a lot of teachers to teach classes out there at night and evening so that's double impact . . . people who are not employed, and then those who were employed, helped them get that second jobs moonlighting.

Coach's statement suggests that we should consider the type of employment and career opportunities created by these complex institutions when evaluating their impact on local communities. While prisons primarily create jobs for correctional officers, their ongoing operation requires the participation of numerous other ancillary professions and services, from accountants to educators and medical professionals.

Among Forrest City's elite, the prison seemed to garner only smiles. Buddy Billingsley affirms, "yeah, the interesting thing is that when I drive by and I see all those lights out there, they say they're unattractive. To me that's very attractive [giggles]!" I probe deeper and challenge this assertion by asking, "well from an architectural point of view prison facilities often aren't the most aesthetically pleasing. What's so attractive about the lights to you?" He replies, "it took ahhh—interrupting himself—jobs! . . . it's also good for the utility companies." While many people find the lights of Paris, New York, or Las Vegas enchanting, and some are infatuated with the glow of sports stadiums, still others—apparently—find the hum of electricity and luminous appeal of the shiny metal and concrete of a correctional facility tantalizing. For some, these bright lights bring big smiles.

Buddy Billingsley's excitement cannot be summed up by trite idioms, like "beauty is in the eye of the beholder." He explains further, "well you're looking at energy corporations supplying electricity and the possibility of another electrical co-op here in Arkansas that would take over supplying energy. That's a real plus to be able to utilize the local corporations to provide utilities be it gas, be it electricity, be it water." For him, the prison was not only a stabilizer to Forrest City. It, and the resources it consumes, represented a wealth of new business and industrial possibilities. Although the new energy corporation has yet to open, the prison has sustained a level of demand for energy that keeps the possibility alive.

The top brass in town so uniformly accepted that the prison had primarily had a positive impact on Forrest City that they seemed shocked when I asked them if the prison limited future development possibilities. I often received blank looks, as if my respondents had never considered the possible negative economic repercussions from building a prison. A response from a female interview subject was typical: she grimaced, then turned her head and retorted, "What do you mean?" as if she had never been asked that question before. But beyond race leaders and the white elite, opinions about prison impact were a little more diverse. Some Forrest City residents regarded the prison as having had a positive economic benefit for a select few, with little benefit for the whole of Forrest City.

Skepticism among the Polity

Despite expressing some concern over the disproportionate rate of imprisonment of black men, very few race leaders found discontent with the prison's presence in Forrest City. One who did was Mrs. Weaver, an ordained evangelist in the Church of God in Christ (COGIC). A proud single mother, she raised five children, all of whom, she proudly proclaims, are professionals. Like Mayor Bryant, she comes from humble beginnings, having grown up in a sharecropper family in Forrest City. She too chopped and picked cotton in the Jim Crow South. Her mother and father never owned their home. In contrast, she and all eight of her siblings own their own homes. For most of her adult life she worked as a union organizer for the AFL-CIO and the IUE, which once recognized her as organizer of the year.

Evangelist Weaver remains active in the NAACP, her COGIC church, and is addressing issues of racial disparities in the criminal justice system in Arkansas. She has served as campaign manager for Arkansas state senator Jack Crumbly on all his campaigns. She is a proud, tough leader who has met every US president since Carter, with the exception—ironically—of President Obama. She has been a representative at the Democratic National Convention for Arkansas since the 1960s and is on a first-name basis with President Bill Clinton and former Secretary of State Hillary Clinton. Although she has not met President Obama, she has met First Lady Michelle Obama, as evidenced by a picture with her among a wall of fame for Arkansas politicians. Mrs. Weaver serves as the District 5 representative of the Saint Francis County Quorum Court and as a Justice of the Peace.

Evangelist Weaver has lived in what she labeled the "hood," or the South End of Forrest City, for all but two of her seventy-eight years. She has a strong attachment to Forrest City, as she "believes in local community" so much so that she rents out property in the South End. She supported the arrival of the prison, like everyone else, believing that it would help the sluggish Forrest City economy. She believed that the prison would not only bring jobs but also spur additional development through spillover effects. The project spillover would impact housing and other job sectors that provide services to the prison. While she has been disappointed by the lack of growth and the prison's impact on housing prices compared to the initial projections, she cannot find any substantive downsides to having a prison. With good reason, Mrs. Weaver seemed more concerned with expunging criminal records of people of Forrest City than prison impact.

Despite unanimous community support, the prison did not live up to race leaders' high expectations for the prison as the remedy for all that ailed Forrest City. A race leader (who chose to remain anonymous) explains that her disappointment with the prison is not about the substance of what was delivered, but about what was advertised. She explained, "it [the prison] did not have nearly the economic impact on the community that it's been expected to have." She continued, arguing that, since Forrest City captured the prison, it should also have captured the lion's share of the benefits. From her perspective, when a federal prison comes, the total of its operations should impact the town. Forrest City, however, was not prepared to receive the full benefit of the prison, especially when it came to housing. She expresses particular unhappiness with the BOP policy that allowed workers to live outside of town. From the beginning, she had been swayed by the idea of the BOP issuing a mandate that employees either live in the town or within a limited distance of the facility. She recalled hearing of a policy like this during the public meeting at the Saint Francis Courthouse and that it might be considered in building the FCFCF. Such a mandate, she thought, would do wonders for the housing market. I do not have other data that confirms or refutes why this mandate was not included with the FCFCF, but in any case, it was not. The result was that, as she explained, "Some guards have an hour's drive, versus coming up with a house and planning a subdivision for them to accommodate the market. We've experienced where the folks who had homes just make a way to profit for themselves, trying to make a killing! In response, these prison folks [people employed by the prison] changed [housing] markets for a larger city! So consequently we only get about 30 percent of the new employees."

She also contends that because so few FCFCF employees live in town, the rates of homeownership are lower, and vacancy rates higher, than the national average. She is also quite clear on where the blame for this development rests. "When I say we should [get the lion's share of benefits], let me be real clear, I'm not talking about the mayor's office, I'm talking about the chamber of commerce . . . to this day I still see no leadership that pushes that agenda to try to come up with housing that would accommodate a future generation of prison employees." She elaborated:

> And so, they [white elites] have not put together a plan that deals with all of that. They haven't put together a housing plan. We [African Americans] don't control the housing, we don't control the property. They could easily put together a housing plan and allow those folks to live here and they might have the opportunity to also do construction and the selling of the housing development contract. . . . We don't own the banks. We don't own the contractors. We don't own any of that, so they're just so narrow-minded, they're so narrow minded.

Her comments demonstrate not only her individual frustration, but also how racial tension, coupled with a lack of vision and leadership, can hinder a town's ability to gain from prison building.

Mayor Bryant expressed similar sentiments regarding the overall welfare of Forrest City and the housing market in particular:

> Resident were so happy the prison was coming and that it was going to bring jobs. In response, homeowners jacked the price up on their property because people were buying some houses. Because property values were artificially inflated now we ended up with white flight in those neighborhoods. Now, [white neighborhoods] are the neighborhoods impacted by white flight because those that didn't get out early couldn't sell after the housing prices were jacked up so high.

Forrest City had already been experiencing white flight after the fall of Jim Crow and the integration of the schools; the location of the prison may have accelerated it.

While some residents believed that the artificially increased costs of homes decreased potential sales in certain areas, everyone agreed that a few more homes were sold in Forrest City as a whole because of the prison. The increased home values had other unanticipated consequences beyond white flight. Larry Bryant, for instance, believed that the announcement of the prison artificially inflated land values:

> I tried to buy 8 feet of property from the lady next door to me and offered her three thousand dollars for 8 feet so I could put a restaurant up and she said no. Before the prison was coming I could buy a whole lot [big enough for a single

family home] for a hundred thousand dollars, some crazy [low] price. . . . You'll find out the housing prices [in Forrest City] is why some people moved to Wynne as the prices were lower.

Mayor Bryant, like many others, believed that prior to the prison, an entire plot of land in town could be purchased on the cheap. After the announcement of the prison, however, even a generous offer for a sliver of land was rebuffed, halting property expansion and squelching potential business developments—in this case, a restaurant that Mayor Bryant was looking to open.

This drastic change in land values also relates to the artificially inflated value of homes in Forrest City, in that it produced a tight rental market. Tight rental markets can push new residents to find cheaper rents in other towns. Many of the residents I spoke with believed the tight rental market in Forrest City caused potential residents to relocate to Wynne and other surrounding communities. I will return to this issue in the next chapter, where I will share how I inadvertently learned about the rental market barriers in Forrest City through my unsuccessful attempts to move my family into town. For now, suffice it to say that barriers to the rental market may well have driven would-be residents to Wynne.

Across all strata of Forrest City, locals repeatedly expressed their disappointment that residents were not hired at the facility at the rate that had been predicted. At the outset, 65 percent of all jobs created at the FCFCF were projected to go to Forrest City locals or people who would relocate to the town. Without the BOP housing mandate, new hires were free to live where they wished. Nearly every respondent believed Forrest City captured less than a third of new positions at the FCFCF, though some were more bothered by this than others. The college-aged cohort, for example, reported being underwhelmed with the prison's impact—no one more so than Crystal. Although she was born in Allen, Texas, Crystal's family is native to Forrest City. Her mother works as a nurse and, following a divorce, she returned to find work near Forrest City while Crystal was in middle school. At the time of the interview, Crystal was attending a historically black college in hopes of entering the medical field as well. While appreciative of the increase in jobs and new people, Crystal saw few tangible, direct benefits going from the prison to locals. When asked where the jobs from the prison were going, Crystal provides perhaps the most thoughtful critique:

CRYSTAL: It was supposed to bring more job opportunities for us and there are people coming from all over the place. And they're more qualified than us.

J. E.: So how does that make you feel?

CRYSTAL: Like man we've been tricked or bamboozled! Like what . . . see ok . . . it's like most people that live in Forrest City most of the jobs they hire for are like you know you work in Wal-Mart and grocery stores. And even if there's a whole other level than that and usually people who work those jobs come from out of town.

Each young adult supported this claim by listing neighbors or congregation members who relocated to Forrest City from Indiana, Louisiana, Mississippi, and Tennessee for work at the prison. Before the prison, there was fierce competition in the labor market and periods of severe unemployment. The arrival of the prison was billed as a way to decrease this competition by making more jobs available. However, as Crystal points out, many residents did not qualify or had to wait to gain enough seniority in the federal system to be placed locally.

Given the segmented labor market in rural southern towns, the specialized, relatively well-paying positions at the FCFCF increased competition among black locals already beleaguered by an evaporating employment base. Because there was no intentional plan to desegregate the job market through the targeted hiring of blacks, the segregated job market was reproduced. The prison jobs that could have been open to black residents were given to outsiders. Crystal's mother, for example, had put in for a nursing position at the prison and had not heard back. After pondering this, Crystal railed against the facility and what it represents—another failure of the local political economy enshrouded in racial tension:

CRYSTAL: There's one like real crazy twisted you know where I'm just like oh OK . . . [she takes a deep breath as her complexion changes to red/orange and the frustration in her voice becomes more palpable] they had no problem with putting a prison here, but um . . . it took years for us to even get a new junior high. But ok so you're saying the prison is more important than the safety of our youth? I was like OK so I hear it's a nice prison but you had to go to a crappy school and the people are like "we want a new school" but others are like "ah taxes, taxes" . . . What are you . . . I was like what's wrong with us . . .

CHARLES [FREEMAN]: It took years to get the millage passed just so we could build a new school.

CRYSTAL: That was so backwards!

CHARLES: Yeah. It was bad. Huh?

CRYSTAL: Then the people voted against a new gym. They voted against so much. They voted against the gym, but then the prison passed? It's kind of hard to pass things because it's like beaten them [whites] up . . .

CHARLES: Their kids live here and it's like they don't want to help. And it was like I know they were going up but it was like a penny?

CRYSTAL: Yeah!

CHARLES: It was a penny tax. And they were going to make a new school with that penny and folks they just don't want to pay.

Although an atypical response to the FCFCF, Crystal's and Charles's recounting of the battle over passing the tax increase articulates a deeply held sentiment by many African Americans about the white elites—that they do not have compassion or concern about the plight of local blacks because of the continual battles over public dollars. Moreover, these comments also reflect their general distrust of whites.

The "penny tax," or millage, to help fund schools is an ongoing issue in cash-strapped rural communities. The annual millage (0.1 percent increase in real estate tax) continues to be at the center of racial tensions in many rural, southern towns. Given the projected windfall of the prison, some believed the annual battle over the millage would be a thing of the past. Improvements in education represent much more than just community pride. Education is billed as the cure for poverty. Race leaders like Evangelist Weaver, who toiled for years trying to increase the funds available to the public school system, saw a practical, concrete, delivery attached to the prison. To them, the prison was a lottery designed to profit the community it sat within.

Nevertheless, the elite felt the prison provided more opportunities for people to stay or move into the greater Forrest City region. Prison impact on population change was a prominent theme that emerged from my interviews. Steve Lindsey, a member of the local brass, contends that, "we've been able to keep some of our younger people because of the maximum hiring age [at the FCFCF] . . . those that could qualify to go to work for them that we might have loss otherwise." Many rural communities experience a demographic hollowing out (Carr and Kefalas 2009) from the flight of young adults. In Forrest City, some business leaders, like Steve Lindsey, believed the prison could help reverse this exodus of young adults by giving preferential hiring to younger people through the maximum hiring age.

The college students I spoke with, in contrast, remained dubious of job opportunities in Forrest City. Charles Freeman confesses that his mother did not want him to return to Forrest City once he completed college. She believed the limited professional opportunities would hinder his life chances and his young adult experiences. Despite the FCFCF providing new employment and diverse professional opportunities, neither Charles nor his cohort at the Saint Francis County CDC returned to the town. Their exit as young adults is indicative of larger trends in rural communities. Charles left school in North Carolina and worked toward his BA and MA in Little Rock before taking a position in a federal agency in Washington.

Unfulfilled Opportunities

When I told informants how I learned firsthand about the tight rental market in Forrest City, they were not surprised. Many believed that Forrest City homeowners did not bother to invest in their properties to make them more attractive. Surrounding communities, like Wynne, maintained coordinated efforts to keep home prices reasonable. This was only one of several ways in which Forrest City's residents believed that Wynne surpassed Forrest City in taking advantage of the prison's location.

Businesses in Wynne, compared to those in Forrest City, were quite aware of and attentive to outsiders. When shopping, employees would ask me if my family was affiliated with the prison. We encountered similar queries at school and church functions. I first passed this off as a function of the highway system. Although many native Forrest City residents can recognize outsiders, business owners cannot assume these outsiders are connected with the prison, because Forrest City is on Interstate 40. Wynne, in contrast, was located twenty miles from the interstate, crossed instead by Arkansas Highways 1 and 64. Visitors from faraway, in other words, are unlikely to arrive in Wynne by accident.

While residents' view of the prison's impact on Forrest City was positive, many believed that Wynne benefited even more. Most believed the housing market in Wynne appeared to benefit more from the prison than did that of Forrest City. One realtor in Wynne, for example, was renting and constructing dozens of new homes in Cross County. He continued to do so despite the national economic recession in 2008, and claims that dozens of FCFCF employees were already renting or had purchased homes from him directly. When my family arrived, we rented near a large plot of land near Highway 1 that was scheduled for development. By the time we left eight months later, the developer had started constructing multifamily rental housing on this land—much to the chagrin of our home-owning neighbors. Most homes near us had been purchased from this same realtor within the previous five years. Transects and interviews suggested that Wynne had more new construction than Forrest City.

Examples from Forrest City and Wynne highlight the importance of the context of reception for benefiting from prison placement. While Wynne seemed to prepare for the long-term benefits of the prison siting twenty miles away by developing rental properties and having a fair and inclusive rental market, Forrest City leaders engaged in an internal power struggle steeped in a bitter racial history. By the time the prison was finally constructed in 1997, Larry Bryant had defeated Danny Ferguson to become the first black mayor in the city's history. Race leaders negotiated minority set-asides during the construction of the prison, but they still faced a white elite unwilling to yield power. This speaks to how racial tension can affect the context of reception. Despite sharing a similar history of bitter racial tension endemic to this region of the South, many residents in Wynne (and Forrest City alike) believe their town is more progressive than Forrest City. To be sure, black residents in Wynne experienced residential segregation and other forms of discrimination. However, neighborhoods experiencing concentrated poverty and residential segregation in Wynne did not have the feel of desperation/nihilism so omnipresent in Forrest City. For example, the schools in Wynne did not feel as repressive as those of Forrest City, in that they did not require uniforms or strict dress codes. Likewise, blight and deteriorating housing stock are not as prevalent in the poorer neighborhoods in Wynne as they are in Forrest City.

Spotting Prison Tourism or Terrorism

A final issue that affects how residents perceive and interact with a prison facility is its location. Combessie (2002) studied a remote French prison town in which, he claimed, the owner of the inn, the shopkeepers, and the townspeople could readily identify prison visitors. The ease of identifying prison visitors created contentious situations in which guards and visitors interacted outside of the prison (Combessie 2002). While this situation may be typical in France, US prison towns differ, in that prisons are not typically built on Main Street. A prison location in the center of town would provide locals with a prominent view of who came and went, allowing prison visitors and staff to be easily identified by local shopkeepers and residents. US prison towns, in contrast, tend to be larger; in the case of the FCFCF, the town is near an interstate. Because prisons are tucked away and hard to reach even for rural residents, the towns coexist alongside the prison. In the United States, most prisons are built in remote, or at least peripheral, loca-

tions, both as a security measure and because of the need to acquire sufficient land. Prisons are, therefore, usually visited only by persons with a need
to conduct business in these inconvenient locations. As a consequence, few
townspeople see the prison on a daily basis; fewer still enter the facility. Even
if they do deal with individuals connected with the facility, their involvement is not usually in any official capacity. For the most part, the prison is
out of sight and out of mind. These spatial aspects of prison facilities make
gauging some types of impact in Forrest City more difficult.

Escapes are one of the more plausible ways that residents might come
into contact with the prison and its related stigmas. In Forrest City this potential negative impact was never taken seriously by anyone I encountered.
Most people, one would think, would be frightened by the idea of someone
living in a hole in the side of a hill covered by thickets of bush and trees in a
residential area, whether or not the person was a prison escapee. In recounting this story of his mother's near encounter with a prison escapee, however,
there was no fear or hesitation in Charles Freeman's voice. Freeman, an
intern at the Saint Francis County Community Development Corporation,
recounted the day shortly after the prison opened:

> I did have one direct encounter or my mama did have one direct encounter
> with the prison. It was a breakout . . . one of the guys was hiding. You know
> where my house is when you come up to the right that path in there. He was
> hiding down in my path and my mama went out walking early in the day. And
> then when the cops came they came and picked him up. If she had drove out
> he might have been able jumped out and get her or whatever. He was right
> there. He was down in that little hole for like a day or so.

The escape involved an inmate driving an ATV out of the ungated, low-
security, correctional facility campus. The *Forrest City Times-Herald* covered
the incident, but locals didn't make much of it; few felt threatened by the
presence of the facility despite the news that an inmate had been found hid-
ing in a ditch in a residential area.

Freeman shared this story among a group of college-aged African Americans. There was a brief silence until a cohort member, Crystal, echoed the
lack of concern with escapees that seemed to be prevalent in Forrest City.
Crystal explained, "Yeah, but it's a federal prison so like if it were any other
prison I probably would not be worried because there are real hardened
criminals there. We do have rapists in the federal prisons, but most of the
criminals in there [FCFCF] do like white-collar crime like money launder-
ing. Not like we got Charles Manson in there or anything like that." These

comments epitomize the pervasive mythology in Forrest City of what kinds of prisoners the FCFCF held, which helps explain how residents cope with the presence of convicted criminals in their midst.

The distance of the prison from town also makes it difficult for residents to evaluate the broader effects that the prison has on the economy, including tourism. Locals are unlikely to pick up on "prison tourism" because of the difficulty in distinguishing between interstate travelers and prison visitors. A few keen observers in the hotel/hospitality industries, however, reported that out-of-state families "coming to visit daddy" would often ask for directions to the prison while checking in. According to informants, many of these families were Latinos who lived outside of Arkansas. Hotel staff members noted two or three Latino families every week. Given the black-white racial social system in Forrest City, Latinos would be easily noticed, whether visiting the prison or not.

Toward a Theory of Prison Impact: What Can Forrest City Teach Us?

How do rural residents make sense of the economic, social, and political impacts of prisons? The evidence presented here suggests that prison building provides some perceived benefit for locals, independent of whether those benefits are substantial or lasting. In direct contrast to the literature on prison impact, locals did not perceive the prison as a nuisance or a burden. In fact, the only disappointment with the FCFCF was that it did not live up to its billing as a panacea for the numerous challenges facing the town.

The perceived differences between Forrest City and Wynne suggest that the context of reception matters for prison impact. Race relations are key to understanding the context of reception in prison towns, as evidence here suggests that racial tension may limit impact. The role of racial tension in limiting the potential positive economic impact of a prison provides further confirmation of the elite-race interaction model (Tomaskovic-Devey and Roscigno 1997), whereas the role of the warden complicates institutional actor theory. I will expand further on both of these implications in the next chapter. If the role of warden is as vital as Mayor Bryant suggested it to be, then prison impact does start at the top of the facility. In communities unfettered by racial tension, however, we should expect the role of a strong warden to diminish as multiple organic ties develop between the prison and the surrounding communities. Regardless, the findings here suggest that wardens are pivotal in setting the tone for how prisons interact with their surroundings, suggesting that future ethnographies of prison towns take this into account in their investigation. Timing, too, matters in understanding how prisons impact places. We should expect to find different levels of perceived impact when measuring across different phases of building, opening, and continued construction.

Most citizens in Forrest City believed they did not directly benefit from the FCFCF. Additionally, while all interviewees viewed the prison beneficially, they did not view it as equally beneficial. Therefore, the meaning of the prison differed depending on the status of individual within a town. A low-skilled worker lacking access to a job at the prison viewed the prison very differently than did the director of the chamber of commerce. From interviews and participant observations, I found differences by race as well. High-ranking black officials did not view the prison the same way as did as high-ranking white business leaders or officials. Some downtown Forrest City shopkeepers have lost hope or interest in benefiting from the prison. The highway bypass effectively routed traffic for the prison away from the center of Forrest City. Many downtown businesses, already struggling before the prison, continue to do so now.

In addition, when considering the relationship between the town and the facility, Forrest City residents did not consider the possibility of escape, and the danger that that might bring, as a real concern. Whether real or imagined, the fear of escape can be a source of stigma, producing negative impacts on a prison town. Moreover, escapes may be a source of stigma that locales are unwilling to confront. To manage their own sense of selves they laugh off the problem (Goffman 1963). If there is a fear of crime associated with the facility in a prison town, evidence from Forrest City suggests that future investigations should examine the role of the prison administration in propagating moral panics by labeling the families of prisoners as gang bangers and potential terrorists. In considering connections between the prison and the surrounding community, evidence here also suggest that the warden may be the central figure in making connections between the prison and the town. While the evidence illustrates the ways that rural residents perceive the impact of prison building on their communities, the implications extend far beyond Forrest City and Wynne. In the next chapter I turn to a more detailed accounting of how prisons slow economic decline in rural communities.

SEVEN

The Tarnished Jewel of the Delta: Continuity and Change in Caste, Class, and Disrepute

During a preview tour of the newly constructed FCFCF, a local resident remarked, "I was completely blown away, I had no idea, first, of the size, and second of all the planning that went into everything. . . . I had no idea that prisoners had so many facilities available to them. One thing that struck me . . . is that what those guys (inmates) have available to them is nicer than what a lot of Forrest Citians have available to them" (*Forrest City Times-Herald* 1997). Drawing comparisons between prisons and disadvantaged communities is not novel (Eason 2012; Wacquant 2002). However, the parallel drawn above speaks volumes about the shape of Forrest City on the eve of opening the FCFCF. If living conditions in a federal prison are comparable or better than conditions for many living in your locale, this is yet another sign that your community suffers from underdevelopment.

We have seen that leaders in Forrest City called for a prison because they thought it might save the town from material disadvantage and social stigma. We have also seen that locals believe the prison buffered against economic decline and improved the town's reputation. But while the FCFCF slowed the city's decline, it could not save the town from continued underdevelopment. The unabated rise of the rural ghetto presented obstacles to development and challenges to rebuilding the reputation of Forrest City. Signs of continued underdevelopment in the town point to the continued caste and class system that maintain the ecology of disrepute. Undoubtedly, the prison improved the town's image, but it is still tainted by the rural ghetto.

The rural ghetto is ever present in Forrest City's structure and culture. Perry Webb argues, "It [the FCFCF] postponed the inevitable just a little bit. And I think maybe it avoided the worst-case scenario for the town. It will never be as bad as it could have gotten." In essence, the city's image is a little better than it would have been without the prison, but it nonetheless remains problematic. The limited positive impact of prison building becomes more evident when Forrest City's situation is compared to that of other disadvantaged communities that did not receive a prison. For instance, the neighboring town Brinkley, Arkansas, is closing public schools because of its dire economic straits. In comparison to Brinkley, Forrest City is prosperous. Compared to towns that were not as deeply stigmatized in the first place, however, like Wynne, Forrest City struggles.

In what follows, I begin by rethinking the prison as an institutional actor. Then, I return to cataloging the use of racial scripts in confining, defining, and controlling the town's poor black residents to demonstrate the enduring salience of race and racism in rural southern towns like Forrest City. Outlining the prominence of disadvantage and stigma, despite the presence of the prison, illustrates continuity and change in the rural ecology of disrepute in communities like Forrest City. To be clear, while the form of racial and economic oppression has changed since the days of Jim Crow, the fundamental function has not—deep racial divides and underdevelopment still mar communities like Forrest City. After that, I use descriptive statistics to compare and contrast how the FCFCF slowed decline in Forrest City and its neighboring city of Wynne. This allows us to move past polarizing debates on the benefits/harms of prisons and instead focus on the depths of inequality within rural communities. I conclude by arguing that continued underdevelopment in communities like Forrest City should be understood as an extension of the hyperghetto (Eason 2012; Wacquant 2002).

Rethinking Impact: The Prison as Institutional Actor

As a forerunner to key sociological concepts like collective efficacy and organizational density, institutional actor theory provides theoretical purchase crucial to explaining prison impact. In *Paths of Neighborhood Change* (henceforth *Paths*), Richard Taub, Garth Taylor, and Jan Dunham (1984) describe institutional actors as organizations that aid in stabilizing or exacerbating individual reactions to environmental uncertainty. Institutional actors are part of the ecological milieu because of their ability to wield clout as employment centers, campaign contributors, and movers of money and people. Many aspects of prisons are comparable to those of such other institutional actors as colleges, hospitals, and shopping centers in maintaining community stability and order. As stigmatized institutions, however, prisons also have certain institutional parallels with incinerators, landfills, nuclear power plants, asylums, and other types of land use planners traditionally labeled as undesirable.

The FCFCF is a major employer in town. Prison officials and employees may serve as key nodes across networks that might allow the town to buttress itself against further economic decline. Residents believe the prison has created well-paid, unionized positions with benefits. They also believe that certain ancillary businesses thrive because of the prison. Goods and services needed by prison employees provide another potential way for a prison to boost the local economy. Prison employees can increase the tax base of a community by moving into town or using local businesses during their commute if they do not live in town. Large institutions moreover provide in-kind services outside of employment. Prison employees are not just workers—if they choose to be, they are involved in the community through volunteering and supporting the churches. While these additional activities are not directly mandated or sanctioned by FCFCF, the benefits to the community can be traced back to the prison.

Paths (1984, 183–84) finds that institutional actors' "economic resources, combined with their preferential tax status, are so great that even a very small proportion of those resources devoted to the appropriate strategies can notably affect neighborhood stability. Corporate actors are able to have an impact on the real estate market and to deploy their personnel at a level that individuals cannot." Institutional actors can provide community stability by taking action, effectively solving the collective action problem and free-rider syndrome, thereby lowering the bar for individual decision makers to enter the community investment process. In Forrest City's case, the arrival of the FCFCF represented a significant investment that may have helped not only to stabilize but also to artificially increase land values in Forrest City.

Another potential institutional economic effect of the prison could exist in prisoners' relationships with family and other visitors. Because prisons are often situated at a sizable distance from prisoners' origins, de facto tourism industries sometimes spring up around prison towns. Whether visiting overnight or just for a single day, local gas stations, hotels, and eateries all stand to potentially benefit. Likewise, visitors to prison towns need transportation. Both journalists and scholars have begun to take note of the thriving busing industry from the major cities to these small towns and the economic and social impact of such activities on the prison town (Christian 2005; Phelps 2012). Forrest City locals, as we have seen, may or may not notice this economic impact given the town's proximity to the interstate and the prison's location on the edge of town.

Prisons and prisoners also impact political representation and access to government funds. Calvin Beale (2006), for example, demonstrates the effect of prisons in changing the statistical demographics of rural counties. Beale found that, during the 1980s, 5 percent of population growth in all US rural communities could be attributed to prison construction. In some states, like Texas and California, prisoners can account for more than ten thousand persons in some counties. Eric Lotke and Peter Wagner (2004) argue that counting the mainly urban prison population in rural communities distorts democracy by skewing political apportionments. Electoral representation at every conceivable level of our democracy (from local dog catcher to the US presidency) is based on population counts. Fiscal apportionments, too, are based on population counts and impact funding from everything from roads to schools. These revenues are possible sources to provide an economic boost to places like Forrest City. Of course, this benefit to rural places comes at a cost to the urban places who disproportionately *lose* residents to prison building. By thinking about the prison as an institutional actor we can account for the myriad of ways prisons impact communities.

Continuity and Change in the Rural Ecology of Disrepute

Forrest City's reputation as a filthy town is not entirely undeserved. In tracing the history of the town, I found that Forrest City's reputation had been tainted long before either the arrival of Mayor Bryant or the FCFCF. Some institutions, especially within the uneven commercial development concentrated in what used to be downtown Forrest City, could definitely be considered filthy. The "filthiness" cannot be considered separately from the material conditions of underdevelopment in Forrest City and long-lasting racial stigma. Many of these uneven or underdeveloped areas can be connected to the neighboring ghetto of the South End, which is within walking distance of downtown. Although I frequented a good proportion of businesses in town, I did not enter every one. The type and condition of commercial establishments downtown signify challenges; they are similar to those in many former industrial centers suffering from macroscale changes like deindustrialization and globalization. Below, I offer a thick description of the underdevelopment that has occurred in rural communities for decades (Falk and Lyson 1988; Lyson and Falk 1993). I begin by describing an eatery, then a handful of small specialty shops, and finally, grocery stores. My intention is to show that commercial areas were struggling well before the arrival of the FCFCF; they continued to struggle afterward.

I Appreciate You, Waffle House

Waffle House is a familiar southern institution enjoyed by diverse crowds. The large yellow sign with black block letters beckons visitors from the highways and the interstates for a great meal. At 3:30 a.m. in a larger southern city, you could run into a professional basketball player enjoying a waffle and chili; at high noon in a small town, a truck driver enjoying a chopped steak dinner; at either location, working girls could stop in anytime to enjoy a cup of coffee after leaving the Holiday Inn up the road. In northern urban areas, hipster coffee houses are often social centers. In Forrest City, Waffle House serves a similar function as a focal social space.

The atmosphere in the Forrest City Waffle House is lively, if somewhat disordered. On this particularly day, a middle-aged, dark-skinned, well-dressed black man seated by the door looked the part of a mayor or high-powered preacher. He was seated with a lady dressed like a Mary Kay rep from the 1980s—pink frilliness, including pink bows on her hat. They chatted up pretty much everyone entering and exiting the restaurant. The cook, a short teen with mousy-brown hair, is quarreling with a thirty-something expeditor. Our young adult black female server informs us that the expeditor is the cook's mom. Lisa, my wife, placed one of the many orders the mother/son combo mishandled. She sent her plate back. The third time she just gave up. Her eggs were awful—runny in parts and overcooked in others, with cheese lumped in one spot. This is not typical of Waffle House. The food is normally tasty—a little greasy but tasty. During one of our many encounters with the server, she told us that the mom—the expeditor—is a former teacher. Expeditor and cook curse loudly while shoveling dishes back and forth at each other—plates clank and rattle loudly almost in sync with their cursing. Perhaps they are not quarreling over orders but continuing a domestic dispute. We absorb the performance as we try to eat.

Before leaving, I take my son, Major, to the restroom. Along the dimly lit hallway, a large clump of napkins and a pile of dirt on the floor adjacent to the cooking area seem to have been undisturbed for some time. With greasy food, a certain level of filth is expected in the restroom, yet even by Waffle House standards, this restroom is filthy. It smells like fresh urine, and most of the floor is muddied with urine. The toilet seat is covered in urine. I lift it up with a shoe trying not to touch anything with my hands. This restaurant bathroom was not the only one in town in this condition.

When we get up to leave our server says "Iaaa-ppreciate-cha." She says it as one word, slow, drawn out. Discussing it as we drive away, Lisa explains that "I appreciate you" is a way to show thanks for patronizing a business or used as a kind farewell. Regardless of the meal, when I think about the atmosphere and warmth of the server, I am reminded of the distinction between southern charm and country ways. I found southern charm is expressed by an individual showing graciousness to others almost as sign of self-respect.

When servers smile and say, "I appreciate you," they are not simply showing you respect but respecting themselves, regardless of the circumstance surrounding them.

In sharing encounters like this with members of the chamber of commerce, they confessed this type of consumer experience has become all to commonplace for many Forrest City businesses since the mid-1980s. This pattern is due in large part to the high supply of unskilled laborers relative to the number of positions available. A poorly trained service staff also speaks to the lack of investment in public education for workforce preparedness. Most importantly, the scenario described here also speaks to the underdevelopment of communities like Forrest City.

The Cat Piss, Good Hair, and Bad Hair Stores

Along with the political landscape, the social and economic landscape in Forrest City had shifted since the 1980s. It is well documented that residents of disadvantaged neighborhoods in large cities have patronized businesses owned by South or East Asian owners since the 1980s (Lee 2002). Jennifer Lee traces the history of the transition from Jewish to Korean ghetto merchants while portraying both groups' dynamic interactions with African American customers. Urban African Americans acclimatize to certain scripts and customs in these shops depending on the ethnic group serving them. Shop owners often hire black employees as way of minimizing tensions, but more savvy owners often deal directly with customers. Although not as well studied, rural black communities have a similar history. One day while shopping for a rather innocuous item, I took note of the settings and scripts in Forrest City. These observations provide a basis for comparing the rural and urban neighborhood economic base. While I found settings familiar to those in urban areas, regional differences seemed to color interactions much as they did in the Waffle House.

I noticed the first shop after leaving the Blue Flame, one of a handful of downtown restaurants. I was drawn to the shop because they advertised school uniforms on a large piece of butcher paper in the window. I had seen similar markers in Chicago "Hair and Wig" shops that often had a large selection of hair picks. As I approached the shop, I felt completely isolated— not a car or another person on the road. As I drew closer, the shop felt even more desolate. It was an overcast fall day, much warmer than forecast. The clouds seemed to hush the chirp of birds and hum of insects. The yellow paint on the wooden storefront was peeling.

I walked up a couple of stairs and gave a slight push to the wooden door that I expected to be heavy. It flung open, and I stumbled in, announcing my unfamiliarity. It felt similar to off-brand dollar shops on Seventy-First Street in Chicago, which are often not well lit, have dark red carpeting, shelves filled with small items in plastic bags, and circular islands filled with poly blend clothing in bright colors. The air in such places is often thick and musty, but the air in this store was particularly foul. Because I smelled the odor at the entrance, I assumed it was emanating from the steps. As I walked around the store, I noticed the smell getting stronger instead of dissipating.

I had become accustomed to a warm greeting in stores in Forrest City, but in this case the South Asian shopkeeper barely acknowledged my presence. In fact, he reluctantly spoke to me only after I inquired if he sold hair picks. He pointed to his limited selection in a basket inside a case. I tried to stomach the smell and began looking around to see if animals were roaming around actively relieving themselves. I began creating excuses in my head justifying the stench—maybe the air conditioning unit was broken. After all, it was an unexpectedly warm day. I left the store convinced that if there were a market for the stench of cat piss, this store would make record profits. The lack of cleanliness reflects poorly on the operator and the customers. Who is shopping for school uniforms under such unpleasant conditions? At this point, it struck me that the "old" downtown of Forrest City was less than a half-mile walking distance from the South End. Given the lack of public transportation in town, residents from the South End could easily walk or bike over to these shops even if they had limited car options.

As I walked in search of another hair-care shop, I passed a furniture store, a pawnshop now closed for business, and a dry cleaner near City Hall. As I approached a glass storefront, I noticed multiple entrances. One near the rear might have been for employees; another faced City Hall, so I chose it, thinking the shop might draw customers from William's Restaurant and the barbershop. I chose wrong. The door was bolted, and I shocked a patron as I yanked it to no avail. Startled, she smiled and pointed toward the entrance that opened. Although the signage on the outside of the building could use an update, the inside was well lit and seemed like any urban "Hair and Wig" shop. Not quite as nice as a Sally Beauty Supply, a leading national chain of hair-care stores, but definitely clean with well-stocked and maintained shelves and baskets on the counter with things like doo-rags, wave caps, and stocking rollers. As I entered, I felt like a conspicuous outsider because I could not open the door, an identity made more obvious once I began speaking. All of the fair number of customers had thick Arkansas accents. After hanging out for about half an hour, I purchased a pick. During that time, I talked with black clerks and the white shop owner. Although a white

"Hair and Wig" shop owner is still commonplace in rural black communities like Forrest City, it would seem peculiar to many students of urban niche markets because so many white owners have abandoned the inner cities (Lee 2002).

The Food Desert of Forrest City

Food deserts have recently been understood as a type of uneven development. Because of the novelty of this concept, the term itself is contested. However, in developing a typology of food deserts, Hillary Shaw (2006) posits disadvantaged rural communities suffer from particular challenges in accessing fresh fruits and vegetables. In comparison to other towns in the area, Forrest City boasts numerous places to shop. Staff members are always cordial and genuinely nice to shoppers, with big smiles and warm and inviting conversations. However, of the four major grocery stores in Forrest City it was not uncommon to find dust on canned items, spoiled or outdated food on the shelves, and floors in need of cleaning. It was also not uncommon for these stores to run out of staple items like bread or milk and to have low limits on the amount of cash ($5–$20) one could receive back when making a purchase with a debit card. The deli counter in one particular grocer persistently smelled like rotting meat. Like urban food deserts, fresh fruits and vegetables were in limited supply. Even when we tried to time our shopping on the day food was delivered, fresh food off the truck was scarce. Conversely, fast food options were numerous, ranging from KFC, Sonic, Wendy's, and a McDonald's all within a square mile on Washington Avenue near Interstate 40. Forrest City is surrounded by farmland, but many residents (especially the poor) lack access to fresh fruits and vegetables. According to Shaw (2006) these conditions are likely to create a food desert for the elderly, single-parent homes, poor minorities, single-car households, and others without cars.

Crime and Health

Food deserts, unkempt eateries, and shopping venues in the central business district and former downtown symbolize the continual underdevelopment of Forrest City despite the arrival of the prison. While these areas present ongoing challenges to the top local brass, signs of uneven development and stigma also seeped into tourist/visitor areas like the hotel campus. It was not uncommon, for example, for bullet holes to scar the windows of the Motel 6 and Best Western. Patrons at these motels were frequently exposed to violence and drug busts. The drug busts and other associated violence/criminal activity in these hotels is related to international and local drug trafficking markets: Interstate 40 is a main trade route for drugs from Mexico to the Midwest and East Coast.

Since the late 1980s, the local drug trade (primarily crack) has flourished in Forrest City due in large part to underdevelopment of the commercial sector and chronic joblessness/unemployment in the ghetto. Understanding this type of local informal economy can help explain the high crime rate (especially the inordinately high murder rate) for a town this size. In addition, Forrest City has an astronomical number of prisoners reentering community life each year. Between 1990 and 2006, over one thousand former Arkansas Department of Correction prisoners came home to Forrest City—more than sixty annually, on average, return to a handful of geographically contiguous blocks in the South End. Therefore, a significant proportion of the South End faces the personal and structural challenges endemic to the population of prisoners returning home, including unemployment, medical needs, frayed family ties, and a discriminatory housing market (Petersilia 2003). While the concentration effects of prison reentry have been examined in urban areas (Clear, Waring, and Scully 2005), little is known about the impact on rural communities (Wodahl 2006). Prisoner reentry is another criminal justice outcome with potentially lasting and meaningful effects on rural communities. Rose and Clear (1998) find that an overreliance on incarceration may weaken community social cohesion and the ability to act collectively, spurring an increase in crime and further social disorganization/disadvantage.

Health disparities are linked to concentrated disadvantage in rural and urban communities alike (Smith and Hattery 2008; Geronimus et al. 2006). According to the University of Arkansas–Little Rock Division of Agriculture Rural Profile of Arkansas 2005, "the health of Arkansas citizens is not as good as the national average" (28). The five-year infant mortality rate is 8.8 deaths per 1,000 births, versus 7 deaths per 1,000 births nationally. The Delta and Saint Francis County have even higher rates for the same time period: 10.5 and 12.1, respectively (Arkansas Department of Health, Saint Francis County Health Facts 2011). Smoking, obesity, and lack of access to health care cause many problems. The 2011 Saint Francis County Health Fact sheet shows that, in Arkansas, more rural than urban residents smoke. Nearly a third of Delta residents smoke and roughly 70 percent are obese (BMI = 0.25). Overall, Arkansas lags behind the national average, with only eighty-three primary care physicians per 100,000 persons; rural areas have only seventy-one, and the Delta, only fifty-nine. While these figures portray a stark reality for Forrest City residents, the HIV/AIDS rate is grimmest. With 1.1 percent of the population between the ages of fifteen and fifty-nine carrying HIV/AIDS, the rate in Saint Francis County is on par with less-developed nations. While these figures are county-level statistics, it is plausible to expect equal if not higher rates of poor health within the South End of Forrest City given the spatial concentration of disadvantage (for example, prisoner reentry) in this neighborhood. Rucker Johnson and Stephen Rafael (2005) find that increases in state incarceration levels predict increases in the incidence of HIV/AIDS, a finding that also supports the probability of HIV/AIDS being concentrated in the South End of Forrest City.

FCFCF Impact on Forrest City and Wynne

Given the multiple ways of measuring prison impact, I can only provide a thumbnail sketch of the FCFCF's impact on Forrest City, by focusing on median family income, median home value, unemployment, and poverty. I use descriptive statistics to provide snapshots of Wynne and Forrest City before and after the prison's arrival. In addition to economic indicators, the descriptive statistics of Forrest City and Wynne include several other indicators, like racial composition and total population. Most importantly, the analysis shows that the FCFCF provided an economic bulwark against further decline.

To think about how the FCFCF improved these communities we should first consider the implications of the increased prison population in Forrest City. While prisoners do not vote or burden services in local communities, their bodies are counted in the local population of the municipality where they are sentenced for governmental policies like "turn back" dollars or state and county apportionments of taxes returned to municipalities. Prisoners therefore, provide benefits to the locales without cost. According to the Arkansas Municipal League, for municipalities alone the state returns about $70 person annually. According to the 2000 census there were 2,394 persons living in correctional facilities in Forrest City. Therefore, prisoners have provided the municipality upwards of $167,580 annually from 2000 until 2009. This annual amount rose to $273,350 as the group quarter population living in correctional institutions mushroomed to 3,905 in 2010. These are sizeable amounts considering Forrest City's annual budget has increased from $6.7 million in 2000 to $10.5 million in 2014. The town also benefits politically, gaining increased representation given that the prisoners make up roughly 20 percent of the total population. Despite these benefits, prisons distort the demography of rural towns by skewing race and sex ratios.

Although we know that prison building is a rare event most likely to occur in the South, Arkansas increased prison building at a pace four times the national average during the prison boom. In addition to two previously existing prisons, Arkansas has opened twenty-six new facilities since 1974. Of those, twenty-one are state operated, five are private, and two are federal. Both the low- and medium-security federal facilities are located in Forrest City. The low-security facility opened in 1997, and the medium-security prison opened in 2004.

While the median home values in Forrest City and Wynne rose at a relatively similar rate between 1980 and 2000, the median family income in Wynne rose roughly 30 percent faster over the same period. From 1980 to 1990 unemployment in Wynne surged roughly 5 percent compared to more than 6 percent for Forrest City. The 1980s proved to be a rough economic time for most of the country, but these towns suffered more than average. While the country overall witnessed an economic turnaround in the 1990s, the economic improvement in Wynne and Forrest City can at least in part be credited to the arrival of the FCFCF. Unemployment dropped by more than 3 percent in Wynne; in Forrest City it only increased by a little more than 1 percent, to just over 16.4 percent. While this may at first seem like a very high rate, it is actually a marked improvement compared to the 30 percent spike that occurred around the time of the Sanyo strike. If asked to explain the differences between the two towns, many residents would agree that these figures demonstrate that both towns have benefited from the prison, but that Wynne has benefited more—primarily due to the context of reception. Wynne, in other words, did a better job at taking advantage of the FCFCF's arrival.

Changes in poverty and population levels across these two cities are more difficult to explain. For instance, poverty increased faster in Wynne between 1980 and 1990, and between 1990 and 2000 poverty fell faster in Forrest City. A similar trend holds for total population. Between 1980 and 1990, the population of Wynne decreased by just 119, whereas Forrest City witnessed the exodus of more than 660 residents. These trends reversed between 1990 and 2000, with Forrest City gaining 1,125 residents and Wynne gaining 412. Many of the "new residents" in Forrest City are undoubtedly prisoners in the FCFCF. Based on observations and interviews, it is plausible to attribute a fair share of the population growth over this period in Wynne and Forrest City to the FCFCF.

Table 7.1. Estimating rural property value, family income, poverty, and unemployment as a function of recent prison building for Forrest City and Wynne, Arkansas, 1980–2000

Variables	1980		1990				2000			
	FC	Wynne	FC		Wynne		FC		Wynne	
	Mean	Mean	Mean	Δ 80–90	Mean	Δ 80–90	Mean	Δ 90–00	Mean	Δ 90–00
Median Home Value ($)	31706	33110	40594	8888	43462	10352	56100	15506	60100	16638
Median Family Income ($)	12653	15023	18812	6159	23345	8322	27432	8620	35714	12369
Poverty (%)	33.86	17.53	40.2	6.34	26.64	9.11	33.37	-6.82	21.44	-5.2
Unemp (%)	9	6.75	15.18	6.18	11.63	4.87	16.41	1.23	8.47	-3.16
Tot population	14337	8374	13674	-663	8255	-119	14799	1125	8667	412
Black (%)	48.85	30.92	55.14	6	32.68	1.76	60.96	5.82	32.95	.27
Hispanic (%)	1.1	.64	.60	-.5	0.92	.28	8.8	8.2	1.8	.88
Owner Occ (%)	54.83	70.41	54.05	-.77	66.24	-4.17	50.97	-3.08	62.43	-3.8
Coll Degree (%)	11.96	9.13	12.19	.22	10.98	1.85	12.4	.21	13.14	2.15
Same Residence (as prior census %)	56.39	56.71	56.49	.1	55.85	-.86	43.12	-13.37	53.71	-2.14

Source: Prison Proliferation data

Owner occupancy and residential stability are correlates of residents' investment in a neighborhood (Taub et al. 1984; Sampson 2012). We should expect communities with higher owner occupancy rates and less residential mobility to have more community stability. Between 1980 and 2000, the percentage of residents who have the same address as in the previous census as well as the owner occupancy rates have declined in both Forrest City and Wynne. Although owner occupancy in Wynne had dropped to 62.43 percent in 2000, it is around the national average for rural communities. It also remains relatively high compared to Forrest City's 51 percent.

The percentage of a community's population over age twenty-five with a college degree typically reflects a community's potential pool of managerial or other skilled white-collar labor. For Wynne and Forrest City, the percent of adults who have completed college consistently hovers between 11 percent and 12 percent in 1990. This number of college graduates is comparable to the national average for all rural towns of 11.5 percent, which suggests that either community could attract and sustain a wide variety of industries, including some that are more technologically driven (map 7.1).

Since 1980, Forrest City's proportion of black residents increased from 49 percent to 61 percent, whereas blacks in Wynne increased from 31 percent to 33 percent in that same span. With respect to Hispanics, Wynne remains under 1 percent. Before the arrival of the prison, Forrest City's Hispanic population was roughly 1 percent as well. After the prison opened, the Hispanic population in prison swelled to nearly 9 percent. Put another way, in 1990, there were only eighty-seven Hispanics living in Forrest City; in 2000, there were more than 1,200. The map below shows that while Hispanics make up roughly one-third of the prison population, the vast majority of Hispanics reside in the FCFCF (map 7.2). Ironically, the prison represents the lone mixed-race census block in Forrest City. Lastly, the overwhelming number of male inmates also distorts the sex ratios of rural locations.

Continuity and Change in Caste and Class

In 1937, John Dollard argued, in the classic *Caste and Class in a Southern Town*, "the lives of white and Negro people are so dynamically joined and fixed in one system that neither can be understood without the other" (1). While rural, southern communities have witnessed immense change over time, the legacy of the two-tier plantation system (white landowners overseeing black labor) still looms large (Davis et al. 1941; Cobb 1994). This system marks neighborhoods through racial residential segregation and concentrated poverty—the rural ghetto emerged under this new system.

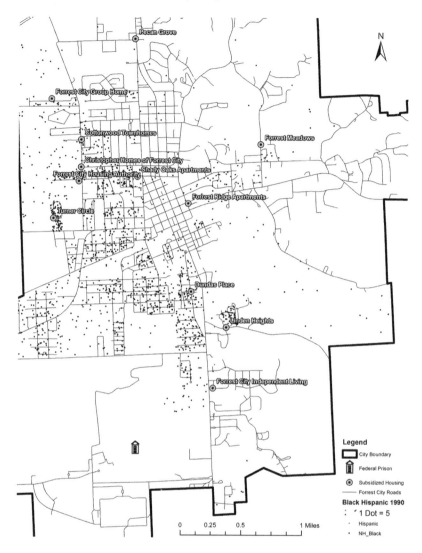

Map 7.1. Black-Hispanic population density by race in Forrest City, Arkansas, 1990

Uneven development across neighborhoods is directly related to the emergence of the ghetto; wealth remains concentrated in the hands of the white elite (Tomaskovic-Devey and Roscigno1997). Forrest City, like many other Deep South or Mississippi Delta communities, continues to operate this way.

As we entered the field in 2006, my family became entangled in a racialized system reminiscent of what Dollard encountered in 1937. In contrast

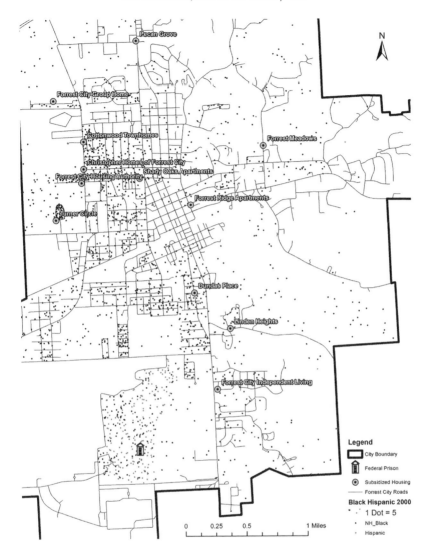

Map 7.2. Black-Hispanic population density by race in Forrest City, Arkansas, 2000

to Dollard's classic study, however, I fully disclosed my role in the study to my subjects (Dollard 1937; Davis et al. 1941). For us, the processes of gaining access and developing relationships produced rich data—specifically, data about the prevailing attitudes of white elites and race leaders toward the growing number of truly disadvantaged (Wilson 1987) in Forrest City. The difference between our findings and Dollard's is that racism is no longer officially sanctioned as state policy but still is practiced.

Racial Script: Better Schools

Being parents of a school-aged child also provided my wife and me with a unique entrée into daily life in Forrest City and Wynne. This perspective allowed us to see how perception does not necessarily mirror reality. We loved the school, and teachers even more, in Wynne. We felt they made great efforts in providing quality education. Our on-the-ground experience with students and teachers in both communities suggests that schooling in Forrest City would have been significantly different. As a first grader in Wynne our son became an unwitting participant-observer, granting unfettered access but also complicating this study. For instance, we learned that there were points when his teacher made him speak in front of his classmates because he lacked an Arkansan accent. His teacher intentionally took this time so that the class could learn "proper" English enunciation without a southern accent. Although his speech had improved by the time we entered the field, ironically, as a kindergartener in the Chicago Public Schools, he was enrolled as a special needs student in speech therapy. We also learned firsthand that Wynne schools had a fair share of poor children. On a school field trip to a sweet potato farm, we observed several of the children spending time with their parents, who were migrant workers. While we did not ask their income, migrant farming in a right-to-work state is an extremely low-paying job. The schools in Arkansas also enlightened us on the impetus for programs aimed at diet and exercise. Physical education in school was once a week, and the free or reduced-price meals that many students at both Wynne and Forrest City schools qualified for were not remotely healthy. Breakfast typically included a biscuit or Pop-Tart, fried (powdered) eggs, or biscuits with gravy. Lunch was equally nutrition-poor, calorie-rich, and lacking in fresh fruits and vegetables.

We frequently heard the phrase "better schools" as a way to differentiate and delineate desirable schools across and within communities in Forrest City and Wynne. Schools are essential to housing markets. Given that we had school-aged children and Arkansas's record of underfunding schools and poor performance on national standardized tests, we approached our move with trepidation. Further compounding our apprehension, Forrest City's test scores were well below the state average. In fact, many schools in the greater Forrest City/Wynne area were not meeting standards set by the state of Arkansas in accordance with the "No Child Left Behind Act." We additionally knew about the constant battles over the millage from my initial interviews. Our perception of the schools was so bad that we considered homeschooling; we also investigated the parochial schools, including a private Christian academy. While the FCFCF delivered numerous benefits, it could not improve the reputation or quality of the local schools. Although Wynne faired better than many school districts in the area, Wynne's test scores, school rankings, and best students were not much different from Forrest City's. "Better schools," in this context, was relative. So why did everyone tell us that Wynne's schools were "better" than Forrest City's?

We found gatekeepers in Forrest City used the phrase "better schools" to us as a racial script not only as a way of saying we (upwardly mobile blacks, clearly not from the area) didn't belong, but more importantly as a way to stigmatize Forrest City. At first, we thought people called Wynne schools "better" because they had higher test scores. However, informants in Forrest City and Wynne gave their opinions of the school systems based on the how they perceived the learning environment, not so much the test scores themselves. Not coincidentally, Wynne public schools are predominantly white, while Forrest City schools are predominantly black. Race was a dominant factor in evaluating school environments. Disadvantage also played a central role in shaping discourse on school environment. Gatekeepers read cues we offered about our family, such as our educational backgrounds, in certain ways, and followed the racial script they thought appropriate for the situation. The script in dealing with upwardly mobile black people—"respectable" folks—was to offer a negative opinion of Forrest City public schools. These cues provide insight into how people viewed the public school systems in Forrest City and Wynne, and how these towns were viewed as well. While Forrest City public schools were constantly disparaged, Wynne schools were consistently heralded as the only viable public option in the area.

When we attempted to move into Forrest City, nearly every informant warned us that the public schools were a major concern. In fact, most people blamed the quality of schools for pushing people out and repelling would-be residents. Local insurance agent and chamber member Steve Lindsey described the complex connections between prison impact, schools, and race on community choice:

S. L.: We've lost a lot of folks that moved here . . . we didn't get the shot in the arm for housing that we should have [from the FCFCF] as we lost a lot of them to Wynne and surrounding areas . . . [long pause] we'd like to have kept them in Forrest City, but that's another story . . .

J. E.: How do you feel about that?

S. L.: Well, it's a problem that has no answer. I think the main reason is the school system in Forrest City it's got its problems. The one thing you can point your finger at one thing why folks have moved to Wynne with the prison so they could go to the Wynne school district. We've lost some good quality folks here that moved 17 miles just to get out of this school district. I'm not sure exactly what the problem is. I think its lack of discipline . . . disruptions in the schools . . . teachers' frustration with all of it . . . and not getting taught as well.

Other informants also characterized Forrest City schools as being over-run by undisciplined "ghetto" children. This issue, too, was discussed in terms of "better schools." "Better schools" were seen as a solution to man-aging ghetto behavior. Perry Webb recalls that while living in Forrest City, the magnet school his children attended, Stewart Elementary, was the best school in the worst part of town (the South End). He recalls that even back then behavioral problems with children were common. Webb's experi-ence at Stewart Elementary is a testament to the existence and continuity of "ghetto" behavior in the schools. Discourse on public education, like public safety, is often used as a catchall for discussing community concerns (Taub, Taylor, and Dunham 1984). Residents in Forrest City and Wynne use discourse on education to signal concerns about their burgeoning ghettos.

A key difference between Forrest City and Wynne schools involved their approach to student discipline. Darrell Smith, the superintendent of public schools in Wynne, claims that the public schools were integrated peace-fully there based on a common vision: "in Wynne, parents, black and white, agreed on two things, education and discipline." To this point, a rarely (if ever) used paddle for spanking hung prominently in my son's classroom as evidence of the focus on discipline as part of the education. Although my son was in first grade, paddles were present in classrooms throughout the elementary school. Some locals claimed that Wynne had fewer disciplinary problems in the public schools than did Forrest City because the school dis-trict still allowed corporal punishment (with parental consent). For Forrest City and Wynne, managing "ghetto" behavior was a crucial part of maintain-ing a suitable educational environment. The Wynne superintendent also claims the focus on education and discipline allowed the schools to enforce rules with little controversy or pushback from parents.

Wynne has not had a parochial school since the Catholic school closed in the 1970s. In Forrest City, in contrast, white elites established a private academy shortly after the US Supreme Court decided the landmark *Brown v. Board of Education* case (based on a claim from nearby Little Rock). In case you missed the point, they named it after Confederate general Robert E. Lee. Southern private schools formed in this era as a backlash to school de-segregation are commonly known as "segregation techs." Some locals used the more pejorative term "redneck tech" to describe Robert E. Lee Academy because of its exclusionary practices against African Americans. The school reportedly remained all white until well after the millennium.

The politics governing the public schools in Forrest City are racially contentious as well. Coach Twillie is not only a former principal of nearby Marianna High School and current director of Christian education at his church, but he also serves on Forrest City school board and on the education advisory committee for the city council. His decades of service and multiple positions avail him a unique outlook on the politics of education in Forrest City. Coach believes that, to be sensitive to the needs of the students, "the school board should reflect the student population." In 2006, he argued that because 90 percent of the students in the Forrest City school district are black, the school board should represent this majority—yet only four of the seven school board members are black. Like many other blacks in town, Coach believes three white school board members symbolize the continuity of white control.

Racial Script: Pull Your Pants Up!

After my formal interviews with Coach Twillie, we met regularly for breakfast or lunch at local establishments to discuss progress on the study, current events in town, and national issues impacting African Americans. We became better acquainted through these chats as Coach waxed eloquent on issues ranging from why devil's food cake is black and angel's food cake is white, to the personal responsibility of blacks in achieving racial uplift. While most of his adult life has been committed to improving condition for blacks in Forrest City, his frustration boiled over one afternoon. It was a sunny, humid day like most in Forrest City in the summer, but inside the Blue Flame Bar and Restaurant it seemed almost like an overcast fall day. On Tuesdays and Thursdays, the restaurant used a counter on the bar to serve a small cafeteria-style lunch. As I picked bits of bacon off the perfectly seasoned and stewed cabbage, flanked by a delicious smothered, baked, quarter chicken, Coach asked, "What do you think about what Bill Cosby said last year"?

He was referring to the controversial "pound cake" speech Bill Cosby made during the fiftieth anniversary celebration commemorating the *Brown v. Board* decision. I responded diplomatically, stating that some people believed the speech was problematic, but given the death of his son and all the hard work he has done for black folks, he has the right to speak his mind. During this address, the philanthropist/comedian scolded poor and middle-class blacks for not upholding the values and victories of the civil rights era. Many commentators characterized this address as, at best, a mean-spirited rant against poor blacks blaming themselves for their position; at worst, it was characterized as racist vitriol spewed by a frustrated aging entertainer. Critics alleged that Cosby degraded poor blacks' lack of parenting, the names they gave their children, their loose morals around sex and dress, and even their speech. Instead of reading Cosby's comments as part of the politics of responsibility, with its litany of "shoulds" and "should nots," Coach heard inspiration. He exclaimed, "Bill Cosby is right! White folks have never taken care of us, so we need to take care of ourselves!" Like Cosby, Coach believed that respectability starts at home.

Cosby peppered his speech with a number of self-help tips for the black community that Coach evidently found inspiring. For instance, Cosby claims, "Now, look, I'm telling you. It's not what they're doing to us. It's what we're not doing . . . we cannot blame white people. White people— white people don't live over there [in our neighborhoods]." Like Cosby, Coach mentioned low-hanging pants; he also added earrings and tattoos as things we just don't need, especially in schools. He then talked about his frustration with the local school board in disputes with parents who refuse to hold their children accountable for poor behavior and dress code violations. He also voiced concern about gang activity and drug selling in the South End. These are all things he feels blacks in Forrest City need to put an end to, and things that can be taken care of in house. This discourse ultimately represents the intraracial tension in the black community when race leaders and the truly disadvantaged meet (Pattillo 2007).

The case of Forrest City, Arkansas, demonstrates that poor blacks' behaviors are policed and stigmatized not only by middle-class blacks through the politics of respectability. Policing poor blacks' behavior is as much a form of social control of seemingly deviant behavior as it is about maintaining southern identity for race leaders. Attempts or calls to correct "ghetto" behavior not only demonize poor blacks but also draw attention from the root causes of these behaviors—continuity in racial and economic inequality through the rural ghetto. Stigma is key to understanding intraracial tensions within a prison town.

Racial Script: Is That a PhD in Street Pharmaceuticology?

It is evident that I am an outsider when I call realtors about available units in Forrest City. At some point when leaving a message or talking with a rental agent, I was sure to mention my key informants' names, my university affiliation, and my student status. As previously discussed, I have an unmistakable black, male, non-southern voice. My partner, who is more adept at mimicry, had better luck than I did in getting the predominantly white realty and rental operations in Forrest City to return her calls. Her ability to adapt her voice helped us understand that realtors received us differently. This interaction clued us in to some racial scripts used to stigmatize ghetto residents in Forrest City—recall that a realtor told her not to live in Forrest City because there are too many coloreds there. While she made headway on the practical goal of securing housing, I was racially profiled as a drug dealer by realtors and rental agents.

In contrast to the work of scholars who have suggested that middle-class blacks can mitigate some of the effects of racial stigma through privilege (Anderson 2001; Lacy 2007), I found that the stigma of blackness made it nearly impossible to find a place to live in Forrest City. My subjective experiences tell an objective story. In seeking an apartment, I could be categorized according to realtors' racial scripts. I use my experiences trying to find a rental property to reveal larger structures and broader patterns of experience at work in Forrest City. My findings provide further evidence that life for blacks in Forrest City continues to be defined through a narrow lens of local whites' racism.

After spending the previous summer living in Forrest City hotels while I conducted research, my wife and I decided to move our family from our home in the urban North to Forrest City. After repeatedly contacting all eight realty agents listed on the Forrest City Chamber of Commerce's website over the course of three months, we had reached a dead end. If I were fortunate enough to talk to a realtor, I was asked questions like, where will you work, what will you be doing here? Some brazenly inquired, why on earth would I move to Forrest City? Following a few innocuous questions, one realtor asked for my social security number. I thought nothing of this until he asked for Lisa and the children's social security numbers and birth certificates. I told him I would have to get that information later. Many middle-income renters would find the use of a form requesting verification of your legal rights as parent insulting. One rental agent used a form application from the National Apartment Association that conflates a potential renter's credit history with his or her criminal history. Some realtors agreed to e-mail pictures of the properties and formal copies of the rental applications, but they rarely followed through and usually did not respond to my calls.

While the agents were clearly worried about my intentions as a renter, I was worried about the use of my personal information. I felt as if I were being profiled or accused of some type of illegal activity (presumably drug dealing) by asking about available units. Realtors were clearly concerned about an outsider looking for a place to live in their town. Perhaps Forrest City realtors were simply acting as gatekeepers by filtering the entry of new blacks or outsiders. This might be racial prejudice. The locals, however, might see it as a reasonable response given examples of northerners, like the Chamberlin boys—these drug dealers operating out of Detroit infamously ran drugs between rural Arkansas and Detroit (Adler 1995).

After months of frustration, we decided to try our luck in person. We again drove nearly half a day, staying several more days in a hotel in search of a rental property. Using the networks of key informants, we found a three-bedroom apartment that was available, but we needed to overnight a deposit in the form of a money order, application, and a letter of recommendation. We did not hear back from the realtor for weeks. After repeatedly calling, the agent we initially contacted answered and cursed at me for inquiring about the apartment. I informed her that she had our deposit in the form of a money order. She calmed down, apologized, and said she was having a stressful day (as if I should console her) and told us the apartment we had sent a deposit to secure was occupied. Moreover, the tenant whom she thought was going to be evicted had paid her rent, so the apartment was no longer available.

On this recent trip, one of the two rental agents who contacted us Googled me and downloaded and read one of my papers before returning my call, as if I were applying to an elite housing cooperative or condominium on Park Avenue in Manhattan instead of an apartment in Forrest City. In New York, the elaborate application and recommendation process signals a constrained housing market based on the demand of extremely wealthy or high-status buyers. Realtors and condo and co-op boards in high-end markets serve as gatekeepers. While the rental market in Forrest City faces constraints, these barriers do not result from the attempts of the extremely wealthy or elite to move in. In contrast, the gatekeeper function of realty agents was quite the opposite.

From the information I had on the rental market from the census data, I had expected better business practices. For example, I had assumed that realtors would return potential renters' phone calls. If nothing were available, the rental agent might inform the caller of the situation. At the minimum, a person should not receive a tongue lashing for checking on the status of a security deposit. Realtors/rental agents in Forrest City not only failed to provide a base level of respect for their potential renters; they were often openly hostile.

I eventually learned that our experiences in the housing market in Forrest City were not isolated incidents. Later, I also discovered that there were other reasons for the constrained rental market. Upon sharing our experiences in the Forrest City rental market with Perry Webb, the former director of the Saint Francis County chamber, he explained:

> When I got to Forrest City, I'd been there about three days and my assistant came in and said, "uh, do you know about our rental list." And I went, "a what?" And she said, "our rental list." We were the clearinghouse—if somebody [white] in Forrest City had a house they wanted rented, they would call the chamber and they kept a notebook listing available houses. My assistant said, and I quote, and she said, "Now, if they sound black, we don't tell them." [long pause and silence] . . . and she said, "if they sound black, we're not supposed to tell them about these." And I said, "well give me that book," and she handed it to me and I just ripped it to shreds right in front of her. And I said, "this program stops, this second. Do you realize what you're doing?" And she went, "oh we're just doing what they want us to do." I said, "no, no." But I get it. I witnessed it. I saw it and that was prevalent and it probably still is you know . . . that was the way it was.

I have every reason to believe that the housing policy Perry Webb removed was reinstated under the new chamber director. When I informed David Dunn of our difficulties finding housing and asked for his assistance in making referrals, he reacted coolly, with neither surprise nor sympathy. Although I was unaware of the policy of denying black renters access to the list of "white" rentals at that time, it would certainly explain the difficulties my wife and I encountered in renting houses in Forrest City. These types of policies are evidence of the continuity in racial caste and class that maintain the segregated neighborhood ecology of disrepute.

Despite Being Tarnished, Some Luster Remains

Dollard (1937, 62) asserts that, "caste has replaced slavery as a means of maintaining the essence of the old status order in the South." Dollard, writing in the 1930s, noted that this new caste system flourished in communities like Forrest City under Jim Crow. In our contemporary era, the rural ghetto has replaced the Jim Crow system as the mechanism for maintaining caste in the rural South. While the arrival of a prison slowed Forrest City's decline, its rural ghetto endures. The endurance and eventual collapse of the rural ghetto presents obstacles to development and challenges to rebuilding the reputation of Forrest City. And yet, things are not as bad as they could be in Forrest City. Prisons can be economically viable, and the presence of the

FCFCF has ensured that Forrest City will survive, even as other towns in eastern Arkansas continue their economic freefall.

Leaders in Forrest City believe that the FCFCF, along with expansion of the East Arkansas Community College (EACC) and vocational tech school, have saved Forrest City's image. Some of them also credit the prison with attracting and retaining the Boar's Head meat-processing plant. Everyone I spoke with agreed that the town is better positioned because of the FCFCF. The evidence presented in this chapter suggests that their impressions are correct: The FCFCF had a countervailing effect on the political economy of Forrest City. These findings suggest that prisons can be considered institutional actors that rural communities can use to slow their economic skid. To be sure, many Forrest City residents continue to suffer deep poverty, and the presence of a rural ghetto continues to challenge the town's reputation, creating barriers to attracting and sustaining development. The policing of the truly disadvantaged through the politics of respectability, by race leaders and white elites, shows that leaders are aware of, and are attempting to combat, this stigma.

Forrest City shows some signs of progress. For example, Buddy Billingsley aided in securing the multi-million-dollar expansion of the East Arkansas Community College Fine Arts wing. Woodruff Electrical Cooperative also opened a facility in Forrest City, representing a hefty investment in capital and an expansion of the local workforce. There are signs of political progress as well. The school board and city council is as integrated as any town's in the South. Challengers to Mayor Larry Bryant in his reelection bid in 2014 were black and white and politically to the left and right of him. These developments also speak to the town's increase in racial diversity as far it being a majority racial minority community. And compared to other places in the area, Forrest City's fortunes don't look nearly so bleak. In follow-up interviews, multiple respondents told me some version of, "It's a shame what's happening here in the Delta." By that, they mean depopulation, along with its accompanying social and cultural shocks. While the public schools remain open in Forrest City, many surrounding communities have lost so many residents that they have had to close their schools—from Helena to Blytheville, things are drying up. And with the closing of the schools, housing values in Helena, Marianna, Parkin, Forrest City, Earle, Wynne, Brinkley, Cotton Plant, and Marvell have declined. Even with its blemished image, in comparison to surrounding communities, Forrest City remains the "Jewel of the Delta."

EIGHT

Bringing Down the Big House: The Political Economy of Prison Proliferation

> In the case of labor power, a person can cease to have economic value in capitalism if it cannot be deployed productively. This is the essential condition of people in the "underclass" . . . above all [they lack] the necessary means to acquire the skills needed to make their labor power saleable. As a result they are not consistently exploited . . . the underclass consists of human beings who are largely expendable from the point of view of the logic of capitalism.
>
> —Wright 1997, 28

This sophisticated Marxist analysis of modern class stratification echoes the simple words of a sage lay leader in a South Side Chicago church basement over a dozen years ago— "you either get a job, or you become a job." Inspired by my experiences as an organizer closing drug houses in Chicago neighborhoods, this book has focused on linking punishment, racial inequality, and neighborhood change to the political economy of rural communities. The study provides nuance to social scientists' understandings of the multiple ways racial inequality and punishment relate to the political economy of, and neighborhoods within, rural communities. To date, scholars have studied punishment primarily by focusing on the causes and consequences of mass imprisonment in urban neighborhoods (Goffman 2014; Jacobs and Carmichael 2001; Jacobs and Kleban 2003; Mauer 2006; Pager 2003; Tonry 1995; Wacquant 2001; Wakefield and Uggen 2010; Western 2006; Uggen and Manza 2002). The small but growing literature on the prison boom finds that prison building increases racial and economic inequality across the rural-urban continuum (Besser and Hanson 2004; Gilmore 2007; Hooks et al. 2004; Hooks et al. 2010; Huling 2001; King, Mauer, and Huling 2003; Schlosser 1998). While the classic criminological literature posits the prison as an institution that should be used to incapacitate, rehabilitate, deter, and enact retribution, I suggest the causes and consequences of the prison boom extend far beyond the typical purposes of the prison.

Big House on the Prairie has explored the causes and consequences of the prison boom from the perspective of town leaders and residents who sought after, and won, a prison for their community. Structural changes in rural communities like Forrest City lead to prison "demand." In showing how this phenomenon operates, I provide a framework linking local community processes of prison placement to the national phenomenon of prison proliferation. Because prisons are stigmatized (Combessie 2002; Goffman 1963), these institutions, and therefore the demand for them, are quite different from the standard story of industrial development. Prisons carry multiple meanings: Prisons are a good, a bad, and are often structurally quite ugly. During the prison boom, building occurred mainly in towns that were themselves stigmatized and therefore more willing to pursue a stigmatized institution like a prison.

Locals use various strategies to frame placement as a way to improve a town's image. For a disadvantaged town like Forrest City, building a prison is often the best of the last development options to manage the town's spoiled identity associated with the rise of the rural ghetto. Forrest City's colorful history certainly makes it a unique case. In many respects, however, Forrest City represents the prototypical town that received a prison during the height of the boom—it is a micropolitan town with a high poverty rate and a high concentration of blacks. In towns like this, black poverty is concentrated into neighborhoods that might best be understood as rural ghettos. The need to combat the stigma of the rural ghetto united two factions that typically battle for political power within a rural southern town—race leaders and white elites. In Forrest City—and, I would argue, other prison towns—these two groups formed a growth coalition to produce a groundswell of support for prison placement by framing the prison as a way to save the community. The notion of the prison being the best of the last options permeated the local discourse as the town pursued and secured the prison. This framing of the prison not only explains why leaders pursue placement, but also affects how locals perceive impact.

Recent qualitative studies of prison towns (primarily by geographers) have begun to tease out the nuances of prison impact (Bonds 2012; Campo Nation 2006; Engel 2007; Morell 2012). All told, the territory covered by the prison boom spans 580 square miles, more than half the size of Rhode Island, with capital costs in construction in the hundreds of billions. Clearly, prisons must have *some* sort of impact on the communities they occupy.

Existing scholarship emphasizes the negative consequences of this building boom. While prior chapters have challenged this depiction through a case study of Forrest City, this concluding chapter tests the theory that prison building slows economic decline in rural communities by tracing national trends in prison impact over time. I demonstrate that the prison acts a stabilizer against turbulent economic times for rural communities, but that impact differs by period of the prison boom. By and large, the trends from Forrest City hold.

These findings suggest several theoretical and policy implications. First, given that prison towns are sites of racial and spatial stratification, examining them provides a way for us to rethink the core purpose of punishment. Second, the policy implications of prison proliferation extend far beyond the facilities or the communities in which they reside. I conclude by exploring these policy implications in more detail. I return to David Garland's description of the new iron cage, in which prison building is justified by, "the system taking on a life of its own, giving rise to adaptive behavior serving secondary interests" (Garland 2001, 179). I redefine the *penal*-industrial complex— "the set of bureaucratic and private institutions that produce and manage jobs around prison building" (Garland 2001, 179)—more broadly as the economic, social, and political institutions related to the causes and consequences of the prison boom.

This distinction allows us to ask different questions regarding prison impact. For instance, if prisons are obsolete, as some scholars and activists argue (Davis 2003), how will the de-escalation of prison building impact rural communities? Should we keep building or renovating facilities? What are the collateral consequences of repealing mass imprisonment for communities of color across the rural-urban continuum? While these questions fall outside the purview of the prison-industrial complex, the concept of the *penal*-industrial complex allows them to be addressed head on. I therefore conclude with the proposition that rethinking the penal-industrial complex is the best approach to understand prison proliferation.

Using this model not only addresses how NIMBY became PIMBY regarding prisons, but also the assumption that prison proliferation is fundamentally racist. To further clarify, I am not arguing that white elites who want prisons cannot be racist. This of course belies structural racism. To be clear, I am suggesting that even if there is structural racism in the placement process, it is not paramount to the desires of local white elites. Again, racism in this instance is a secondary effect rather than a primary cause. That being said, in no way should arguments here be used to defend private contractors seeking profits from prison beds in the recent spike in immigrant detention facilities. Although there has not been empirical evidence illuminating their intentions (whether ill or null), on face value alone development activities in this sector are extremely exploitative. If prison placement is not a direct result of racism in the criminal justice system, one could ask if racism plays a role at all. The simple answer is yes. Understanding the role of underdevelopment as a part of this new system of racial and economic subordination that maintains the racial hierarchy in southern towns provides a basis for asserting that the rural ghetto (not mass imprisonment) has effectively replaced Jim Crow.

The Economic Impact of Prisons

The impacts of prison proliferation are not simply limited to where prisoners are from or where prisons are constructed. Expanding how we think about prison impact broadens our ability to explore the link between prison proliferation and inequality. Prison proliferation is a pressing question not only for scholars of crime and punishment, but also for scholars of rural economic development and urban poverty. The prison boom should be understood, at least in part, as a product of the power structures between and within rural and urban communities.

To date, prison impact studies have primarily focused on the advantages or disadvantages provided by prison building in rural communities (Hooks et al. 2004; Hooks et al. 2010; King, Mauer, and Huling 2003; Huling 2001; Glasmeier and Farrigan 2007). These studies focus on measures of employment growth and poverty alleviation as central economic indicators. While Glasmeier and Farrigan (2007) find that prisons provide little economic benefit to the most disadvantaged communities, the scholarly consensus is that prisons are bad for rural communities (Hooks et al 2004; Hooks et al 2010; King, Mauer, and Huling 2003). In fact, some work suggests (implicitly or explicitly) that prison stigma negatively impacts rural communities by limiting other types of development beyond future prison facilities (Gilmore 2007; Hooks et al. 2004; Hooks et al. 2010; King, Mauer, and Huling 2003; Huling 2001; Schlosser 1998).

There are several reasons to question the harmful effects of prisons to rural communities. First, many of these studies are based on a single state over a short period (Gilmore 2007; King, Mauer, and Huling 2003). Second, most studies only consider economic growth (Hooks et al. 2004; Hooks et al. 2010; King, Mauer, and Huling 2003; Glasmeier and Farrigan 2007). This limited approach does not provide clarity on the more crucial policy question of whether or not prisons slow economic decline. Third, the unit of analysis is not standardized in quantitative studies of prison towns—some measure counties (Hooks et al. 2004; Hooks et al. 2010; Huling 2001), while others measure US census places (Glasmeier and Farrigan 2007).

Furthermore, the demographic impact of prisoners cannot be understated for the political economy of prison towns. While prisons may not have an effect on electoral races as direct campaign contributors, they can still wield considerable political clout through their ability to mobilize people and money. On the local level, some have found that because prisoners are counted by the census as residents in the locale of the prison, states are redistricting seats based on minority inmates, skewing population counts (Tilove 2002; Lotke and Wagner 2003). The census also helps determine governmental funding for communities such as Community Development Block Grants.

In short, these studies fail to consider whether prisons and the new jobs they bring slow economic decline or other ways that prisons may benefit rural communities. Although prisons may not solve all the economic woes facing most disadvantaged rural communities, they may offer a reprieve from an economic downturn. More to the point, we lack empirically grounded theories to conceptualize the links between the prison boom and disadvantage in rural towns. By examining prison impact at the national and local levels we can better grasp the mechanisms and processes of racial and economic stratification across the rural-urban continuum. This approach allows us to consider how the modern prison has become not only a means of social control but also a form of poverty management, exploitation, and stigma.

Measuring Prison Impact

Until recent qualitative studies (Bonds 2012; Campo Nation 2006; Engel 2007; Morell 2012), investigations into prison impact lacked methodological diversity. In a key piece on prison impact, Blankenship and Yanarella (2004) suggest a powerful rubric for measuring prison impact on communities. They propose that a prison with a positive impact would (1) create high-quality jobs within the local economy, (2) preserve local capital, (3) improve local public infrastructure and increase the local tax base, and (4) improve or maintain local social capital and civic culture.

To date, no study has taken this holistic approach as a framework for measuring the pros and cons of prison building. Several studies have, however, attempted to provide sophisticated approaches to understanding economic impact. Hooks and colleagues (2004; 2010), for instance, provide a county-level spatial economic analysis of prison impact over time for all US prisons (rural and urban), including controls for established prisons. The authors found that "prisons impede economic growth in counties growing at the slowest pace, [which] flies in the face of the widely held view that prison construction can assist struggling local areas" (Hooks et al. 2010, 51). These findings support the claim that prior prisons create an agglomerative prison economy, driving away other types of future developments. I build on this finding by investigating the role of prior prison placement in future prison building.

Studies of prison towns vary widely in their unit of analysis. Although many studies use the county as the unit of analysis (Hooks et al. 2004; Hooks et al. 2010; Huling 2001), increasingly scholars of rural communities use the town or US census place (Eason 2010; Glasmeier and Farrigan 2007). Each unit of analysis presents unique advantages and challenges for interpreting outcomes. While county-level analyses have provided better and more reliable data over time, they tend to obfuscate prison impact on the rural locales that are arguably most disadvantaged. Town-level demographics offers a more nuanced assessment of the prison boom (McShane, Williams, and Wagoner 1992; Besser and Hanson 2004). Glasmeier and Farrigan (2007) took the town-level analysis further by using town-level predictors to measure the economic impact of prisons. Their contribution of clear, standardized measures of propinquity to prior prisons makes their work an innovative approach to studying rural prison impact. The absence of controls for region, state, and race in these studies is problematic, given that other studies have found these factors to be significant predictors of prison building. Nevertheless, these initial studies provide a good description of overall trends.

One potential problem with these studies is their reliance on mailing address data from the American Correctional Association (ACA). ACA data alone cannot be used to geocode prisons because more than 150 prisons list addresses at a location five or more miles away from the prison facility. An alternative is to use US census places as a unit of analysis. In my own analysis, I improved on the ACA data by verifying each prison's US census place (see the methodological appendix for a more detailed description of this process). Although US census places are usually considered too limited in size to capture employment and well-being outcomes, they nevertheless provide a good avenue for understanding the relationship between concentrated disadvantage and the prison boom. The US census place, or rural town, allows an appropriate spatial scale for this analysis. Much like neighborhoods in urban areas, rural US census places refract extreme concentrations of racial and economic disadvantage, as evidenced by high rates of concentrated poverty (Lichter et al. 2008) and residential segregation (Lichter et al. 2007a and b).

As I have demonstrated previously (Eason 2010), race, region, population density, poverty, unemployment, degree of rurality, and prior placement are correlates of prison placement. I consider these factors in predicting prison impact. While Hoyman and Weinberg (2006) measure poverty and Gregory Hooks, Clayton Mosher, Thomas Rotolo, and Linda Lobao (2004; 2010) measure employment as outcomes, I examine both. Building from the framework of prison impact established in the prior chapters, I analyze how newly constructed prisons impact places across different periods of the prison boom. In considering the relationship between prison building and political economy I assess the impact of newly constructed prisons on (1) median home values, (2) median family income, (3) poverty, and (4) unemployment of rural towns.

Prison Impact across the Boom

For detailed analysis see, "Estimating Impact across the Prison Boom, 1980–2000," in Appendix B. Findings demonstrate that prison building slows economic decline and stabilizes prison towns and other surrounding communities. Overall, prisons provide a short-term economic boon in some periods for rural communities compared to communities that do not build prisons. While prison building in the earliest period increased median home value, reduced unemployment, and eased poverty, these effects are not lasting. Examining the effects of prisons across different periods of national economic hardship (1980s) and prosperity (1990s) allows a discussion of how broader economic trends impact rural towns. While prisons may increase or decrease unemployment depending on the period of building, the findings also suggest that prisons replace jobs lost across struggling rural communities. In other words, towns that built prisons between 1989 and 1998 experienced a less pronounced economic decline than similarly situated towns. Moreover, in favorable economic conditions, prisons provide a boost to local economies by reducing unemployment. However, the impact of a prison on unemployment does not seem to carry over from prior decades, suggesting a decay effect. This decay effect may be linked to broader downward economic shifts in rural communities. Because the impact of prison building on poverty in 1980 is statistically insignificant in 1990 and 2000, the effect of prisons on poverty may decay over time as well. The lagged effects of mass imprisonment and prison building help shape the context of early versus late adopters of prison placement. Prison building not only lessened the economic strain from poverty and unemployment for towns that built prisons during the trying economic times of the 1980s but also improved their economic conditions by improving median family income and home values.

Overall, I find that towns that adopted prisons earlier in the prison boom received a short-term boon compared to those that did not build, but these effects were not lasting. For early adopters, prison building increased median home value and median family income while easing poverty and bumping up unemployment. Later in the boom, prison building protected towns against further economic decline by slowing unemployment. There is no evidence supporting the claim that prison building has negative consequences on rural communities. We should therefore consider the prison as a stabilizing force for rural communities headed toward the precipice of economic and social despair.

The FCFCF follows the national trends in prison impact. In fact, my findings suggest that Wynne and Forrest City may have benefited more than the average prison town during the period of the boom. Given that prisons may not necessarily produce dire consequences in rural communities, how should we make sense of prison impact? Understanding that rural towns use prisons to ease economic hardships not only speaks to prison "demand," but also how we understand placement, impact, and proliferation.

Conclusion: Bringing Down the Big House?

The prison town is an important site to explore the confluence of criminal justice expansion, racialized social systems, and neighborhood change. The complex process of prison building is far too often reduced to a by-product of imprisoning urban minorities for the benefit of rural whites (Gilmore 2007; Lotke and Wagner 2003; Mauer 2006; Schlosser 1998). In this scenario, the complicated process of prison placement is reduced to a zero-sum game where rural white towns win prisons at the expense of urban black and Hispanic neighborhoods. From this perspective, one could argue that economic progress in rural white communities is a linear outcome of urban arrests of blacks and Latinos (Alexander 2010; Davis 2003; Gilmore 2007; Jacobs 2005).

The racial and economic exploitation described in this scenario is palpable. Nevertheless, I do not believe that it fully accounts for the local context of decision makers in rural communities. This book has shown that prison building and cordoning off zones for the so-called underclass is not just a phenomenon that impacts urban communities. Instead, the stratification of poor, rural, minority communities is a necessary but not sufficient precursor to prison building. If prison building could simply be explained as a function of urban economic and racial stratification, then how can we reconcile the benefits prisons provide to rural communities of color? A fair number of prison jobs go to people of color in rural communities. For example, in 2000, African Americans and Latinos respectively made up 22 percent and 7 percent of correctional officers in the United States (Ward 2006). The presence of a significant number of blacks and Hispanics in correctional officer positions in rural communities complicates a central theme of racial dominance in the prison boom literature. In addition to social control, poverty management, racial exploitation, and stigma, prisons appear to offer jobs to disadvantaged rural communities of color. The costs and benefits of prisons must include the preferences of rural communities that most often site them.

My findings challenge existing paradigms about prison placement and impact. The sorts of rural communities of color that disproportionately site prisons are frequently alienated, yet this social exclusion does not appear in a literature that overwhelmingly presents prison siting as a form of environmental racism (Huling 2001; King, Mauer, and Huling 2003). We can rethink this prior literature using Ward (2006, 67–68): "research has been less attentive to ethnoracial group agency in justice processes, including the ways race and ethnicity relate to policy interests, organizational cultures, levels of influence, and eventual distributions of services and sanctions within justice systems themselves. Imbalanced attention to the subjectivity of marginalized groups in justice processes and neglect of actual and potential group agency not only limits appreciation of the complex dynamics of radicalized social control but may also reinforce stereotypes about and its racial dimensions."

Unlike Loïc Wacquant (2011, 607), I am not attempting to "slay the chimera of the 'Prison Industrial Complex.'" Instead, I am constructing a more empirically based, theoretically driven, methodologically rigorous framework to advance the study of prison proliferation. This line of research situates the study of prison impact within a theoretical perspective that anchors the rural prison town at the center. From this perspective, I suggest that the prison, as a complex institution, should be understood as neither panacea nor pariah for rural towns. The context of reception becomes essential to understanding placement and impact. Scholars like Joseph Donnermeyer and Walter Dekeseredy (2008) advocate for a new rural criminology focusing on context. This inquiry serves as an anchor for a new critical rural criminology focused on the context of crime and criminal justice outcomes. We can further this theoretical perspective by considering prison building as fundamental to the political economy of punishment. We can moreover highlight the salience of the political economy of depressed rural communities of color to prison proliferation. In doing so, the normative claims of the prison-industrial complex model can be reframed from a more positive perspective as a *penal*-industrial complex focusing on the private and governmental agencies managing and producing jobs around prison building. Fully understanding the penal-industrial complex requires that we delve deeper into the political economy of local, state, and federal actors and institutions that drive prison proliferation. This approach makes the direct policy implications of studying prison proliferation more apparent.

Distinguishing the causes and consequences of the prison boom from mass imprisonment makes a significant contribution to how we understand criminal justice outcomes. Disentangling mass imprisonment from prison proliferation allows us to examine how inequality is produced and reproduced in rural communities of color. If we want to discontinue our over-reliance on mass imprisonment, we need to consider the interventions needed in rural communities of color to minimize their further stratification. This is a critical move, because we do not fully understand why communities allowed 1,152 prisons to be constructed in their backyards in just over thirty years. A better understanding of the benefits and challenges presented by prison building can also help us understand why those towns wanted these stigmatized facilities. This book is an attempt to better understand the benefits of prison building that have led to increased demand for them as economic engines in depressed rural areas.

These findings raise questions about whether state governments should close prisons, maintain or renovate their facilities, or continue to build them. This knowledge base provides predictive power to understand potential outcomes for rural communities as the pressure mounts to roll back imprisonment. The debate over de-carceration, or the rollback of imprisonment, is already taking shape in states like New York, where Governor Cuomo has closed over a dozen facilities in only a few years. While closings have increased in New York because of budget deficits over the past decade, prison construction has altogether ceased in the state of New York.

From Texas governor Rick Perry to former Speaker of the US House of Representatives Newt Gingrich, to black activist Angela Davis, a growing number of conservative politicians and activists agree our spending on corrections is out of control. In March 2009, amid reasonable calls for the reduction of the number of those imprisoned and moratoriums on prison building by prison abolitionists, US senator Jim Webb offered a plea to middle Americans, titled "Why We Must Fix Our Prisons," in *Parade Magazine*. Like many other scholars and activists before him, he argues that our criminal justice system flies in the face of America being a free and fair nation. "With so many of our citizens in prison compared with the rest of the world," he wrote, "there are only two possibilities: Either we are home to the most evil people on earth or we are doing something different—and vastly counterproductive. Obviously, the answer is the latter" (5). Senator Webb also challenges us to think about the costs of imprisonment in terms of lost opportunities and tax dollars.

Discussions of correctional spending primarily focus on annual operating budgets, specifically the annual cost to lock up an individual. Capital costs, especially of building prisons, are usually ignored. In analyzing the impact of prison building on gross state product across the United States, I find that despite the economic boost to rural communities, prison building is a drag on state economies. That is to say that prison building is costly to states. In light of recent budget shortfalls, many states are considering closing prison facilities. Many well-intentioned activists and scholars are similarly advocating for prison abolition (Davis 2003; Gilmore 2007; Jacobs 2005). The implications of these policies, however, have not been fully thought out. Closing prisons will not solve the problems of poor minorities, rural, urban, or otherwise, and may in fact produce unanticipated collateral damage. Prison abolition efforts may inadvertently harm vulnerable populations within the very African American and Hispanic communities they are trying to protect. At the risk of implying that racism is not a problem in prison towns (it is), activists need to understand the damage from racism does not come from attempts to exploit urban communities, but rather from rural ghettos within the prison town itself. These communities suffer from prison reentry, racial profiling, and disproportionate minority involvement in the criminal justice system, the same as their urban counterparts.

Despite theoretical and substantive advances in scholarship on mass imprisonment, mass imprisonment remains invisible in the lives of mainstream white Americans and means very little to that segment of society (Western 2006). In contrast, for poor, uneducated blacks and Hispanics, the criminal justice system has become omnipresent, shaping nearly every experience (Goffman 2009; Pager 2003; Uggen and Manza 2002; Wildeman 2009). For many rural poor communities of color, prison proliferation represents another shift in the purpose of the prison. We cannot forget that mass imprisonment is not limited to northern urban areas—rural towns of color have also experienced mass imprisonment (Lynch 2010; Perkinson 2010). While we await further study of prison impact, our understanding of the prison system must be informed by the benefits and costs to rural towns as well urban communities.

One example, in 2015, a riot forced a prison in a Texas town to close. According to the Willacy County commissioner, Beto Guerra, in the "worst scenario, we'll lose about $2.3 million annually, which is about 23 percent of our [the county's] income" (Burnett 2015). The article goes on to describe a town that is in many ways similar to Forrest City. Cursory descriptions of the town suggest that it, too, suffers from the same type of concentrated disadvantage and spoiled reputation that drove Forrest City to seek a prison. Instead of a rural ghetto, one could imagine a rural barrio driving prison "demand," given the high percent of Latinos in town. The effects of this closing could be devastating, especially to poor people of color.

To be clear, I am not advocating for the construction of prisons as a poverty reduction or economic growth strategy. I am, however, suggesting that the discontinuation of prison building or an outright reduction in the number of prisons in rural communities may have collateral consequences, including increasing poverty in rural communities of color. Given the urban focus of most research on penal expansion, the long literature documenting the deleterious impact of the criminal justice system on low-income communities of color, and the stigma associated with prisons, it should not be surprising that the positive impacts of prison building on rural communities remain unseen. These benefits, however, are not trivial, and could help to explain why prison expansion, despite considerable declines in crime and the cost of imprisonment in a time of relative fiscal constraint, remains attractive to prison towns, particularly in southern states. In many ways, prison construction serves as a state-sponsored public works program for disadvantaged rural communities of color.

This study highlights the salience of prisons to poverty policies in rural communities. Over the past forty years, the prison has become essential to the economic survival of some distressed rural communities. Given the insatiable demand for economic development in depressed rural communities, will prison building continue at the feverish rate of recent decades? Or will states succumb to austerity measures aimed at cutting costs through closing prisons? To curb rural prison "demand," we must provide alternatives to the perverse economic incentives of prison building. Eric Schlosser posits that

> The spirit of every age is manifest in its public works, in the great construction projects that leave an enduring mark on the landscape. . . . All across the

country new cellblocks rise. And every one of them, every brand-new prison, becomes another lasting monument, concrete and ringed with deadly razor wire, to the fear and greed and political cowardice that now pervade American society. (Schlosser 1998, 10)

Some rural communities of color, devastated by the rise of the rural ghetto and mass imprisonment, cling to prisons as life rafts. The very real economic impact of prisons in these towns points to a sobering reality.

The United States has devoted a massive acreage to prison construction over the past forty years. How will we ultimately define the prison boom and how will prison proliferation define this era? Over the past three years, imprisonment in the United States has finally leveled off. And yet, the *Sentencing Project* estimates that, without sweeping sentencing reforms and policy changes, it would take almost ninety years to get us back to the prison population of 1980. Given the complicated relationship between mass imprisonment and prison proliferation, neither sound scholarship nor political rhetoric alone will resolve these high-stakes issues for disadvantaged communities of color.

ACKNOWLEDGMENTS

Many believe that research (especially ethnography) results from a lone scholar going off into a community and returning to tell his or her tales. This project was possible primarily because of the collaboration of many people in the field and throughout the writing process. To this end, I must first and foremost recognize the people of Forrest City, Arkansas. While there are far too many to identify by name here, I do use the real names of informants in the manuscript. These individuals gave their time, and without them there would not be a story to tell. In addition to naming these individuals in the manuscript, I would also like to recognize their contribution here. Although there are some informants who chose to remain anonymous (and others that I did not feel comfortable identifying), I need to thank each of them for sharing their stories. I am forever indebted to each of these individuals.

I especially need to thank André Stephens and the staff of the Saint Francis County Community Development Corporation. Without their help, I would not have been able to build the necessary inroads to effectively conduct interviews in Forrest City. Cecil Twillie and John Alderson provided bridges across the racial divides that existed during my fieldwork. In addition, many key pieces of secondary data were either gathered by or found under the direction of Kendall Owens of the *Forrest City Times-Herald*, George Brewer at the Arkansas Department of Corrections, and Sharon Rose (Judah) Donovan at the Arkansas Department of Health. Their professionalism and timeliness made the iterative process of data analysis across multiple methods possible.

Omar McRoberts, Richard Taub, and Bruce Western provided encouragement, support, patience, and the vision to drive toward an unrelenting adherence to the scientific method. The theoretical foundation of this project was established at the Probing the Penal State Conference at the University of California, Berkeley. Hosts Loïc Wacquant and Bruce Western assembled amazing participants like David Garland, Mona Lynch, and Jonathan Simon to provide constructive comments to a community that included several junior scholars. This workshop was key in cultivating my thinking on punishment and inequality. My mentors at Duke University, Eduardo Bonilla-Silva and Linda Burton, and William "Sandy" Darity, inspired me to carve out a space for discourse between several disparate subfields. David Brady, Tyson Brown, and Sherri Lawson-Clark each took a keen interest and provided useful feedback on chapters during my time at Duke University as well. When writing got tough and I needed encouragement most, David Ferguson, Jason Greenberg, Angela Hattery, Joseph Jewell, Andrea Leverentz, Janice Williams Miller, Reuben Miller, Zandria F. Robinson, Earl Smith, Andrew Papachristos, and Christopher Wildeman could always find kind, encouraging words to help me clarify things for the reader.

The late Calvin Beale, Peter Wagner, and Marc Mauer were incredibly gracious in taking time to speak by phone early in my graduate career. They gave me sage advice on how to overcome the challenges in compiling and properly managing prison building data early on in this project. Looking back on the time they so unselfishly gave to me I am humbled. Without their encouragement I would not have been able to amass the quantitative data for this project. Furthermore, key to completing the fieldwork was the Dissertation Fellowship from the Center for the Study of Race, Politics, and Culture at the University of Chicago. In my tenure there I received support and encouragement from Waldo Johnson, Tracye Mathews, Theresa Mah, and Jessica Sparks. Thank you. Over the life of this project Jason Beckfield, Mary Campbell, Larry Hedges, Pat Rubio-Goldsmith, and Rafe Stolzenberg provided invaluable methodological feedback on quantitative modeling. Gabriel Amaro, Rufus Barner, Robert Fornango, Mark Fossett, Eric Hedberg, Neal Patel, and Chris Winters provided valuable assistance with secondary data management, cleaning, coding, mapping, and analysis. Vanessa Barker, Randol Contreras, Matt Desmond, William Falk, Joe Feagin, Shaun Gabbidon, Larry Griffin, Gregory Hooks, Linda Laboa, Dan Lichter, Damian Martinez, Reuben May, Alex McIntosh, Andrew McNeeley, Alex Murphy, Mary Pattillo, Jon Wynn, and all my colleagues in the Department of Sociology at Texas A&M provided comments and substantive feedback throughout the development of this manuscript.

Over the years I have presented chapters at a multitude of other workshops and conferences. Each of these forums helped refine/reshape my thinking—most recently at the Yale Urban Ethnography conference. I have found this be a special gathering and I would especially like to thank Eli

Anderson, Charles Gallagher, Colin Jerolmack, Marcus Hunter, Forrest Stuart, and Waverly Duck. Corey D. Fields, Adam L. Horowitz, Tomás Jiménez, and Aliya Saperstein from the Race Workshop in the Sociology Department at Stanford University also provided invaluable comments during my time there. I would like to also acknowledge participants from the rich workshop culture at the University of Chicago, including the Crime and Punishment workshop, Urban Structure and Process workshop, Race and Racial Ideologies workshop, and the Department of Sociology Paper Writing seminar. The University of Chicago supported, nurtured, and challenged key theoretical contributions in this project. I would especially like to thank Andrew Abbott, the late Donald Bogue, Andrew Dilts, Bernard Harcourt, Elizabeth McGhee-Hasserrick, Eric Hedberg, Sylvie Honig, Fen Lin, Sheldon Lyke, Tracey Meares, Thomas Miles, William Parish, Xuefei Ren, Fabio Rojas, David Schaliol, Mario Small, Jolyon Ticer-Weir, and Danielle Wallace. I would also like to recognize the contributions of William Martin and Joshua Price at the SUNY Binghamton Justice Project workshop participants and the SUNY Binghamton Decarceration Working Group. With their encouragement I never took my eye off the policy implications of this study.

I also have to recognize Doug Mitchell, Tim McGovern, Kyle Wagner, Dawn Hall, and the rest of the staff at the University of Chicago Press for shepherding this project through. Moreover, I cannot give enough praise to Audra Wolfe for helping completely restructure this manuscript based on the suggestions of Fred Wherry and an anonymous reviewer. Writing concisely can prove difficult for the verbose, and they provided great advice along the way.

In closing I need to also recognize support for this project by the American Sociological Association Funds for Advancement of the Discipline, the Institute for Social Science Research at Arizona State University, and the Texas A&M University College of Liberal Arts Seed Grant.

Lastly, and most importantly, this project is made possible through the hard work and dedication of my wife, Lisa Ellis, and children, John Major Eason Jr. and Zuri Eason. Without their sacrifice and effort as fieldworkers this project would not be possible. Lisa not only took pictures but also field notes. Major provided constant questions that kept me clear on why we were in the field. My family's deep involvement in the project gave me the inspiration and perseverance to complete the manuscript.

The Multiple Imagined Positionalities of the Black Scholar in the Deep South

In this appendix I detail my multiple negotiated and conflicting positions. My position-refracted conflicts arose across an imagined family geography, imagined genealogy, the imagined role of the "good" black family man, and as a researcher. By traversing these multiple imagined positionalities, I was granted greater access, but also required greater reflexivity to remain neutral (yet internally critical) in interactions, writings, analyses, and interpretations. My multiple, often conflicting, roles gave me access to real experiences in the field. In fact, how I observed and was observed was different as a solo researcher as opposed to the roles of husband and father. As a solo researcher, I was constantly in observation mode. With my family, I was more of a participant because of the responsibilities involving life matters. The standard of least harm used by institutional review boards to evaluate the impact of social scientific work is less than satisfactory when involving one's family in research. As parents, we are supposed to provide the best for our children, even if that means sacrificing ourselves. While these competing interests were the greatest source of tension in my fieldwork, they also provided the most insight about the field site.

While I adopted the ethnographic convention of using pseudonyms to protect the identity of vulnerable or disadvantaged subjects, I used the actual names of public officials because their highly visible position would make anonymization nearly impossible. Because many of the study participants were proud Forrest City citizens who held positions representing the town in public or nongovernment organizations, their opinions were often a matter of public record, so there was no need to protect their identity. More importantly, there was no desire on their behalf to be kept anonymous, as they felt that by sharing their story they would help to illuminate the struggles of Delta communities. Most study participants did not give their time for self-aggrandizement. Instead, they willingly participated in hopes that I would provide a fair representation of the plight of their beloved community. I cannot thank each of them enough. By extension, I also used the real name of the town because a pseudonym would obscure how much race and racism have defined this town from its inception. For these purposes, I will describe the overarching research design after discussing the importance of reflexivity and representation in research. Ultimately, I hope this methodological appendix serves as a record of transparency for the people of Forrest City/ Wynne that gave their time by participating in this study.

Brick House to Outhouse: Decoupling the Many Souths from Variations in "Country"

In studying southern communities, Zandria Robinson (2014) demonstrates the importance of how reflexive practices differ depending on the researcher, subjects, and site. In relocating my family to rural Arkansas, reflexivity was key, given the social and physical proximity between my research home and the field. Like Robinson (2014), my race and gender proved important in garnering data. However, my unfamiliarity with, and need to learn about, southern culture was significant to discoveries in the field. Not only did I face the kinds of obstacles any researcher faces through the ethnographic process, but there were also plenty of additional roadblocks to using the rural South as a laboratory. Although I had my own hesitations, I found that others freely expressed their reservations. Some colleagues warned that given the difficulties of moving, the rural South may not want to be studied. Other colleagues suggested that there was enough statistical data on the universe of southern prison towns for a quantitative project, rather than a more qualitative one. This suggestion was usually followed with advice that I minimize the hardship of relocating to what they saw as a miserable place. My six-year-old son was even clear in articulating his initial displeasure with moving to the rural South. After our first few weeks in the field he asked, "Did someone make us come here? Why are we here? Why do they call this place Forrest City if there are no tall buildings?" These comments reflect the bias against (and stigmatization of) the South among academics, but also the difficulties that they placed on my family. By keeping a log of remarks like these I became sensitized to my own biases about the South and attempted to mitigate them.

By describing my stance toward the subjects and field site I hope to explain how I mitigated my own biases. At the conscious (and unconscious) level, researchers always have a stance toward their subjects. The nature of our subjects also influences our epistemological position, so one should consider reflexivity as a tool to combat bias. Being aware of and mitigating bias is even more salient with stigmatized subjects and spaces. Ethnographers keep our positions in attempting to understand how our own socio-economic and cultural dispositions inform our data collection. Awareness of stance and position in writing and observing creates better data and analysis leading to more informed theory.

In attempts to mitigate my bias, I frequently reflected on how I came to learn about the South. My orientation to the rural South began years before graduate school. Like many black natives of the Chicago area, my family came from the Deep South. Despite my family originating from the greater Memphis area, I had never spent significant time in the region until I traveled with my then (at the time) girlfriend to Texas and Louisiana. My family, like others since the great migrations, understood that Chicago was a step off the train from Mississippi and Arkansas. As these migrants evolved into urban northerners, they attempted to shed "country" or rural ways. In this process, "countryfied" talk and mannerisms were conflated with southern customs, deemed unacceptable to advancing, and policed as such. I can recall, for example, from my childhood relatives disparaging each other for "country" ways, including the innocuous use of words like "ain't" and "fixin' to." Policing of this sort was not just a form of the politics of respectability. Nor was this just about the use of these contracted verbs—but instead, the intonation and over emphasis of certain vowels produces a twang that did not resonate with the urban neighborhood colloquialism. These cultural boundaries were even starker when considering common nouns like the use of "soda" instead of "pop" or describing sneakers as "tennis shoes." To say "soda" or "tennis shoes" with too much twang was to risk ridicule in Chicago. This was seen by "other" southerners as backward. Like many black Chicagoans, I was raised with this view and recognized just how problematic this was long before conducting research in Forrest City. Like most stigmas, this conflation of South and country was rooted in my lack of experience in the region. For example, in the process of gathering documents for our pending nuptials, my then fiancée requested an original copy of her birth certificate from the county recorder in her hometown of Leesville, Louisiana. To our surprise, "colored" was originally typed in the category for race with a line struck through it with "black" handwritten above. In addition to providing a laugh, this correction rehashed views of the South I learned while growing up.

Fortunately, exposure changed my view of the South. Shortly after our marriage, my partner's cousin held a wedding of her own in their rural hometown. Little did I know that during this visit not only would the distinction between "country" and southern be clarified, but I would also come to understand there are degrees of rurality as well. During the reception my partner's uncles openly joked about the "country" ways and appearance of guests in attendance. The jokes continued well into the night. Having heard enough, and fueled by celebratory drinks, I inquired, "we are sitting in Leesville, Louisiana [population 10,000] and you'll keep talking about how other folks are so 'country.' How does that make sense? I thought this was the country?" One of my partner's uncles placed one of his large welder's hands on my shoulder as he patiently explained, "You don't understand! We are sitting in a brick house. We have indoor plumbing and heat. Theses folks probably have an outhouse and cure their own meat." As the room erupted with laughter, this simple, elegant statement complicated my preconceived notions of southern and "country." After years of conflating the two, this comment crystallized the differences by demonstrating how native southerners differentiated degrees of rurality.

This point was further enhanced by talking with a resident of Colt, Arkansas, a town midway between Forrest City and Wynne. She explained that in the town paved roads are standard. However, in the real "country" dirt roads were a sign of a higher degree of rurality. Of course, there were also sections in the "country" where there was literally no road. This is the rare occasion where one drives through fields. Simply put, the degree of rurality depends on the condition of the road (or the lack of it). Adjusting one's lens is difficult as a researcher because one needs to be able to understand phenomenon on multiple scales and across multiple intersections. Perhaps even more important than the complexity of race, class, and gender that complicate field sites, my bias as an urban northerner had to be constantly checked as to how it influenced my research process.

For one example of how this plays out in a qualitative research study, let me spend a moment on description. Ethnography is often based upon richly detailed illustrations of interactions, people, and scenes (Wynn 2011) and, in describing Forrest City, I was faced with the dilemma of illuminating the "dirty" conditions while trying not to reinforce stereotypes of rurality or the South. However, if I did not portray the lived conditions of this place, I feared that I could not accurately trace the plight of the town, and especially residents in the rural ghetto. I was able to appropriately manage my biases by understanding what Robinson (2014) refers to as the multiple Souths differentiated along space and time. In her study of Memphis, she reminds readers that southern places can vary widely along the rural-urban continuum: the New South and Old South, and different variations of the region are constantly being born and razed. Whenever I engaged with other scholars, my extended family, and my informants, adjusting my perceptions along these multiple lenses kept me grounded as I took notes, transcribed interviews, and evaluated and interpreted data.

Breaking into a Prison Town: Position, Privilege, and Power

Navigating one's own biases and dispositions is just one facet of the researcher's dilemma, of course. To effectively navigate the research design detailed below one undoubtedly needs a diverse research skill set, but a stroke of luck is even better. Having a common surname for this region of the Delta provided numerous unintentional fictive kinships among African Americans in Forrest City. I realized this in a most innocuous way—at the local recreation center. Following a particularly hard-fought pick-up basketball game where my team went down in defeat, Kenneth Taylor, director of the recreation center, exclaimed, "you were going against your cousin really hard in that game!" Ironically, I had not met the young man in question before that day. Despite informing Mr. Taylor during an earlier interview that I did not have any direct connections to Forrest City, he, like so many others, assumed I had numerous local relatives given my prominent surname. This demonstrates how fictive kinships can grant researchers insider status.

My roots to the "old country" can be traced to the Delta. My surname and family ties to the Delta region run deep. While my grandfather hails from Memphis, my grandmother was born in nearby Como, Mississippi, and my father was born in Senatobia, Mississippi. Senatobia and Como are less than fifty miles south of Memphis and within a two-hour drive of Forrest City. My symbolic connection to the region ran even deeper as I shared the same name as a recently deceased local Arkansas state senator, also named John Eason. I would often encounter residents in Forrest City acquainted with him/her. Within most of these introductions the informant would acknowledge that I also resembled him. Because of this, it was all too common for people to ask if we were related when I introduced myself. This coincidence provided a very unconventional inroad because several interviewees met to explore my potential connection to the late senator with a few questioning whether I was a long-lost relative. However, as far as I know, aside from the coincidence of namesake and resemblance, we had no familial connections. This perceived family tie granted me a good deal of entrée. Although I was known as "the guy writing a book on Forrest City," this imagined tie allowed access to multiple social spheres in Forrest City. In conjunction with the assistance of key informants, I used this privileged position to gain access to interviews and exploit a level of comfort and connection respondents felt, even if that tie was unconscious or mistaken.

Rapport with subjects was also developed by the regular presence of my family in community activities, functions, and daily life. In addition to my surname, the heteronormative trappings of a wife, two children, and employment as a graduate student also allowed community members to overcome my outsider status. Not only did whites view me as nonthreatening but also as trustworthy and honest. This privilege is best exemplified through an interaction during a traffic stop on a Sunday afternoon. I was nearly 20 miles per hour over the speed limit with my wife in the passenger seat and the children in the rear of a late model black SUV when I noticed the blue lights behind me. As the officer walked up I rolled down the window, handing him my license, insurance, and registration while apologizing for speeding, explaining that I was distracted by my daughter. As if on cue, she looks up at the officer smiling and giggling from her car seat. The young white officer returns my identification and kindly asked us to drive on after a very polite warning including a smile.

This was not my first (or last) experience with law enforcement, nor do I have a Pollyannaish view of the police. And in no way are my goals here to diminish the effects of disproportionate minority contact with the police through racial profiling, nor am I minimizing the increased likelihood of poor treatment rendered to blacks/Latinos by officers during these stops. However, one could argue that the social order of the rural South is so oppressive that the politics of respectability can alter street-level bureaucracy wherein rare instances those appearing to be race leaders can, in fact, be treated as human by police officers. After this experience, I took notice of how fathers who appeared responsible—dare I say younger black fathers in particular?—were treated quite kindly by whites and blacks in town. Because black children are more likely to grow up in a single female-headed household than a two-parent household, I was led to investigate the local statistics on family and community structures. Strong favorable reactions to my presence as a seemingly responsible black husband and father coupled with observations led me to believe the Forrest City/Wynne area would have an even higher percentage of single female-headed households. Unlike the use of single female-headed households indicating a so-called culture of poverty, I feel that this indicator is another reason for how I gained greater access in the field. The role of a "God fearing, church-going" father and husband provided capital in both black and white circles. Several interactions like this one demonstrated how, in some respects, my family provided better credentials than my academic institution ever could. My family dined with residents and engaged in other social activities around school and church that further normalized our presence. My solidified role as a "family man" put many subjects at ease during interviews and other social encounters. Nearly every informant told me that I could relate to a host of innocuous events as "a family man." I was, in some way, a familiar and accessible person, nurturing candid responses and comfortable interviews.

Being perceived as trustworthy and nonthreatening was also based on the role and status of the interviewee vis-à-vis the ethnographer. In most community studies the researcher holds a more privileged position than his/her subjects. That is to say (with few exception) ethnographers typically study disadvantaged groups. In the case study of Forrest City, I was primarily studying elites. Their role as white elites within a traditional rural southern town (see Cobb 1994; Roscigno and Tomaskovic-Devey 1994; Tomaskovic-Devey and Roscigno 1997) allowed them to exercise privilege in a way that is rarely captured in an era of political correctness. As such, informants would often take liberties in objectifying me during interviews while expressing their opinions about local poor blacks.

This juxtaposition came in the form of comments differentiating my educational success as a young black man from how they viewed the average local. While simultaneously congratulating me on being a decent black for working on my doctorate, the average local black male was vilified. David Dunn, for example, felt compelled to make this distinction in our interview, saying, "see you wanted somethin' better for yourself. These folks don't." In essence, he was saying, "you may be black, but you're not like the one's around here." Cues or comments like this were quite common in my conversations with many whites, demonstrating the palpability of race in this town. This typifies racial scripts used to stigmatize locals, simultaneously setting me apart as an exception only to prove the rules in their minds, as they set about governing blacks in their daily lives.

Likewise, being perceived as a BUMPY (Black Upwardly Mobile Young Professional) was especially beneficial in gaining access to key black informants. Many race leaders held a similar view of me. Interestingly, both white and black leaders saw my research as "advancing the race" as they charged me with letting the world know about the plight of the Delta from the southern perspective. In closing interviews, occasionally respondents would express how they enjoyed our talk then would stress the importance of completing this research project as a credit to my race.

Because informants recognized me as part of the black middle class, they assumed I subscribed to the politics of respectability and held so-called middle-class American values. Therefore, this was yet another imagined position granted access to privileged conversations often centering on the politics of respectability from a very heteronormative position. This insider status meant that I could observe middle-class blacks (aspirational actors and achieved) along with whites partake in the shaming ritual of poor blacks that do not follow the rules dictated by the politics of respectability. Racial scripts are often used to stigmatize the behavior of blacks that do not subscribe to the politics of respectability. The politics of respectability is not just about sagging jeans that expose one's hindquarters—it is also a broader cultural critique rooted in doing away with the so-called culture of poverty. We can learn from observations in Forrest City that poor blacks' behaviors are policed and stigmatized as a form of social control, spatial practices of confinement (Martin and Mitchelson 2009), and maintaining southern identity for race leaders. While the politics of respectability are usually practiced within the black community as a form of boundary maintenance against poor blacks, I was somewhat surprised at the prevalence and untethered use among southern white elites during interviews. However, Robinson (2014) explains that in the South cultural practices meant as boundary maintenance are often blurred along racial and regional boundaries.

During interviews some white informants confessed that their family was among the original settlers of Forrest City. This admission was done in such a casual manner one could infer they were proud to admit (just shy of a boast) their family is linked to the founding of the Ku Klux Klan. Not surprisingly, many white informants dismissed structural race prejudice as the cause of local residents' lack of mobility. Many still used the so-called culture of poverty argument to blame local residents' lack of mobility. So the casual, matter-of-fact tone assumed as they schooled me on the rural South seemed to be born out of their historic position of power—a position with clear ties rooted in the foundations of Jim Crow in the Delta.

At this point, it should be clear that my position relative to many informants provided numerous interactions where comments on my status refracted racial and economic schisms in the local social structure. Given that I was a graduate student and many informants held positions of power and influence, I learned that if I remained neutral in my responses (no matter how I felt about their statements), respondents would more freely provide greater details to justify their racism, further revealing the depths of race and class bias inherent in the local culture. These encounters produced a *standpoint crisis* (Contreras 2012). As I began analyzing data, I wrote memos criticizing myself as a coward for letting respondents off the hook by not challenging them enough on their racist views. However, if I pushed back too much as an advocate of racial equality, respondents (black and white) may have shut down, concealing their true feelings, and limiting the richness of data. I was trapped between what Gary Alan Fine (1993) describes as an "unobtrusive" and "kindly" ethnographer — a researcher that blends into the setting, writing about subjects in a manner sympathetic to their plight.

This was incredibly difficult because, as an African American male studying the very institution designed to confine, define, and control me and others like me, I was profoundly conflicted. Despite local perception, I was not a BUMPY. In fact, despite being raised in the affluent city of Evanston, Illinois, my family lineage is akin with many of the folk living on the South End in Forrest City. Given my family background, I was quite familiar with the collateral consequences of mass imprisonment. Long before my academic career, my grandfather, Robert Lee Eason, a middle-school dropout, fled law enforcement in rural Mississippi for Chicago before his oldest son Robert Lee Eason Jr.'s, second birthday. Cattle rustling was among the myriad of criminal offenses leading to this involuntary relocation—a nice way of saying he was run out of town by local law enforcement. Although my grandfather aged out of his criminality before I was born, he did not desist for some time. In fact, he was arrested during the second semester of my father's senior year of high school. He pleaded with my father from his jail cell to abandon school and take up a full-time job to support his eight siblings. My father obliged. I believe this decision altered my father's trajectory. Upon my grandfather's return, my father married my mother and began having children. I am the sixth of seven children. Although my dad was a skilled carpenter, a large family requires a sizable income. As a high school dropout, legal means to achieve this goal were limited. After our home entered foreclosure, my father turned to illegal means of acquiring money and was incarcerated for selling cocaine when I was eleven years old. My parents became estranged during this process, as did my remaining sibling. Having lost our home, we lived in abandoned buildings, with grandparents, other family, and friends for nearly a year. Once we settled, I began working multiple jobs (despite being on public assistance) to help make ends meet, effectively becoming the "man" of the house at age eleven. I would complete high school, become the first of my siblings to attend a major university and the only one to earn an advanced degree.

This biography has a profound effect on my life—teaching me that context, not just individual choices, mattered for the social determinants of criminal justice outcomes. These life experiences influenced my decision to enter community and political organizing and inform my academic interests and approach to topics. Given that my adult life has been dedicated to research aimed at improving life for the most vulnerable populations caught between the intersections of racial and economic exploitation and the criminal justice system, I initially found it difficult to write about people with political power in a sympathetic way.

As admitted juvenile delinquents, Victor Rios (2011) and Randol Contreras (2012)[1] write about street-level criminality as former insiders in a way that triggers a standpoint crisis. For me, the source of my standpoint crisis lingered in direct contrast to dilemmas described in these works. I was more concerned about representing the multifaceted nature of rural southern communities while trying to maintain a critical distance of those in power given my close contact. This is a difficult task without being perceived as doing the bidding of local power players who are believed to rationalize prison building as a way to continue the racist practice of mass imprisonment. This was also a struggle because most ethnographers fancy themselves as champions of the dispossessed, making the voice of the subjects critical in how their communities are represented. The danger with my subjects is that they are very atypical in ethnography. With few exceptions (Davis et al. 1941; Dollard 1937; Duncan 1999; Falk 2004; Stack 1996), ethnographers do not typically represent the voice of rural southerners. This is further complicated because many of my subjects are neither poor nor powerless. In fact, they are quite the opposite, and therein lies the danger in representing a privileged subject because one can be seen as advocating for people and policies that reinforce systems of stratification. In addition, being perceived as too kindly or overly sympathetic to unpopular, powerful subjects can cast an unflattering light on the ethnographer.

This ethnographic dilemma presented itself in several ways. First, if I showed that local elites were racist through their everyday comments and actions, I could be accused of demonstrating that they only wanted the prisons based solely on a racists' needs to control black bodies. This is a common-held belief reifying a stereotype of rural communities' demand for prisons (Davis 2003; Huling 2001; King, Mauer, and Huling 2003; Schlosser 1998; Street 2002). Yet if I downplayed white elite and race leader's racism toward poor blacks, then I could be accused of white washing their role in perpetuating disadvantage. Second, if I wrote about my subjects as an unobtrusive observer, I could be accused of ignoring how my position affected my findings. Yet if my role was too pronounced, I could be accused of auto-ethnography or lacking critical distance. Either way, I could be called out for lacking analytical rigor. Third, as respondents regularly expressed problematic (especially racist) views to me, but not necessarily about me, I felt as if I should intervene but did not. Not only did I have to endure the statements as they happen but also suffer being charged with being an accessory to drive-by racism. By not correcting problematic speech/actions I provided tacit approval/support of their position. As an ethnographer subjected to racist speech/actions and expected to be the bearer of said talk in the book there is an assumption by elite respondents (based in privilege) that I will represent and defend their position.

For these reasons, I too faced a triple-representation dilemma (Contreras 2012). However, as an ethnographer my chief responsibility is to use theory as a tool for interpreting social reality. In doing so, I was challenged with adhering to the methodological rigor imparted during my graduate school training in properly representing subjects. Reflexivity was a necessity in balancing between characterizing subjects as one-dimensional racist cartoons and avoiding romanticizing the complex figures in Forrest City as lovable, misunderstood, "Archie Bunker" types.

All ethnographic data collection is messy in some way, but to balance these conflicting imagined and real research identities, I paid careful attention to my biases while in the field and maintained reflexivity in writing and representing subjects and myself through the analysis and writing process. So far I have detailed how my position furnished privilege in Forrest City. What follows is an example of perils I encountered in prison town research.

Nearly Incarcerated Ethnographer

This day began pretty much like any other in the field. I got up trying to piece together notes from the late conversations in the Memphis Blues bars with a key informant and made phone calls to set up other interviews. I was excited about visiting the prison to meet the warden in hopes of establishing a rapport by explaining how nonthreatening my study was to her. In fact, I hoped to sell her on the idea of being interviewed as a matter of public relations because of the nature of my study. Unfortunately, by high noon I was offered more than I bargained for. It was already above 90 degrees as I left my hotel around eleven. I thank Coach for the ride out, as we get into his car—a late-modeled Lexus with leather seats worn from the intense heat of the Arkansas sun—and drive. His radio is tuned to a more contemporary R&B station than one would expect for a man sixty-one years young, and he drives pretty fast for an older gentleman, as well. We are at the prison complex in no time.

The parking lot outside of the meeting is filled with cars. The cool air from the facility greets us as we enter. On particularly steamy days, air conditioning feels exhilarating even after a short jaunt from the car. A female guard asks if we are attending the community meeting, and after we respond affirmatively, she asks us to sign in. We print our names, then our signatures, at 11:35 a.m. On our way in a younger black man in his mid-thirties introduces himself, but I did not hear his name clearly (is this Sterling, the incredibly patronizing assistant of the warden I spoke to on the phone?). Coach introduces himself. I walk behind Coach, and as he introduces himself, again to someone else, I nod politely and follow him into the room. The room is filled with people. There is a large conference table in the middle surrounded by chairs. There are lines for food in two different places.

Someone jokes that there are a lot of people at today's meeting and maybe they should not have moved it from the regular meeting room. This room does seem a little more confining, and I am generally discombobulated as I try to figure out the food lines and the food, the latter of which consists of hefty portions of beefsteak, tater tots, and a rather rancid-looking salad. While the food left much to be desired, particularly because I did not eat beef, I piled a few tater tots on a plate so as not to appear rude. I scan the crowded room for an open seat between the various drinks, purses, and other personal effects acting as placeholders. I am prompted by a gentleman to find a seat at the table, and I respond, saying that it does not look as if there are any available. He motions to a man moving his suit coat, gesturing toward the now open seat, which is right next to Coach Twillie.

Marking the location of the open seat, I go to the salad table, still confused about how the line works. As I attempt to dip salad without spilling, another man approaches me and asks, "Do you want to put your bag in the corner, get a little more comfortable?" I respond, "Ah, I'd rather not. I have a notebook in there that I would like to write on. I'll keep it under my chair, if that's okay." He walks away.

Alas, I am seated, plate piled with a few tater tots and a relatively aged salad. I place my water bottle onto the table, but before I can set my plate down, a tall, dark-skinned black woman hurries over to me and confronts me angrily. Even apart from her stature, her presence is intimidating. She is wearing shiny black, chunky-heeled, shoes, and a pants suit. Her face is stern, and she looks like the type that would not be a stranger to glasses. Her skin was very dark and stunning so it did not seem to require much makeup. She stood at least five feet eight without shoes but was more like five eleven with them. In a gravely voice she says: "And what is your name?"

I tell her, as I am taken aback.

"No wonder why could we not figure out who you were."

Still surprised by her demeanor, as well as reeling from the heat, the confusing food, and lines, I begin to respond, "and who are . . . ,"

But she cuts me off and retorts, "I am the warden. What are you doing here? Didn't I refuse your request to conduct a study?"

"No, not to my knowledge . . . besides I am guest of Mr. Twillie's at what I thought was a community meeting."

"It's by invitation only. We need to talk in my office. It is right over here."

I follow her as she walks hastily by with what seems like a pack of people (including Coach Twillie) in close pursuit, out of the conference room, through a foyer of administrative offices, and into her executive office. The warden then calls on Sterling, her executive assistant, in a patronizing voice meant to cover his ass, "yes, I told you that yesterday on the phone that your request to conduct your study was refused." I retort, "first of all, the study itself was a separate issue, I was requesting a photo of the facility and a meeting." The warden then ends the brief discussion by accusing me of subverting their process and instructs guards to remove me. "I refused your study," she stated simply, adding, "Please escort him out of the facility." Coach Twillie's face drops, and he is left attempting to explain the situation to her as I am being escorted out.

There is a stout Latino guard, whose name is preceded by "Captain" on his name badge, walking behind me who stops and stands at the sign-in desks; he says, "you need to leave the facility now!" The two female guards at the desk raise their eyebrows in surprise and confusion, to which I shrug my shoulders, purse my lips at them, and raise my eyebrows in return. I put my arms up on both sides, turn, and drop them as I take a deep breath and ask, "can you call me a cab?" He snaps toward the two ladies, "Call him a cab," and he directs me, "you need to move out." I go outside and stand in the shade of the facility where the temperature is in the low 90s. The guard calls after me, "you need to head over to start walking toward the highway where the cab can pick you up or else the Forrest City Police will be here to pick you up." I raise an eyebrow and glare at him. I tell him, "I'll call for a ride." I phone André Stephens and tell him that I need a ride immediately from the prison. He says he's sending one of his employees, and hangs up. I stand in the shade waiting in silence.

The guard is on the other side of the entrance, seething. Without looking at me, he asks, perhaps rhetorically, "why didn't you put down your backpack when they told you to?" I nod my head, smile, and say, "No one told me to. They asked me if I wanted to put my bag in the corner to get more comfortable. I have a $2,000 computer in the bag and a $400 iPod," I say neglecting to calculate the depreciated value of the laptop. "Would you just lay your bag in a corner if some stranger asked you to?"

We return to silence. He talks into his radio. My ten minutes have expired, but luckily the police have yet to arrive. A short while later, a white guard with close-cropped hair appears. The short guard is asking Captain Vasquez what's going on. Captain explains, "That guy [pointing at me] was trespassing." I don't say anything, but I feel the short guard looking with at me with his small, slanted eyes. He sneers. The captain walks inside, while the white guard proceeds with his own set of questions:

"Where are you from?"

"Chicago."

"Don't you know not to walk on federal property uninvited?"

"This is all a misunderstanding that got blown out of proportion."

He sneers again and chuckles, "What were you doing?"

"My ride is inside. I was trying to attend a community meeting. They put me out."

He sneers again, "Don't you know you don't come out here unless you have an appointment or someone has invited you?"

While I hope that my ride beats the cops, I try to make the most out of the situation. I talk with the guard about how hot it is, ask him where he's from, and inquire as to whether the guards live in town. For a minute or so he acts civil. Then, he asks me again with a nasty tone if I know better than to walk on federal property. I ignore his question again. A squad car approaches, and a tall, wide forty-year-old black cop gets out and waddles up to us as if he were carrying the sun itself and asks begrudgingly in a thick Arkansas accent, "Ah right now, what seems to be the problem?" I explain, "I rode out here with Coach Twillie and they don't want me in this meeting. Now I'm waiting on a ride." His forehead wrinkles and his eyes squint. Coach Twillie walks out of the facility. The situation seems defused. We jump in his car and drive off.

When I spoke with Mr. Stephens about the incident, he jokingly said, "they wanted you to walk? You didn't even have a hat, right? You would've suffered heat exhaustion or heat stroke out there today," chuckling, as he adds, "you would've wandered into the road and ended up as road kill, man!" While in hindsight I found humor in this encounter, returning a smile to Mr. Stephens, at the time it seemed deadly serious. Although he was relieved that I survived the ordeal, he expressed the real threat of arrests from Forrest City Police or the option of facing dangerous conditions (dehydration, vehicular homicide) of an isolated, desolate rural highway without a sidewalk on a 100-degree day with the promise of at least a seven-mile walk back to town. Almost a third of that walk was across facility grounds, with a strong chance of a guard asking me to prove that I'm not an escapee. Mr. Stephens also, half jokingly, noted that over that distance a black man would have surely been pegged as an escapee and shot.

While some might describe the incident as simply an encounter with a jerk or a bully, Everett Hughes (1945) would characterize this encounter as a contradiction and dilemma in status. Elijah Anderson (2011) describes encounters like these as *nigger moments*: "acute disrespect based on race." While these are apt characterizations, a deeper etiology is required to explore not only if race matters but how race matters, because my presence clearly posed a threat to the authority of Warden Linda Sanders and upset the local order. Recounting trepidation from this episode can also shed light on challenges in conducting fieldwork as well as the structures of prison towns reinforcing racialized social systems.

Much as some scholars (Christian 2005; Comfort 2007) consider how the prison shapes the lives of visitors, others (Carroll 1974; Walker 2016) consider how prisons functions as "race-making institutions" for prisoners. My encounter demonstrates how the prison is a race making institution for *visitors*. Analyzing this encounter using contemporary theories of race, racism, and racialization sheds light on how these processes are central to shaping space in the institutional space of the prison. I will pay particular attention to the role of racial minorities in maintaining white institutional space. Within racialized social systems, actors at key nodes can grant the benefit of the doubt for misunderstandings or diminish life chances of an individual. Eduardo Bonilla-Silva (1996, 470) argues, "The social system produced tends to increase the life chances of the dominant group (whites) while diminishing others." Knowingly putting me in harm's way based on a clerical misunderstanding potentially diminished my life chances. Ultimately, Linda Sanders is serving the interests of white domination because her position as warden allows her to replicate white dominance (Moore and Bell 2010). This power is exercised by controlling black and brown bodies within (and outside) the prison.

Her power resides in her supports and role within a racialized social system. By throwing me out, Warden Sanders reinforced her power. Her abuse of power is a reasonable reaction given that my presence as a scholar was a threat to her power. My presence exemplified her engagement in an act of white power. My presence threatened her power because I had power to say something about how she ran the prison. While theoretically fruitful, this lesson came at the cost of duress of bodily harm under a racist regime. Using Wendy Leo Moore and Joyce Bell's (2010) work, one can argue that a black woman racializing, and therefore discrediting me, maintains the existing hierarchy and is a way the woman can advance her position. Anderson (2012) reminds us that incidents like these also to remind middle-class blacks of "who they are," putting them on notice "that as black people they occupy a perpetually provisional status" (12). At that time the FCFCF was a minimum-security prison. The pay, prestige, and rank of wardens increase with responsibility, typically corresponding with the security level of their facility. By publicly shaming me as a black male she demonstrated that she is a team player in maintaining the racial hierarchy. Some would argue that Warden Sanders was even solidifying her position and, potentially, advancing her career through actions like these that maintained the racial hierarchy.

The encounter further underscores the importance of the warden in setting the tone for how prisons interact with their surrounding communities. My experience suggests that the title of "community meetings" should have been rethought by Forrest City Federal Correctional Facility's administration. Despite this episode, I doubt that this level of tension exists between most correctional facilities and host communities. During my tenure I found the prison provided the community with an undeniable level of economic stability. By assuming an adversarial role with the community, Warden Sanders created a hostile environment with both the sitting mayor and the community at large.

By arriving with Coach, I was initially granted status as an insider evidenced by the warm greeting from Sterling, the warden's assistant, on the way into the meeting. However, once the warden "exposed" me, effectively challenging my status, Sterling completely changed his demeanor by claiming that he informed me of her rejection. This misrepresentation was without hesitation despite Sterling's knowledge that Warden Sanders had no authority over my study, as I had explained to him on the phone (and via e-mail) that the institutional review board at my university had already approved the study so she did not have a procedural role in the study. She could choose to participate or not. Her abhorrent reaction to my presence provided a clear answer to this question. Clearly, the warden has total authority on who can come on facility grounds. However, given her lack of professionalism and ignorance of the research process she has no regard for such procedures.

Moreover, Coach explained on the ride back that while I was being removed she confessed her fear of me having an audio recorder in my bag. I reminded Coach that I indeed had a recorder (as I recorded my interviews with him), but that I was not unscrupulous enough to record the meeting without permission. I reminded him of when I first interviewed him:

I read the standard protocol aloud and had him sign a waiver before our interviews. We talked extensively about the importance of conducting ethical research in the black community given the sordid history of scientific exploitation evidenced in research projects like the Tuskegee experiment. Furthermore, I reminded him that he agreed I could accompany him to the meeting so he could introduce me to the warden. As we drove back to his home he seemed to still be in shock from the exchange.

But who could blame him? Even with great distance and time out of the field, I still struggle to grasp the motivations behind her reaction. One has to wonder if she would have reacted the same way to the presence of a white researcher. I cannot say with certainty that she would have given a white ethnographer the same choice between arrest or severe heatstroke or even death. But her disdain toward people of color demonstrated that it is not a stretch to think she would not.

Privilege and Peril in Prison Town Studies

Examining life in a prison town can teach us much about stigma and the continuity of disadvantage as it maintains the hyperghetto in rural form. Recounting trepidation from the episode at the FCFCF can shed light on challenges in conducting fieldwork as well as the structures of prison towns reinforcing racialized social systems. The interaction with the warden also informed my theoretical understanding of prison impact and the role of the warden in that process. Partly based on the encounter at the correctional facility, I came to understand prison impact as the economic, political, and social benefits/costs for a host community. The warden can mediate the relationship between the prison and it's host community. My brief encounter and her explanation of what a "community meeting" is provides evidence of why there was very little relationship between the prison and Forrest City during her tenure. Local informants described the relationship between the prison and community as being the most distant and problematic under her tenure. My encounter provides evidence of this rift and the underlying racist practices under her administration contributing to the poor relations.

There are many other valuable lessons my encounter at the FCFCF can teach us. Chief among these are lessons in doing fieldwork. It is well known that ethnographic research is rife with pitfalls. This incident is telling of doing research in a white dominated institutional space. Accessing institutions like prisons has always proven difficult. However, I had already been cleared by the Institutional Review Board at my university and did not need approval from the warden. Formal approval does not keep researchers safe from informal institutional practices. Furthermore, traumatic incidents in the field have retired many from ethnographic fieldwork or made others cut their studies short. The encounter with Warden Sanders happened within the first ninety days of observations. Although the experience was disheartening, I shared this experience with a few key informants at critical junctures during interviews to get them to open up more on their views about the current relationship between the town and the prison. This strategy proved especially fruitful in detailing the role of the warden within the larger study.

The fieldwork encounters here are emblematic of how one's subjective experiences can lead to an objective story about local culture and structure. By examining the role of the ethnographer we can see how stigma is pervasive in a prison town. Ethnographers should not only be reflexive about what they observe and what they are told when interviewing subjects, but also what happens to them directly. That is to say, that by acknowledging the peril and privilege of my unique position I could dig deeper to shed light on mechanisms responsible for my treatment in a given encounter. These same mechanisms are part of the dynamic process stratifying local residents' life chances. The process of doing ethnography in a prison town allows insight into how racialization and stigmatization maintain the continued caste system in places like Forrest City.

Interview Guide for Forrest City, Arkansas

Questions

1. How long have you lived/worked in Forrest City?
2. What does Forrest City mean to you?
   —What do you value most (or what is most valuable) about Forrest City?
   —Why is Forrest City worth saving/defending?
3. What was life like before the prison?
4. What is it like to have a prison in your community?
5. Has the prison affected jobs?
   —How?
6. Has the prison affected the general economy of the community?
   —How?
   —How has the prison affected the government? How?
7. What kinds of businesses open up because the prison is here?
8. Who gets the jobs at the prison?
   —In town vs. out of town?
9. Are there any downsides of having the prison?
10. Describe the people who come to visit the prison.
11. Were you in favor of the prison coming to town?
    —Why or why not?
12. In your opinion, has anyone benefited from the prison coming to town?
    —Has any group suffered since the prisons arrival?
13. Organizational affiliation
    —Are you on any boards or the chambers of commerce?

Demographics

Age:
Race:
Sex:
Country of Origin:

Research Design

Rural communities (especially those of color) do not often benefit from careful examinations using tight linkages between grounded theory and broad-based empirical research. W. E. B. Du Bois pioneered this terrain through his studies "The Negroes of Farmville, Virginia" and "The Negroes of Dougherty County, Georgia" that bookended the classic *Philadelphia Negro*. I build on this model of scholarship by traversing description (what is) and function (what it does). I unearth structural characteristics of a prison town using urban ecological models. This research design articulates a classic Chicago school approach to studying rural communities. By Chicago school, I mean the use of multiple methods to investigate a local phenomenon linking micro- and macroprocesses. The current Chicago school approach stems from a long tradition of ethnographic studies based in black communities (Drake and Cayton 1945; Frazier 1957; Pattillo 1999) that can be traced to the original blueprint laid out by Du Bois (1898; 1899; 1901). This study returns to this original blueprint of community studies using a rigorous methodological approach to explore prison building by focusing on: (1) context, especially place; (2) community and city properties as social systems; (3) variations in social organizations as opposed to population attributes or composition; (4) neighborhood change and spatial dynamics; (5) public affairs and improvement of community life; and (6) an integrating theme (Sampson 2002, 217). While this research design is now common in urban areas, I extend this analytical frame to rural settings in the form of a case study.

Robert Yin (2003) defines the case study: "a research strategy comprises an all-encompassing method—with the logic of design incorporating specific approaches to data collection and data analysis" (13). Case studies are useful research tools when answering "why" or "how" research questions.

While investigating how the FCFCF was originally designed as an explor-
atory case, it is ultimately an explanatory case study of prison placement.
The flexibility incorporated into this research design was born out of the
need to understand the contemporary events (surrounding prison impact)
and historical events (in how the FCFCF was built). As a way to integrate
themes across context, reflexivity was used to inform different methodological approaches at each stage. For example, to choose a field site for the ethnographic study I first used quantitative methods to map the demographics of the US prison boom. Some argue that reflexive practices should be
applied independent of qualitative or quantitative methodology (DeSouza
2004; Ryan and Golden 2006). Given that my research questions surrounding the prison boom originated while I was a community organizer, I was
faced with a dilemma—either fight with the social facts my analysis provided or except them and forge a new research agenda. I originally believed
that small towns' desire for prisons were based in a false consciousness of
their leaders being duped by the prison-industrial complex. In essence, the
leaders of these small towns were victims of a system of control much like
the prisoners now residing within their city limits. This was logical given the
stigma attached to these institutions. But it must surely outweigh any immediate economic benefit and in the long run would have more damaging
social costs that would outweigh the short-run economic benefits.

Choosing the Case

By mapping prison towns, I came to understand the breadth and contours
of this phenomenon and gained a sense of town-level characteristics that
produce conditions for prison placement. Moreover, this initial analysis
also provided a baseline of comparison to evaluate potential sites. Most
importantly, this analysis furnished a plausible rival hypothesis to the dominant narrative on the prison boom supplying convincing evidence for me to
change my perspective on the mechanisms driving prison building. Because
findings suggested that the prison town occurs most often in the South,
I changed my original plans to study a prison town in Illinois and began
searching for recently constructed prisons in the South for the case study.
Furthermore, quantitative analysis measuring prison impact in the conclu-
sion was informed by theories derived from interviews and fieldwork in
earlier chapters. Specifically, the fixed-effect regression analysis was used
because interview data suggested that a comparison between towns that get
prisons versus those that do not would produce more robust results.

Forrest City is representative of most new prisons constructed during the prison boom because it is in a southern state and it has roughly the average poverty rate for a town siting a prison. However, Forrest City has a much higher than average percent of blacks and much lower percent of Hispanics and whites than the average prison town. The fact that this case is not in Texas, Georgia, or Florida provides some control for the over-representation of prisons sited by these three states.

After establishing key informants in the spring of 2006, I moved to Forrest City that summer without my family. I was originally considering a comparative ethnography between the southern town of Forrest City, Arkansas, and the midwestern town of Tamms, Illinois. Both sited federal facilities in the late 1990s. Tamms is a super maximum-security facility while Forrest City Federal Correctional Facility was originally minimum security. Tamms is more representative of the average US rural town demographically than Forrest City as well. In addition to regional differences and demographics, I believed facility type would make a strong basis for comparing these towns. After my experience in Forrest City during the summer of 2006, I refocused the study to a single case, working on a theoretical frame for a rural ghetto.

While Forrest City is representative of prison towns because of region and larger percent of African Americans, it is a unique case study for several reasons. First, despite the large majority of prisons being state operated, Forrest City successfully sited a federal facility after considering both state and private facilities. Second, the symbolic irony of a town named after the founder of the Ku Klux Klan that is majority African American requires no explanation. Third, this site was also chosen in large part because of access—my colleague, Richard Taub, established informants in Forrest City during the construction of the facility while conducting research for *Doing Development in Arkansas*. While Forrest City fit several within the universe of potential case studies, there are other significant determinants of choosing a case. Ultimately, for ethnographers, establishing a reliable entrance into a site can be the most challenging part of conducting research.

Tracing Placement and Impact

To analyze interview data, I transcribed the digital recordings using Express Scribe. Alongside this process, I also took field notes during interviews in the field. Next, I coded interviews and notes writing memos based on these codes. In perusing these memos, patterns emerged. I used these patterns as evidence supporting the claims in each chapter. Analysis was done as I collected data. This allows for analysis to influence further data collection. However, a substantial amount of interpretation was revisited once I left the field. This was an iterative process as I checked back in with key informants periodically, even sending them material to read. While exploring hypotheses around stigma, I also used qualitative data in characterizing the local social structure and building theory. Given the history of stigma associated with penal institutions, I thought understanding how stigma works conceptually would be key in investigating how different social groups within a prison town view the world. Conceptually, stigma provided an excellent backdrop for economically depressed, rural, African American communities to be compared or contrasted with the urban communities. I then traced the codes emerging from field observations and puzzled pieces together with common themes from the site. Next, I used these themes and codes to speak to existing literature around punishment and inequality, creating a micro-macro theoretical link. Simply put, I used an inductive and deductive methodological approach in this field study. I slightly revised my interview guides through the data collection process to account for differing populations and to confirm or dispel information gleaned in other interviews.

To this end, I specifically looked at the town's key network of relationships influencing community decisions to understand how the choice to obtain a prison was made and to garner their perceptions on the prison's impact on the community over time. I used interviews in particular when investigating the political, cultural, and social meaning of the prison to rural communities. Qualitative methods allowed for a more interpretive analysis, along with the use of frame analysis in-depth interviews and participant observation. The in-depth interviews, in particular, in this ethnographic/ historical approach allowed key public officials, civic leaders, religious leaders, business leaders, and residents to share their perspectives on the prison over time.

During the initial interviews I was often shocked at the impassioned support of prison building—this was especially true for race leaders. My facial expressions and body language left no doubt about this, as I would sometimes fidget in my chair, scratching my head while asking the study participants to explain why. This strategy worked very well as participants walked me through the process by explaining why and how supporting the prison made sense to them. This completely reshaped my research in terms of theory, questions, and the way I navigated the field. As I confess in the opening of the manuscript, I went into the field thinking, why would anyone want a stigmatized institution, and literally came out with the opposite answer. I was not a shocked and naive ethnographer as much as the dominant narrative in the literature was just contrary to what I found in the field.

In constructing the town's social history centering on the placement of the federal correctional facility I also conducted archival research using census data, print and electronic media (primarily newspaper), governance and town-meeting minutes/newsletters, chambers of commerce newsletters/ meeting minutes, and museum records. The Saint Francis County Community Development Corporation, the Saint Francis County Museum, Forrest City Hall, Forrest City Chamber of Commerce, the *Forrest City Times-Herald*, and the East Arkansas Community College all aided in this archival research. I pored over documents and microfiche ranging from Federal Bureau of Prison's impact reports, needs assessment studies conducted by private consulting firms for the city of Forrest City, documents containing family lineages, photographs from the prison's groundbreaking, to the weeks of multiple full-page advertisements in the newspaper welcoming the prison and employees to Forrest City. While generally perusing documents at first to get a sense for how things used to be in the area, keyword searches through microfiche of the *Forrest City Times-Herald* newspaper were conducted in collecting the bulk of the records.

Key questions from the interview guide were used to analyze historical data, including: (1) What was life like before the prison? (2) What is it like to have a prison in your community? (3) How has the prison affected the community? Since the bulk of data consisted of newspaper articles, I looked for patterns describing how people viewed Forrest City prior to the prison coming to the town, how they perceived the prison, and how they felt life has been since the prison was constructed. Many of the articles in the local newspaper contained interviews of public officials with direct quotes or a close paraphrasing of comments on an issue. I used these direct quotes as I would interview data to confirm past views on the prison siting as well as supporting claims about how the prison and town have been perceived. To many in Forrest City, the *Times-Herald* serves as the official meeting minute-keeping device for most public meetings. While the *Forrest City Times-Herald* is not nationally recognized for its quality of journalism, locally it is a well-respected source of information.

Measuring Placement and Impact

For quantitative analysis I use information collected by the United States Census Bureau, United States Department of Agriculture, the United States Department of Justice, Bureau of Prisons, East Arkansas Community College, the University of Arkansas Little Rock Institute for Economic Advancement, the Arkansas Department of Corrections, the Arkansas Department of Health, the Forrest City Housing Authority, the United States Department of

Housing and Urban Development, and the Federal Bureau of Investigations Uniform Crime Report. Stata analysis include Rare Event Logistic Regression (Relogit), a Fixed-Effects model using Stata, and descriptive statistics. For graphing I used Microsoft Excel, Numbers, and R. Graphic Information Services Mapping was completed on ARC-GIS.

With support from the American Sociological Associations Funds for the Advancement of the Discipline, the Arizona State University Institute for Social Science Research, and the College of Liberal Arts at Texas A&M University, the Prison Proliferation Project combines a unique blend of housing, economic, political, and demographic data at the state, county, and US Census place and block level from 1970 to 2010, including all 1,663 prisons facilities geocoded into municipalities across the rural-urban continuum. The primary sources of the prison data were the 2010 Directory of Adult and Juvenile Correctional Departments, Institutions, Agencies, and Probation and Parole Authorities (American Correctional Association 2010; hereafter, the ACA directory) and the Inter-University Consortium for Political and Social Research (ICPSR) data holdings. The latter includes a listing of the 1,600-plus US prison facilities by latitude and longitude coordinates, US census place, name of facility, year of facility construction, and a limited sample of year of facility renovations. The ACA directory is a compilation of data on institutions throughout the United States, its territories, and military facilities overseas.

The directory includes data on facility name, street and mailing addresses, opening date, capacity, security level, average daily population, gender of population, adult or juvenile indicators, number of full-time and part-time staff, cost of care per day, and other information. This source was recommended as the "gold standard" of prison locations by a contact at the United States Bureau of Prisons; even so, its use of mailing addresses introduces the potential for error. I have improved on the ACA data by using an extensive verification process in assigning each prison to the US census place identified by the Bureau of Prisons or state department of corrections.

An extensive process was necessary as prior studies reproduced a measurement error in using mailing address data from the American Correctional Association (ACA). ACA data alone cannot be used to geocode prisons because more than 150 prisons list addresses located five or more miles from the prison facility. I improved on the ACA data by using an extensive verification process in assigning each prison to the US census place identified by the Bureau of Prisons or state department of corrections.

Entries from the ACA directory were reviewed by trained coders and entered into a database. The current data includes adult facilities operated by federal and state governments, Native American governments, and private contract facilities. The database entries were then checked in their entirety for errors and duplicate entries. Due to differences in record keeping across jurisdictions, entries in the ACA directory exhibit some inconsistencies with respect to the types of data provided and the format of those data. Where data were missing, researchers contacted either the facility itself or the state department of correction to attempt to obtain proper figures. I also used the ICPSR data to reconcile some latitude/longitude coordinates and used Google Maps to obtain the latitude and longitude coordinates for facilities with adequate information and checked street addresses again. For those ACA entries that provided only a mailing or PO box address, researchers again used Google Maps with satellite view to obtain visual confirmation of the facility and to collect the latitude and longitude coordinates. The location of each facility was then verified using the Coding Accuracy Support System, a location verification system used by institutions like the United States Postal Service, and each case was reconciled a third and final time.

These data were augmented and merged with Geolytics' decennial US Census demographic and economic data using GIS software. To date, this process has resulted in a data set with every US census place from 1970 to 2000 normalized to 2000 decennial boundaries (N = 25,150) and 1,663 prisons spread across all fifty states. Unlike most data on prisons, these data are not a sample of prisons or towns—the data set includes every adult prison facility and every municipality in the United States. These data were then merged with files containing US state-level economic and program transfer data covering the years 1980–2011 as maintained by the University of Kentucky Center for Poverty Research (UKCPR). The UKCPR data include such state-level predictors as party affiliation of governor and both chambers of the legislature, as well as state-level demographic, poverty, and employment variables.

The data are additionally delineated along the rural-urban continuum according to the Beale Rural Urban Classification Codes (RUCC). The RUCC designates the degree of rurality (9 the most rural) or urbanity (1 the most urban) for each census location in every period of the analysis, with 1974, 1983, 1993, and 2003 as designated years for determining rural-urban classifications. Because of the potential for prison populations to tip the RUCC designation from rural to urban, I used 1974 as a baseline for this analysis.

Analyzing Impact in Prison Towns vs. Rural Towns

Prior to 1969, only roughly 1.3 percent (or 177) of all rural towns sited prisons. Sixty-seven different towns gained a prison in the next decade alone, with fewer than 1 percent of rural towns building a prison between 1979 and 1988. This rate doubled in the following decade, with 1.9 percent of all rural towns building at least one prison. Between 1999 and 2008, the rate of prison building fell to a preboom low, as only 108 rural towns constructed prisons. Prison building is rare in any period. Southern states built more prisons in every period than the next two regions combined. Almost two-thirds of the prisons built in rural towns between 1989 and 1998 were erected in southern states. There was not a period during the prison boom where the South built fewer than 45 percent of all rural US prisons.

There are substantial differences between prison towns and other rural towns. In comparison to towns that did not construct a prison, the median home value was $5,200 higher on average in towns building prisons between 1969 and 1978. The population of a town building a prison during that same period was 4,679 greater than other rural towns. Differences between prison and nonprison towns were even more pronounced in the South than elsewhere in the country, with southern prison towns having twice the total population of other rural towns. Curiously, however, in this period the percentage of black and Hispanic residents in towns building prisons was lower than that of towns that did not site prisons.

Towns that constructed prisons between 1979 and 1988 resembled rural towns that did not build prisons more than in any other period. During this period, the most significant difference between towns that built prisons and other rural towns was the rate at which median home values changed. In the prior period, towns that did not site a prison compared to those that did had lower median home values. This period witnessed a reversal in the trend. This change was most notable in the South, where median home values increased by 38 percent from the prior period for all rural southern towns, compared to a 24 percent increase for rural southern prison towns. While poverty increased in all rural towns from the first to the second period of prison building, the shift was greater in towns that built prisons compared to those that did not. Southern towns building prisons experienced nearly an 8 percent increase in poverty from the prior period, whereas towns that did not witnessed a modest 2.5 percent increase in poverty. The racial composition of towns building prisons also changed between these periods, with increases in black and Hispanic populations. Similar to trends in poverty levels, the percentage of minority populations grew faster in towns that constructed a prison compared to those that did not. Most notably, the percentage of black residents between 1969 and 1978 in southern towns that built prisons was 25.72 percent. During the 1979 to 1988 period, 35.13 percent of the population was black in southern towns that constructed a prison.

Table B.1. US housing and demographic trends prison vs. rural towns, 1980–2000

Variables	1980		1990		2000	
	Prison Towns	Rural Towns	Prison Towns	Rural Towns	Prison Towns	Rural Towns
Median Home Value ($)	37137	31925	47835	49129	62310	70445
Median Family Income ($)	16679	15892	26249	25842	35006	37326
Poverty (%)	17.74	18.42	22.85	21.71	20.62	20.1
Unemployment (%)	8.01	7.48	9.83	8.58	7.78	8.80
Total Population	13571	8892	10122	9599	9875	10634
Black (%)	13.8	15.28	18.55	16.6	19.87	17.86
Hispanic (%)	3.89	5.74	5.98	6.5	12.19	6.78
Owner Occ (%)	65.8	69.36	64.02	66.05	64.2	62.11
College Deg (%)	13.3	10.96	12.4	12.52	13.22	15.08
Same residence prior census (%)	54.6	55.86	52.46	55.41	53.68	54.11

Source: Prison Proliferation data

Table B.2. Southern housing and demographic trends prison vs. rural towns, 1980–2000

	1980		1990		2000	
Variables	Prison Towns	Rural Towns	Prison Towns	Rural Towns	Prison Towns	Rural Towns
Median Home Value ($)	32382	27871	42389	44508	62310	63689
Median Family Income ($)	15801	14569	23213	24222	35006	34300
Poverty (%)	19.09	22.07	26.99	24.53	20.62	23.3
Unemployment (%)	6.8	6.52	9.11	8.4	7.78	8.59
Black (%)	19498	9021	10693	10059	9875	10774
Hispanic (%)	25.72	26.37	35.13	27.67	19.87	33.28
Owner Occ (%)	4.06	4.94	3.7	6.12	12.19	5.51
College Deg (%)	66.99	70.6	64.87	67.4	64.2	62.32
Same residence prior census (%)	11.25	9.9	11.55	11.53	13.22	14.02
	56.11	58.6	54.56	57.62	53.68	55.44

Source: Prison Proliferation data

In the period prior to 1980, prison towns held only a nominal advantage in median family income when compared to other rural towns. However, between 1989 and 1998, this trend shifted, with prison towns having lower median family incomes. With respect to racial composition, both rural towns and prison towns became more black and Hispanic over the prison boom. The fastest change occurred in prison towns, where the percentage of Hispanic residents has tripled since the first period. In nonprison rural towns, the average percentage of black residents in rural towns has only increased 2.58 percent between the first and third period; in prison towns, it increased from nearly 14 percent to 20 percent. No periods show any significant difference regarding unemployment between prison towns and rural towns.

Estimating Impact across the Prison Boom, 1980–2000

In this section, I move from descriptive data to predictive data in describing how prison building affects the local economy of rural towns across different periods of the prison boom. In considering the impact of prisons built between 1969 and 1978 on median home values in 1980, prison building is associated with an increase of $2,560 in median home value.[1] Although this may seem like a nominal amount for home values, adjusted for inflation in 2014 dollars this increase would be more than $7,300. This is not a trivial amount in rural areas, where poverty is higher and median family income is lower than in metropolitan areas. Prison building between 1969 and 1978 is associated with an increase in median family income in southern rural towns in 1980 as well. Again, adjusting for inflation, an increase in median family income of roughly $1,200 in 1980 equals more than $3,400 in 2014 for a town that received a prison versus one that did not. Prison building in this period provided a boost to median home values.

Overall, the impact of newly constructed prisons is not associated with poverty in 1980. However, prison building reduces poverty in rural southern towns that build versus those that do not. Prison building prior to 1969 also has a positive and statistically significant association with median home values in 1980. This suggests that the towns most likely to build, prior to the prison boom, were already on a downward economic trajectory. While prior research shows that there is a large, positive, and statistically significant relationship between prison building and unemployment (Besser and Hanson 2004; Hooks et. al. 2004; Hooks et al. 2010), I found no statistically significant relationship between prison building and unemployment in this period. Results from this period also demonstrate that when prisons have

Table B.3. Fixed-effects analysis of US and southern prison building impact, 1980–2000

Variables	1980 Prison Towns		1990 Prison Towns		2000 Prison Towns	
	US	South	US	South	US	South
Median Home Value ($)	2560*	3529**	-278	-2487*	-681	-358
Median Family Income ($)	659	1233**	-35	-339	-304	-358
Poverty (%)	-.21	-1.71*	1.67*	1.01	0.89	.94
Unemployment (%)	.05	.04	.62	-.12	-1.01*	-.49*

Source: Prison Proliferation data

negative impacts on rural communities, these impacts are not as devastating as prior research suggests.

Comparing towns building prisons from 1979 to 1988 with those that adopted prisons in the earlier period shows a drastic shift from prisons providing a boost in median home value, to decreasing median home value in rural southern towns. While early adopters reaped benefits, prison building offered little economic reprieve to towns siting during this period. Overall, prison building is not a strong predictor of outcomes in this period. The only silver lining for southern towns building prisons in the 1980s is that building prisons reduced unemployment. The move from a positive association of prisons and unemployment to a negative association is the most significant relationship in the final period of the prison boom. In the final period (1989 to 1998), prison building has limited economic impact. It reduces unemployment in rural towns only minimally. Here, prison building seems to have a more protective effect, compared with the rise in unemployment these same towns experienced in the first period. The negative trend in median home values in prison towns versus nonprison towns continues through this final period.

NOTES

PREFACE

1. John Eason, "Mapping Prison Proliferation: Region, Rurality, Race, and Disadvantage in Prison Placement." *Social Science Research* 39, no. 6 (2010): 1015–28.

CHAPTER ONE

1. "Both liberal and conservative, who have used the fear of crime to gain votes; impoverished rural areas where prisons have become a cornerstone of economic development; private companies that regard the roughly $35 billion spent each year on corrections not as a burden on American taxpayers but as a lucrative market; and government officials whose fiefdoms have expanded along with the inmate population" (Schlosser 1998, 51). "Correctional officials see danger in prison overcrowding. Others see opportunity. The nearly two million Americans behind bars—the majority of them nonviolent offenders—mean jobs for depressed regions and windfalls for profiteers" (Schlosser 1998, 51).

2. "Prisons as sources of economic growth have also become vital to the development strategy [of] many small rural communities that have lost jobs in recent years but hold the lure of cheap land and a ready workforce. Communities that once organized the siting of new prisons now beg state officials to construct new institutions in their backyards. Add to this the rapidly expanding prison privatization movement focused on the 'bottom line' of profiting from imprisonment. In the words of one industry call to potential investors, 'While arrests and convictions are steadily on the rise, profits are to be made—profits from crime. Get in on the ground floor of this booming industry now'" (Mauer 2006, 11).

3. Critical Resistance, http://www.criticalresistance.org/index.php?name=materials #pic, accessed January 15, 2007.

4. Scott D. Camp and Gerald G. Gaes, Growth and Quality of U.S. Private Prisons: Evidence from a National Survey. *Federal Bureau of Prison, US Department of Justice,* 2001, http://www.bop.gov/news/research_projects/published_reports/pub_vs_priv /oreprres_note.pdf, accessed November 1, 2007.

5. Ibid.

6. In the early 1990s, the *Journal of Crime and Delinquency* dedicated an entire issue to prison building. Farrington (1992) finds the prison is not a total institution as originally conceived by Goffman, but rather is a semitotal institution that has a semiotic

relationship with its surroundings. Schicor (1992) reviews prison town literature, hypothesizing future prison siting would occur in poor, small communities where prisons are already constructed. Martin (1992) uses a survey of a California community to challenge the view that prisons are LULUs (Locally Undesirable Land Use). The author finds many community residents view prisons as benign. Carlson (1992) builds on Martin using another case study, concluding local perception of prisons is based on the siting process. Sechrest (1992) concludes that in contrast to widespread belief, there is no empirical evidence that prisons siting decreases public safety, land values, and economic development. McShane and Williams (1992) critique prison siting measures and begin to provide a methodological framework for measuring prison impact.

7. Richard Taub is the colleague who brokered my meeting with Mr. Stephens. They met while Richard conducted research for: Richard Taub, *Doing Development in Arkansas: Using Credit to Create Opportunity for Entrepreneurs Outside the Mainstream* (Fayetteville: University of Arkansas Press, 2004).

CHAPTER FOUR

1. Census of State and Federal Correctional Facilities, 2000, holds that 79 percent of US correctional facilities were state operated, 15.85 percent privately run, and 5 percent were federally operated (http://www.ojp.usdoj.gov/bjs/abstract/csfcf00.htm).

METHODOLOGICAL APPENDIX A

1. Contreras's (2012) critique of *cowboy ethnographers*; the perceived use of subjects for exploitation "for their own professional or narcissistic end. In other words, researchers who are taught to glorify themselves at the expense of the study participants (p. 26)." Rios's (2011) exposition of the *jungle book trope* where the ethnographer goes into the mythical bush to conquer their savage subjects and live to tell the tale.

METHODOLOGICAL APPENDIX B

1. Controlling for both US census place-level demography including total population, percent of residents residing in town from previous census, poverty, percent black, percent Hispanic, owner occupancy, and prison building in prior periods.

Adler, William. 1996. *Land of Opportunity: One Family's Quest for the American Dream in the Age of Crack*. New York: Penguin Books.

Aiken, Charles S. 1985. "New Settlement Pattern of Rural Blacks in the American South." *Geographical Review* 75 (4): 383–404.

———. 1987. "Race as a Factor in Municipal Underbounding." *Annals of the Association of American Geographers* 77 (4): 564–79.

———. 1990. "A New Type of Black Ghetto in the Plantation South." *Annals of the Association of American Geographers* 80 (2): 223–46.

———. 1998. *The Cotton Plantation South since the Civil War (Creating the North American Landscape)*. Baltimore: Johns Hopkins University Press.

Alexander, Michelle. 2010. *The New Jim Crow: Mass Incarceration in the Age of Colorblindness*. New York: New Press.

Allen-Smith, Joyce E., Ronald C. Wimberley, and Libby V. Morris. 2000. "America's Forgotten People and Places: Ending the Legacy of Poverty in the Rural South." *Journal of Agricultural and Applied Economics* 32 (2): 319–29. doi: http://www.saea.org/currentback-issues-indexes/.

Anderson, Elijah. 1978. *A Place on the Corner*. Chicago: University of Chicago Press.

———. 1990. *Streetwise: Race, Class, and Change in an Urban Community*. Chicago: University of Chicago Press.

———. 2001. "The Social Situation of the Black Executive: Black and White Identities in the Corporate World." In *Problem of the Century: Racial Stratification in the United States*, edited by Elijah Anderson and Douglas Massey, 405–36. New York: Russell Sage Foundation.

———. 2004. "The Cosmopolitan Canopy." *Annals of the American Academy of Political and Social Science* 595 (1): 14–31.

———. 2011. *The Cosmopolitan Canopy: Race and Civility in Everyday Life*. New York: W. W. Norton.

———. 2015. "The White Space." *Sociology of Race and Ethnicity* 1 (1): 10–21.

Bacon, Lloyd. 1973. "Migration, Poverty, and the Rural South." *Social Forces* 51 (3): 348.

Barker, Vanessa. 2006. "The Politics of Punishing: Building a State Governance Theory of American Imprisonment Variation." *Punishment and Society* 8 (1): 5–32.

———. 2009. *The Politics of Imprisonment: How the Democratic Process Shapes the Way America Punishes Offenders*. New York: Oxford University Press.

Beale, Calvin L., and Glenn V. Fuguitt. 1990. "Decade of Pessimistic Nonmetro Population Trends Ends on Optimistic Note." *Rural Development Perspectives* 6 (3): 14–18.

Beale, Calvin L., and Robert M. Gibbs. 2006. "Severity and Concentration of Persistent High Poverty in Nonmetro Areas." *Amber Waves* 4 (1): 10.

Beaumont, Gustave de, and Alexis de Tocqueville. 1833. *On the Penitentiary System in the United States: And Its Application in France; With an Appendix on Penal Colonies, and Also, Statistical Notes.* Philadelphia: Carey, Lea, and Blanchard.

Benford, Robert D., and David A. Snow. 2000. "Framing Processes and Social Movements: An Overview and Assessment." *Annual Review of Sociology* 26 (August): 611–39.

Bentham, J. 1791. *Panopticon; or, The Inspection-House: Containing the idea of a new principle of construction applicable to any sort of establishment, in which persons of any description are to be kept under inspection, etc.* London: Thomas Payne.

Besser, Terry L., and Margaret M. Hanson. 2004. "Focus on Rural Economic Development." *Community Development* 35 (2): 1–16.

Beveridge, Andrew A. 2008. "A Century of Harlem in New York City: Some Notes on Migration, Consolidation, Segregation, and Recent Developments." *City and Community* 7 (4): 358–65.

Blankenship, Susan E., and Ernest J. Yanarella. 2004. "Prison Recruitment as a Policy Tool of Local Economic Development: A Critical Evaluation." *Contemporary Justice Review* 7 (2): 183–98. doi: 10.1080/1028258042000221184.

Blokland, Talja. 2008. "From the Outside Looking In: A 'European' Perspective on the Ghetto." *City and Community* 7 (4): 372–77.

Bonds, A. 2012. "Building Prisons, Building Poverty: Prison Sitings, Dispossession, and Mass Incarceration." In *Beyond Walls and Cages: Prisons, Borders, and Global Crisis*, edited by J. Loyd, M. Mitchelson, and A. Burridge, 129–42. Athens: University of Georgia Press.

Bonilla-Silva, Eduardo. 1997. "Rethinking Racism: Toward a Structural Interpretation." *American Sociological Review* 62 (3): 465–80.

———. 2006. *Racism without Racists: Color-Blind Racism and the Persistence of Racial Inequality in the United States.* Lanham, MD: Rowman and Littlefield.

Braman, Donald. 2001. "Families and Incarceration." In *Invisible Punishment: The Collateral Consequences of Mass Imprisonment*, edited Marc Mauer and Meda Chesney-Lind, 117–35. New York: Free Press.

Bullard, Robert D. 2000. *Dumping in Dixie: Race, Class, and Environmental Quality.* Vol. 3. Boulder, CO: Westview Press.

Bullard, Robert D., P. Mohai, R. Saha, and B. Wright. 2008. "Toxic Wastes and Race at Twenty: Why Race Still Matters after All of These Years." *Environmental Law* 38 (2): 371–411.

Burnett, John. 2015. "Closure of Private Prison Forces Texas County to Plug Financial Gap." Accessed March 25, 2016, National Public Radio, http://www.npr.org/2015/03/26/394918220/closure-of-private-prison-forces-texas-county-to-plug-financial-gap.

Bursik, Robert J., Jr. 1989. "Political Decision Making and Ecological Models of Delinquency: Conflict and Consensus." In *Theoretical Integration in the Study of Deviance and Crime*, edited by Steven Messner, Marvin Krohn, and Allen Liska, 105–17. Albany: State University of New York Press.

Burton, Linda M. 1997. "Ethnography and the Meaning of Adolescence in High-Risk Neighborhoods." *Ethos* 25 (2): 208.

Burton, L. M., R. Garrett-Peters, and John M. Eason. 2011. "Morality, Identity, and Mental

Health in Rural Ghettos." In *Communities, Neighborhoods, and Health*, edited by Linda Burton and others, 91–110. New York: Springer.

Butterfield, Fox. 2008. *All God's Children: The Bosket Family and the American Tradition of Violence*. New York: Vintage Books.

Byrne, John. 1986. "At Sanyo's Arkansas Plant the Magic Isn't Working." *Business Week*, 14.

Campo Nation, Patricia Ann. 2006. *Reported Impact of a Correctional Facility's Presence on Community Solidarity*. Dissertation prepared for the PhD degree, University of North Texas, Dallas.

Čapek, S. M. 1993. "The 'Environmental Justice' Frame: A Conceptual Discussion and an Application." *Social Problems* 40 (1): 5–24.

Carlson, Katherine A. 1992. "Doing Good and Looking Bad: A Case Study of Prison/Community Relations." *Crime and Delinquency* 38 (1): 56–69. doi: 10.1177/0011128792038001004.

Carr, Patrick J., and Maria Kefalas. 2009. *Hollowing Out the Middle: The Rural Brain Drain and What It Means for America*. Boston: Beacon Press.

Carroll, Leo. 1974. *Hacks, Blacks, and Cons: Race Relations in a Maximum Security Prison*. Lexington, MA: Lexington Books.

Chaddha, Ammol, and William Julius Wilson. 2008. "Reconsidering the 'Ghetto.'" *City and Community* 7 (4): 384–88.

Chicago Crime Index. 2007. Chicago Metropolis 2020. Downloaded from http://www.prisonpolicy.org/scans/2006CrimeandJusticeIndex.pdf.

Chrisman, Robert. 2013. "Black Prisoners, White Law." *Black Scholar* 43 (3): 33–35.

Christian, Johnna. 2005. "Riding the Bus: Barriers to Prison Visitation and Family Management Strategies." *Journal of Contemporary Criminal Justice* 21 (1): 31–48.

Clark, Sherri Lawson. 2002. "Where the Poor Live: How Federal Housing Policy Shapes Residential Communities." *Urban Anthropology and Studies of Cultural Systems and World Economic Development* 31 (1): 69.

Clark, Terry Nichols. 1968. *Community Structures and Decision-Making: Comparative Analysis*. San Francisco: Chandler Publications.

Clear, Todd. 2001. "The Problem with 'Addition by Subtraction': The Prison Crime Relationship in Low-Income Communities." In *Invisible Punishment: The Collateral Consequences of Mass Imprisonment*, edited by Marc Mauer and Meda Chesney-Lind, 181–94. New York: Free Press.

Clear, Todd R., Elin Waring, and Kristen Scully. 2005. "Communities and Reentry: Concentrated Reentry Cycling." In *Prisoner Reentry and Crime in America*, edited by Jeremy Travis and Christy Visher. Cambridge: Cambridge University Press.

Clemmer, Donald. 1940. *The Prison Community*. Boston: Christopher Publishing House.

Clotfelter, Charles T. 2004. "Private Schools, Segregation, and the Southern States." *Peabody Journal of Education* 79 (2): 74–97.

Cobb, James C. 1992. *The Most Southern Place on Earth: The Mississippi Delta and the Roots of Regional Identity*. New York: Oxford University Press.

Combessie, P. 2002. "Marking the Carceral Boundary." *Ethnography* 3 (4): 21.

Comfort, Megan. 2009. *Doing Time Together: Love and Family in the Shadow of the Prison*. Chicago: University of Chicago Press.

Contreras, Randol. 2012. *The Stickup Kids: Race, Drugs, Violence, and the American Dream*. Berkeley: University of California Press.

Cornfield, Daniel B., and Mark V. Leners. 1989. "Unionization in the Rural South: Regional Patterns of Industrialization and the Process of Union Organizing." In *Research in Rural*

Sociology and Development, vol. 4, edited by William Falk and Thomas Lyson, 137–52. Greenwich, CT: JAI Press.

Coursey, Don L., John L. Hovis, and William D. Schulze. 1987. "The Disparity between Willingness to Accept and Willingness to Pay Measures of Value." *Quarterly Journal of Economics* 102 (3): 679–90.

Cromartie, J. B., and C. L. Beale. 1980. "Increasing Black-White Separation in the Plantation South, 1970–90." *Racial/Ethnic Minorities in Rural Areas: Progress and Stagnation, 1980–90.* Economic Research Service (USDA), Washington, DC, 60.

Dahl, Robert. 1961. *Who Governs?: Democracy and Power in an American City*. New Haven, CT: Yale University Press.

Darity, William. 1983. "The Managerial Class and Surplus Population." *Society* 21 (1): 54–62. doi: 10.1007/BF02694971.

Davidson, Osha G. 1990. *Broken Heartland: The Rise of America's Rural Ghetto*. New York: Free Press.

Davidson, Pamela, and Douglas L. Anderton. 2000. "Demographics of Dumping II: A National Environmental Equity Survey and the Distribution of Hazardous Materials Handlers." *Demography* 37 (4): 461–66.

Davis, Angela. 2003. *Are Prisons Obsolete?* New York: Seven Stories Press.

Davis, Allison, Burleigh B. Gardner, Mary R. Gardner, and W. Lloyd Warner. 1941. *Deep South: A Social Anthropological Study of Caste and Class*. Chicago: University of Chicago Press.

Dawson, Michael C. 1994. *Behind the Mule: Race and Class in African-American Politics*. Princeton, NJ: Princeton University Press.

DeSouza, R. 2004. "Motherhood, Migration, and Methodology." *Qualitative Report* 9 (3): 462–82.

Dollard, John. 1937. *Caste and Class in a Southern Town*. New Haven, CT: Published for the Institute of Human Relations by Yale University Press.

Domhoff, G. William. 1967. *Who Rules America? Power and Politics, and Social Change*. Boston: McGraw-Hill.

Donnermeyer, Joseph F., and Walter DeKeseredy. 2008. "Toward a Rural Critical Criminology." *Southern Rural Sociology* 23 (2): 4.

Drake, John C. 2011. "Locked Up and Counted Out: Bringing an End to Prison-Based Gerrymandering." *Washington University Journal of Law and Policy* 37 (1): 237–65.

Drake, St. Clair, and Horace R. Cayton. 1945. *Black Metropolis: A Study of Negro Life in a Northern City*. New York, Harcourt, Brace.

Du Bois, William E. B. 1898. "Negroes of Farmville, Virginia: A Social Study." US Bureau of Labor. Reprinted in *W. E. B. Du Bois on Sociology and the Black Community*, 165–96. Chicago: University of Chicago Press, 1995.

———. 1899. *The Philadelphia Negro: A Social Study*. Philadelphia: University of Pennsylvania Press.

———. 1901. "The Negroes of Dougherty County, Georgia." Reprinted in *W. E. B. Du Bois on Sociology and the Black Community*, 154–64. Chicago: University of Chicago Press, 1995.

Duncan, C. M. 1996. "Understanding Persistent Poverty: Social Class Context in Rural Communities." *Rural Sociology* 61 (1): 103–24.

Duncan, Cynthia M., and Robert Coles. 1999. *Worlds Apart: Why Poverty Persists in Rural America*. New Haven, CT: Yale University Press.

Duneier, M. 2000. "Race and Peeing on Sixth Avenue." In *Racing Research, Researching Race:*

Methodological Dilemmas in Critical Race Studies, edited by France Winddance Twine and Jonathan Warren, 215–26. New York: New York University Press.

Duneier, Mitchell, and Ovie Carter. 1999. *Sidewalk*. New York: Farrar, Straus and Giroux.

Eason, J. 2010. "Mapping Prison Proliferation: Region, Rurality, Race, and Disadvantage in Prison Placement." *Social Science Research* 39 (6): 1015–28. doi: 10.1016/j.ssresearch .2010.03.001.

———. 2012. "Extending the Hyperghetto: Toward a Theory of Punishment, Race, and Rural Disadvantage." *Journal of Poverty* 16 (3): 274–95.

Engel, Matthew R. 2007. "When a Prison Comes to Town: Siting, Location, and Perceived Impacts of Correctional Facilities in the Midwest." Dissertation presented to the faculty of the Graduate College at the University of Nebraska in partial fulfillment of requirements for the degree of Doctor of Philosophy in Geography.

Falk, William W., Larry L. Hunt, and Matthew O. Hunt. 2004. "Return Migrations of African-Americans to the South: Reclaiming a Land of Promise, Going Home, or Both?" *Rural Sociology* 69 (4): 490–509. doi: 10.1526/0036011042722831.

Falk, William W., and Thomas A. Lyson. 1988. *High Tech, Low Tech, No Tech: Recent Industrial and Occupational Change in the South*. Albany: State University of New York Press.

Farrington, Keith. 1992. "The Modern Prison as Total Institution? Public Perception Versus Objective Reality." *Crime and Delinquency* 38 (1): 6.

Fine, Gary Alan. 1993. "Ten Lies of Ethnography: Moral Dilemmas of Field Research." *Journal of Contemporary Ethnography* 22 (3): 267–94.

Fitchen, Janet M. 1991. *Endangered Spaces, Enduring Places: Change, Identity, and Survival in Rural America*. Boulder, CO: Westview Press.

———. 1994. "Residential Mobility among the Rural Poor." *Rural Sociology* 59 (3): 416–36.

———. 1995. "Spatial Redistribution of Poverty through Migration of Poor People to Depressed Rural Communities." *Rural Sociology* 60 (2): 181–201.

Foote, Kenneth E. 2003. *Shadowed Ground: America's Landscapes of Violence and Tragedy*. Austin: University of Texas Press.

Forrest City Times-Herald. 1997; 2011.

Foucault, Michel. 1975. *Discipline and Punishment; The Birth of the Prison*. New York. Vintage Books.

Foulkes, Matt, and K. Bruce Newbold. 2008. "Poverty Catchments: Migration, Residential Mobility, and Population Turnover in Impoverished Rural Illinois Communities." *Rural Sociology* 73 (3): 440–62.

Foulkes, Matt, and Kai A. Schafft. 2010. "The Impact of Migration on Poverty Concentrations in the United States, 1995–2000." *Rural Sociology* 75 (1): 90–110. doi: 10.1111/ j.1549-0831.2009.00002.x.

Frazier, E. Franklin. 1957. *Black Bourgeoisie*. New York: Simon and Schuster.

Frey, William H. 2001. "Migration to the South Brings US Blacks Full Circle." *Population Today* 29 (4): 1.

Fuguitt, Glenn Victor, John A. Fulton, and Calvin L. Beale. 2001. *The Shifting Patterns of Black Migration from and into the Nonmetropolitan South, 1965–95*. Washington, DC: US Department of Agriculture, Economic Research Service.

Gans, Herbert J. 2008. "Involuntary Segregation and the Ghetto: Disconnecting Process and Place." *City and Community* 7 (4): 353–57.

Garland, David. 1990. *Punishment and Modern Society: A Study in Social Theory*. Chicago: University of Chicago Press.

———. 2001. *Mass Imprisonment: Social Causes and Consequences*. Thousand Oaks, CA: Sage Publications.

Geolytics CensusCD 1970. 2010. East Brunswick, NJ: GeoLytics, Inc.

Geolytics CensusCD 1980 in 2000 Boundaries. 2010. East Brunswick, NJ: GeoLytics, Inc.

Geolytics CensusCD 1980 in 2000 Boundaries. 2010. East Brunswick, NJ: GeoLytics, Inc.

Geolytics CensusCD 2000. 2010. East Brunswick, NJ: GeoLytics, Inc.

George, Lance, Leslie R. Strauss, and Mark Kudlowitz. 2008. *Connecting the Dots: A Location Analysis of USDA's Section 515 Rental Housing and Other Federally Subsidized Rental Properties in Rural America*. Washington, DC: Housing Assistance Council.

Geronimus, Arline T., Cynthia G. Colen, Tara Shochet, Lori Barer Ingber, and Sherman A. James. 2006. "Urban-Rural Differences in Excess Mortality among High-Poverty Populations: Evidence from the Harlem Household Survey and the Pitt County, North Carolina Study of African American Health." *Journal of Health Care for the Poor and Underserved* 17 (3): 532.

Gilmore, Ruth Wilson. 2007. *Golden Gulag: Prison, Surplus, Crisis, and Opposition in Globalizing California*. Berkeley: University of California Press.

Glasmeier, Amy K., and Tracey Farrigan. 2007. "The Economic Impacts of the Prison Development Boom on Persistently Poor Rural Places." *International Regional Science Review* 30 (3): 274–99. doi: http://irx.sagepub.com/archive/.

Goffman, Alice. 2009. "On the Run: Wanted Men in a Philadelphia Ghetto." *American Sociological Review* 74 (3): 339–57.

———. 2014. *On the Run: Fugitive Life in an American City*. Chicago: University of Chicago Press.

Goffman, Erving. 1959. *The Presentation of Self in Everyday Life*. Garden City, NY: Anchor.

———. 1961. *Asylums: Essays on the the Social Situation of Mental Patients and Other Inmates*. New York: Random House.

———. 1963. *Stigma: Notes on the Management of Spoiled Identity*. Englewood Cliffs, NJ: Prentice-Hall.

———. 1974. *Frame Analysis: An Essay on the Organization of Experience*. Boston: Northeastern University Press.

Gottschalk, Marie. 2006. *The Prison and the Gallows: The Politics of Mass Incarceration in America*. Cambridge: Cambridge University Press.

———. 2014. "Democracy and the Carceral State in America." *Annals of the American Academy of Political and Social Science* 651 (1): 288–95.

Hattery, Angela, and Earl Smith. 2007. "Social Stratification in the New/Old South: The Influences of Racial Segregation on Social Class in the Deep South." *Journal of Poverty* 11 (1): 55–81. doi: 10.1300/J134v11n01_03.

Haynes, Bruce D. 2001. *Red Lines, Black Spaces: The Politics of Race and Space in a Black Middle-Class Suburb*. New Haven, CT: Yale University Press.

Haynes, Bruce, and Ray Hutchison. 2008. "The Ghetto: Origins, History, Discourse." *City and Community* 7 (4): 347–52.

Higginbotham, Evelyn Brooks. 1993. *Righteous Discontent: The Women's Movement in the Black Baptist Church, 1880–1920*. Cambridge, MA: Harvard University Press.

Hirsch, Arnold R. 1983. *Making the Second Ghetto: Race and Housing in Chicago, 1940–1960*. Cambridge: Cambridge University Press.

Holloway, Steven R., D. Bryan, R. Chabot, D. M. Rogers, and J. Rulli. 1998. "Exploring the Effect of Public Housing on the Concentration of Poverty in Columbus, Ohio." *Urban Affairs Review* 33 (6): 767–89.

Hooks, Gregory, Clayton Mosher, Thomas Rotolo, and Linda Lobao. 2004. "The Prison

Industry: Carceral Expansion and Employment in U.S. Counties, 1969–1994." *Social Science Quarterly* 85 (1): 37–57. doi: 10.1111/j.0038–4941.2004.08501004.x.

Hooks, G., C. Mosher, S. Genter, T. Rotolo, and L. Lobao. 2010. "Revisiting the Impact of Prison Building on Job Growth: Education, Incarceration, and County-Level Employment, 1976–2004." *Social Science Quarterly* 91 (1): 228–44.

Hoyman, Michele, and Micah Weinberg. 2006. "The Process of Policy Innovation: Prison Sitings in Rural North Carolina." *Policy Studies Journal* 34 (1): 95–112. doi: 10.1111/j.1541–0072.2006.00147.x.

Hughes, Everett C. 1945. "Dilemmas and Contradictions of Status." *American Journal of Sociology* 50 (5): 353–59.

———. 1962. "Good People and Dirty Work." *Social Problems* 10 (1): 3.

Huling, Tracy. 2001. "Building a Prison Economy in Rural America." In *Invisible Punishment: The Collateral Consequences of Mass Imprisonment*, edited by M. Mauer and M. Chesney-Lind, 197–13. New York: Free Press.

Hunt, Larry L., Matthew O. Hunt, and William W. Falk. 2008. "Who Is Headed South—U.S. Migration Trends in Black and White, 1970–2000." *Social Forces* 87 (1): 95.

Hunter, Albert. 1993. "Local Knowledge and Local Power: Notes on the Ethnography of Local Community Elites." *Journal of Contemporary Ethnography* 22 (1): 36–58.

Isserman, Andrew M. 2001. "Competitive Advantages of Rural America in the Next Century." *International Regional Science Review* 24 (1): 38–58.

———. 2005. "In the National Interest: Defining Rural and Urban Correctly in Research and Public Policy." *International Regional Science Review* 28 (4): 465–99.

Jackson, John L., Jr. 2001. *Harlemworld: Doing Race and Class in Contemporary Black America*. Chicago: University of Chicago Press.

———. 2005. *Real Black: Adventures in Racial Sincerity*. Chicago: University of Chicago Press.

———. 2010. *Racial Paranoia: The Unintended Consequences of Political Correctness: The New Reality of Race in America*. New York: Basic Books.

Jacobs, David, and Jason T. Carmichael. 2001. "The Political Sociology of the Death Penalty: A Pooled Time-Series Analysis." *American Sociological Review* 67 (1): 109–31.

Jacobs, David, and Richard Kleban. 2003. "Political Institutions, Minorities, and Punishment: A Pooled Cross-National Analysis of Imprisonment Rates." *Social Forces* 82 (2): 725–55.

Jacobs, James B. 1977. *Stateville: The Penitentiary in Mass Society*. Chicago: University of Chicago Press.

Jacobs, Jane. 1961. *The Death and Life of Great American Cities*. New York: Vintage.

Jacobs, Michael. 2005. *Downsizing Prisons: How to Reduce Crime and End Mass Incarceration*. New York: New York University Press.

Jargowsky, Paul. 1997. *Poverty and Place: Ghettos, Barrios, and the American City*. New York: Russell Sage Foundation.

Johnson, Rucker C., and Steven Raphael. 2009. "The Effects of Male Incarceration Dynamics on Acquired Immune Deficiency Syndrome Infection Rates among African American Women and Men." *Journal of Law and Economics* 52: 251–93.

Katznelson, Ira. 1976. "The Crisis of the Capitalist City: Urban Politics and Social Control." In *Theoretical Perspectives on Urban Politics*, edited by Willis D. Hawley and others, 214–29. Englewood Cliffs, NJ: Prentice-Hall.

King, R. S., M. Mauer, and T. Huling. 2003. *Big Prisons, Small Towns: Prison Economics in Rural America*. The Sentencing Project Report. http://www.sentencingproject.org/Admin/Documents/publications/inc_bigprisons.pdf, accessed July 2, 2014.

Kusenbach, Margarethe. 2009. "Salvaging Decency: Mobile Home Residents' Strategies of Managing the Stigma of 'Trailer' Living." *Qualitative Sociology* 32 (4). 399–428. doi: 10.1007/s11133–009–9139-z.

Lacy, Karen R. 2007. *Blue-Chip Black: Race, Class, and Status in the New Black Middle Class.* Berkeley: University of California Press.

Lang, Robert E., and Diane Dhavale. 2004. "Micropolitan America: A Brand New Geography." *Metropolitan Institute at Virginia Tech Census Note 05:01.*

Lawrence, Sarah, and Jeremy Travis. 2004. *The New Landscape of Imprisonment: Mapping America's Prison Expansion.* Urban Institute report downloaded on November 1, 2007, from http://www.urban.org/UploadedPDF/410994_mapping_prisons.pdf.

Lawson Clark, Sherri. 2002. "Where the Poor Live: How Federal Housing Policy Shapes Residential Communities." *Urban Anthropology and Studies of Cultural Systems and World Economic Development* 31 (1): 69–92.

———. 2007. "Migration for Housing: Urban Families in Rural Living." Final Policy Report. Center for Rural Pennsylvania.

Lee, Jennifer. 2002. *Civility in the City: Blacks, Jews, and Koreans in Urban America.* Cambridge, MA: Harvard University Press.

Lee, Matthew R., and Graham C. Ousey. 2001. "Size Matters: Examining the Link between Small Manufacturing, Socioeconomic Deprivation, and Crime Rates in Nonmetropolitan Communities." *Sociological Quarterly* 42 (4): 581.

———. 2005. "Institutional Access, Residential Segregation, and Urban Black Homicide." *Sociological Inquiry* 75 (1): 31–54.

Lemann, Nicholas. 1991. *The Promised Land: The Great Black Migration and How It Changed America.* New York: Random House.

Lichter, Daniel T., and G. V. Fuguitt. 1980. "Demographic Response to Transportation Innovation: The Case of the Interstate Highway." *Social Forces* 59 (2): 492–512.

Lichter, Daniel T., and Kenneth M. Johnson. 2007. "The Changing Spatial Concentration of America's Rural Poor Population." *Rural Sociology* 72 (3): 331–58.

Lichter, Daniel T., Domenico Parisi, Steven Michael Grice, and Michael Taquino. 2007a. "Municipal Underbounding: Annexation and Racial Exclusion in Small Southern Towns." *Rural Sociology* 72 (1): 47–68.

Lichter, Daniel T., Domenico Parisi, Steven Michael Grice, and Michael C. Taquino. 2007b. "National Estimates of Racial Segregation in Rural and Small-Town America." *Demography* 44 (3): 563–81. doi: http://link.springer.com/journal/volumesAndIssues/13524.

Lichter, D. T., D. Parisi, M. C. Taquino, and B. Beaulieu. 2008. "Race and the Micro-Scale Spatial Concentration of Poverty." *Cambridge Journal of Regions, Economy, and Society* 1 (1): 51–67. doi: 10.1093/cjres/rsm010.

Lobao, Linda M., Gregory Michael Hooks, and Ann R. Tickamyer. 2007. *The Sociology of Spatial Inequality.* Albany: State University of New York Press.

Logan, John R., and Harvey L. Molotch. 1987. *Urban Fortunes: The Political Economy of Place.* Berkeley: University of California Press.

Lotke, E., and P. Wagner. 2003. "Prisoners of the Census: Electoral and Financial Consequences of Counting Prisoners Where They Go, Not Where They Come From." *Pace Law Review* 24 (2): 587.

Lynch, Mona. 2009. "Punishment, Purpose, and Place: A Case Study of Arizona's Prison Siting Decisions." *Studies in Law, Politics, and Society* 50: 105–37.

———. 2010. *Sunbelt Justice: Arizona and the Transformation of American Punishment.* Stanford, CA: Stanford University Press.

———. 2011. "Mass Incarceration, Legal Change, and Locale." *Criminology and Public Policy* 10 (3): 673–98.

Lynd, Robert S., and Helen M. Lynd. 1929. *Middletown: A Study in Contemporary American Culture*. New York: Harcourt Brace.

Lyson, Thomas A., and William W. Falk, eds. 1993. *Forgotten Places: Uneven Development in Rural America*. Lawrence: University Press of Kansas.

MacTavish, Kate, and Sonya Salamon. 2001. "Mobile Home Park on the Prairie: A New Rural Community Form." *Rural Sociology* 66 (4): 487–506.

MacTavish, Kate, M. Eley, and S. Salamon. 2006. "Housing Vulnerability among Rural Trailer-Park Households." *Georgetown Journal on Poverty Law and Policy* 13 (1): 95–117.

Martin, Lauren L., and Matthew L. Mitchelson. 2009. "Geographies of Detention and Imprisonment: Interrogating Spatial Practices of Confinement, Discipline, Law, and State Power." *Geography Compass* 3 (1): 459–77.

Martin, Randy. 1992. "Community Perceptions about Prison Construction: Why Not in My Backyard?" *Crime and Delinquency* 38 (1): 265–94.

Massey, D. S. 2007. *Categorically Unequal: The American Stratification System: The American Stratification System*. New York: Russell Sage Foundation.

Massey, D. S., and G. Lundy. 2001. "Use of Black English and Racial Discrimination in Urban Housing Markets: New Methods and Findings." *Urban Affairs Review* 36 (4): 452–69. doi: 10.1177/10780870122184957.

Massey, Douglas S., and Nancy A. Denton. 1993. *American Apartheid: Segregation and the Making of the Underclass*. Cambridge, MA: Harvard University Press.

Massey, Douglas S., and Mitchell L. Eggers. 1990. "The Ecology of Inequality: Minorities and the Concentration of Poverty, 1970–1980." *American Journal of Sociology* 95 (5): 1153.

Mauer, Marc. 2006. *Race to Incarcerate*. Rev. and updated 2nd ed. New York: New Press; distributed by W. W. Norton.

McAdam, D., and H. Boudet. 2012. *Putting Social Movements in Their Place: Explaining Opposition to Energy Projects in the United States, 2000–2005*. Cambridge: Cambridge University Press.

McAdam, Doug, H. S. Boudet, J. Davis, R. J. Orr, W. Richard Scott, and R. E. Levitt. 2010. "'Site Fights': Explaining Opposition to Pipeline Projects in the Developing World." *Sociological Forum* 25 (3): 401–27.

McShane, M. D., F. P. Williams III, and Carl P. Wagoner. 1992. "Prison Impact Studies: Some Comments on Methodological Rigor." *Crime and Delinquency* 38 (1): 105.

Mills, Charles W. 2000. *The Sociological Imagination*. New York: Oxford University Press.

Minchin, T. J. 2000. "Torn Apart: Permanent Replacements and the Crossett Strike of 1985." *Arkansas Historical Quarterly* 59 (1): 30.

Mohai, Paul, and Robin Saha. 2006. "Reassessing Racial and Socioeconomic Disparities in Environmental Justice Research." *Demography* 43 (2): 383.

Monteiro, Circe. 2009. "Enclaves, Condominiums, and Favelas: Where Are the Ghettos in Brazil?" *City and Community* 7 (4): 378–83.

Moore, Wendy L., and Joyce M. Bell. 2010. "Embodying the White Racial Frame: The (In) Significance of Barack Obama." *Journal of Race and Policy* 6 (1): 123–38.

Morrell, A. R. 2012. "The Prison Fix: Race, Work, and Economic Development in Elmira, New York." PhD diss., City University of New York.

Morris, Norvall, and David J. Rothman. 1997. *The Oxford History of the Prison: The Practice of Punishment in Western Society*. Oxford: Oxford University Press.

Murphy, Alexandra K. 2007. "The Suburban Ghetto: The Legacy of Herbert Gans in Understanding the Experience of Poverty in Recently Impoverished American Suburbs." *City and Community* 6 (1): 21–37. doi: 10.1111/j.1540–6040.2007.00196.x.

Neal, Zachary P. 2011. "From Central Places to Network Bases: A Transition in the U.S. Urban Hierarchy, 1900–2000." *City and Community* 10 (1): 49–75. doi: 10.1111/j.1540–6040.2010.01340.x.

Pager, Devah. 2003. "The Mark of a Criminal Record." *American Journal of Sociology* 108 (5): 937–75.

Park, Robert E., Ernest W. Burgess, and Roderick D. McKenzie. 1984. *The City*. Chicago: University of Chicago Press.

Pattillo, Mary. 1999. *Black Picket Fences: Privilege and Peril among the Black Middle Class*. Chicago: University of Chicago Press.

———. 2007. *Black on the Block: The Politics of Race and Class in the City*. Chicago: University of Chicago Press.

Pattillo, Mary, David Weiman, and Bruce Western. 2004. *Imprisoning America: The Social Effects of Mass Incarceration*. New York: Russell Sage Foundation.

Pellow, David N. 2000. "Environmental Inequality Formation toward a Theory of Environmental Injustice." *American Behavioral Scientist* 43 (4): 581–601.

Perkinson, Robert. 2010. *Texas Tough: The Rise of America's Prison Empire*. New York: Metropolitan Books.

Petersilia, Joan. 2003. *When Prisoners Come Home: Parole and Prisoner Reentry*. New York: Oxford University Press.

Phelps, Michelle S. 2012. "The Place of Punishment: Variation in the Provision of Inmate Services Staff across the Punitive Turn." *Journal of Criminal Justice* 40 (5): 348–57.

Quillian, Lincoln. 1999. "Migration Patterns and the Growth of High Poverty Neighborhoods, 1970–1990." *American Journal of Sociology* 105 (1): 1–37.

Reed, John S. 1993. *My Tears Spoiled My Aim, and Other Reflections on Southern Culture*. Columbia: University of Missouri Press.

Rieder, Jonathan. 1987. *Canarsie: The Jews and Italians of Brooklyn against Liberalism*. Cambridge, MA: Harvard University Press.

Rios, Victor M. 2011. *Punished: Policing the Lives of Black and Latino Boys*. New York: New York University Press.

Rivera, Lauren A. 2008. "Managing 'Spoiled' National Identity: War, Tourism, and Memory in Croatia." *American Sociological Review* 73 (4): 613–34.

Robinson, Isaac A. 1990. "The Relative Impact of Migration Type on the Reversal of Black Out-Migration from the South." *Sociological Spectrum* 10 (3): 373–86.

Robinson, Linda Louise. 1972. "Durkheim's 'Two Laws of Penal Evolution': Translated and Annotated." PhD diss., Case Western Reserve University.

Robinson, Zandria F. 2014. *This Ain't Chicago: Race, Class, and Regional Identity in the Post-Soul South*. Chapel Hill: University of North Carolina Press.

Roscigno, Vincent J., and Donald Tomaskovic-Devey. 1994. "Racial Politics in the Contemporary South: Toward a More Critical Understanding." *Social Problems* 41 (4): 585–607.

Roscigno, Vincent J., and M. Keith Kimble. 1995. "Elite Power, Race, and the Persistence of Low Unionization in the South." *Work and Occupations* 22 (3): 271–300.

Rose, Dina R., and Todd R. Clear. 1998. "Incarceration, Social Capital, and Crime: Implications for Social Disorganization Theory." *Criminology* 36 (3): 441.

Rusche Georg, and Otto Kirchheimer. 1939. *Punishment and Social Structure*. New York: Russell and Russell.

Ryan, L., and A. Golden. 2006. "'Tick the Box Please': A Reflexive Approach to Doing Quantitative Social Research." *Sociology* 40 (6): 1191–200.

Salamon, Sonya. 2003. *Newcomers to Old Towns: Suburbanization of the Heartland*. Chicago: University of Chicago Press.

Sampson, Robert J. 1987. *Crime in Cities: The Effects of Formal and Informal Social Control*. Chicago: University of Chicago Press.

———. 1991. "Linking the Micro- and Macrolevel Dimensions of Community Social Organization." *Social Forces* 70 (1): 23.

———. 1997. "What Community Supplies: Recasting Theories of Social Organization." In *Urban Problems and Community Development*, edited by Ronald Ferguson. Washington, DC: Brookings Institution.

———. 2002. "Organized for What? Recasting Theories of Social (Dis)organization." In *Crime and Social Organization*, edited by Elin Waring and David Weisburd. New Brunswick, NJ: Transaction Publishers.

———. 2004. "Networks and Neighbourhoods: The Implication of Connectivity for Thinking about Crime in the Modern City." In *Network Logic: Who Governs in an Interconnected World?*, edited Helen McCarthy, Paul Miller, and Paul Skidmore, 157–66. London: Demos.

Sampson, Robert J. 2012. *Great American City: Chicago and the Enduring Neighborhood Effect*. Chicago: University of Chicago Press.

Sampson, Robert J., and Stephen Raudenbush. 2004. "Seeing Disorder: Neighborhood Stigma and the Social Construction of 'Broken Windows.'" *Social Psychology Quarterly* 67 (4): 319–42.

Sampson, Robert J., Stephen W. Raudenbush, and Felton Earls. 1997. "Neighborhoods and Violent Crime: A Multilevel Study of Collective Efficacy." *Science* 277 (5328): 918.

Sampson, Robert J., and Patrick Sharkey. 2008. "Neighborhood Selection and the Social Reproduction of Concentrated Racial Inequality." *Demography* 45 (1): 1–29. doi: http://link.springer.com/journal/volumesAndIssues/13524.

Sampson, Robert J., and William J. Wilson. 1994. "Toward a Theory of Race, Crime, and Urban Inequality." In *Crime and Inequality*, edited by J. Hagan and R. Peterson. Stanford, CA: Stanford University Press.

Shichor, D. 1992. "Myths and Realities in Prison Siting." *Crime and Delinquency* 38 (1): 70–87.

Schlosser, Eric. 1998. "The Prison-Industrial Complex." *Atlantic* 282 (6): 51.

Schoenfeld, H. 2011. "Putting Politics in Penal Policy Reform." *Criminology and Public Policy* 10 (3): 715–24.

Sechrest, D. K. 1992. "Locating Prisons: Open Versus Closed Approaches to Siting." *Crime and Delinquency* 38 (1): 88.

Selznick, Philip. 1949. *TVA and the Grass Roots: A Study in the Sociology of Formal Organization*. Berkeley: University of California Press.

Shaw, Hillary J. 2006. "Food Deserts: Towards the Development of a Classification." *Geografiska Annaler: Series B, Human Geography* 88 (2): 231–47.

Sherman, Jennifer. 2009. *Those Who Work, Those Who Don't: Poverty, Morality, and Family in Rural America*. Minneapolis: University of Minnesota Press.

Sims, Mario. 1999. "High-Status Residential Segregation among Racial and Ethnic Groups in Five Metro Areas, 1980–1990." *Social Science Quarterly* 80 (3): 556–73.

Small, Mario L. 2002. "Culture, Cohorts, and Social Organization Theory: Understanding Local Participation in a Latino Housing Project." *American Journal of Sociology* 108 (1): 1–54.

———. 2007. "Is There Such a Thing as 'the Ghetto'?" *City and Community* 11 (3): 413–21.

———. 2009. *Unanticipated Gains: Origins of Network Inequality in Everyday Life.* Oxford. Oxford University Press.

Small, Mario L., David Harding, and Michelle Lamont. 2010. "Reconsidering Culture and Poverty." *Annals of the American Academy of Political and Social Science* 629 (1): 6–27.

Smith, Earl, and Angela J. Hattery. 2006. "The Prison Industrial Complex." *Sociation Today* 4 (2): 1–28.

———. 2008. "Incarceration: A Tool for Racial Segregation and Labor Exploitation." *Race, Gender, and Class* 15 (1/2): 79–97.

Snipp, M., H. Horton, L. Jensen, J. Nagel, and R. Rochin. 1993. "Persistent Rural Poverty and Racial and Ethnic Minorities." In *Persistent Poverty in Rural America*, by the Rural Sociological Society's Task Force on Persistent Poverty, 173–99. Boulder, CO: Westview Press.

Sorokin, Pitirim Aleksandrovich, and Carle C. Zimmerman. 1929. *Principles of Rural-Urban Sociology.* New York: Henry Holt.

Spear, Allan H. 1967. *Black Chicago: The Making of a Negro Ghetto, 1890–1920.* Chicago: University of Chicago Press.

Squires, Gregory D., and others. 1987. *Chicago: Race, Class, and the Response to Urban Decline.* Philadelphia: Temple University Press.

St. Jean, Peter K. B. 2007. *Pockets of Crime: Broken Windows, Collective Efficacy, and the Criminal Point of View.* Chicago: University of Chicago Press.

Stack, Carol B. 1974. *All Our Kin: Strategies for Survival in a Black Community.* New York: Harper and Row.

———. 1996. *A Call to Home.* New York: Basic Books.

Street, Paul. 2002. "Color Blind." In *Prison Nation: The Warehousing of America's Poor*, edited by T. Herivel and P. Wright, 30–40. New York: Routledge.

Suttles, Gerald. 1972. *The Defended Neighborhood in the Social Construction of Communities.* Chicago: University of Chicago Press.

Sutton, John R. 1991. "The Political Economy of Madness: The Expansion of the Asylum in Progressive America." *American Sociological Review* 56 (5): 665–78.

Sykes, Gresham. 1958. *Society of Captives: A Study of a Maximum Security Prison.* Princeton, NJ: Princeton University Press.

Tansey, Oisín. 2007. "Process Tracing and Elite Interviewing: A Case for Non-Probability Sampling." *PS: Political Science and Politics* 40 (4): 765.

Taub, Richard. 2004. *Doing Development in Arkansas: Using Credit to Create Opportunity for Entrepreneurs Outside the Mainstream.* Fayetteville: University of Arkansas Press.

Taub, Richard P., D. Garth Taylor, and Jan D. Dunham. 1984. *Paths of Neighborhood Change: Race and Crime in Urban America.* Chicago: University of Chicago Press.

Tilove, Jonathan. 2002. "Minority Prison Inmates Skew Local Populations and States Redistrict." *Newhouse News Service*, March 12.

Tolnay, Stewart, and E. M. Beck. 1992. *A Festival of Violence.* Urbana: University of Illinois Press.

Tomaskovic-Devey, Donald, and Vincent J. Roscigno. 1996. "Racial Economic Subordination and White Gain in the U.S. South." *American Sociological Review* 61 (4): 565.

———. 1997. "Uneven Development and Local Inequality in the U.S. South: The Role of Outside Investment, Landed Elites, and Racial Dynamics." *Sociological Forum* 12 (4): 565.

Tonry, Michael. 1995. *Malign Neglect: Race, Crime, and Punishment in America.* Oxford: Oxford University Press.

———. 2004. *Thinking about Crime: Sense and Sensibility in American Penal Culture.* New York: Oxford University Press.

Uggen, Christopher, and Jeff Manza. 2002. "Democratic Contraction? Political Consequences of Felon Disenfranchisement in the United States." *American Sociological Review* 67: 777–803.

Venkatesh, Sudhir A. 2002. *American Project: The Rise and Fall of a Modern Ghetto.* Cambridge, MA: Harvard University Press.

———. 2009. *Off the Books: The Underground Economy of the Urban Poor.* Cambridge, MA: Harvard University Press.

Vigil, D. 2008. "Barrio Genealogy." *City and Community* 7 (4): 366–71.

Voss, Paul R. 2007. "Demography as a Spatial Social Science." *Population Research and Policy Review* 26 (5–6): 457–76.

Wacquant, Loïc. 2001. "Deadly Symbiosis: When Ghetto and Prison Meet and Merge." *Punishment and Society* 3 (1): 95–134.

———. 2002. "From Slavery to Mass Incarceration: Rethinking the 'Race Question' in the US." *New Left Review* 13 (13): 41–60.

———. 2004. "Decivilizing and Demonizing: The Remaking of the Black American Ghetto." In *The Sociology of Norbert Elias,* edited by S. Loyal and S. Quilley, 95–121. Cambridge: Cambridge University Press.

———. 2011. "A Janus-Faced Institution of Ethnoracial Closure." In *The Ghetto: Contemporary Issues and Controversies,* edited by R. Hutchison & B. Haynes, 1–31. Boulder, CO: Westview Press.

Wahl, Ana-María González, and Steven E. Gunkel. 2007. "From Old South to New South? Black-White Residential Segregation in Micropolitan Areas." *Sociological Spectrum* 27 (5): 507–35. doi: 10.1080/02732170701434674.

Wakefield, Sarah, and Christopher Uggen. 2010. "Incarceration and Stratification." *Annual Review of Sociology* 36: 387–406.

Walker, Michael L. 2016. "Race Making in a Penal Institution." *American Journal of Sociology* 121 (4): 1051–78.

Ward, Geoff K. 2006. "Race and the Justice Workforce." In *The Many Colors of Crime: Inequalities of Race, Ethnicity, and Crime in America,* edited by Ruth Peterson, Lauren Krivo, and John Hagan, 67–90. New York: New York University Press.

———. 2012. *The Black Child-Savers: Racial Democracy and Juvenile Justice.* Chicago: University of Chicago Press.

Watkins, A. M., and S. H. Decker. 2007. "Patterns of Homicide in East St. Louis." *Homicide Studies* 11 (1): 30–49. doi: 10.1177/1088767906296020.

Webb, Jim. 2009. "Why We Must Fix Our Prisons." *Parade* magazine, March.

Weiss, Jackie. 1990. "Public Says 'Yes' to Prison Plan: Overflow Crowd Backs Effort to Boost Local Economy." *Forrest City Times-Herald,* January 12.

Western, Bruce. 2006. *Punishment and Inequality in America.* New York: Russell Sage.

Wherry, Frederick F. 2012. *The Culture of Markets.* Cambridge: Polity.

Wildeman, Christopher. 2009. "Parental Imprisonment, the Prison Boom, and the Concentration of Childhood Disadvantage." *Demography* 46 (2): 265–80.

Wilkes, Rima, and John Iceland. 2004. "Hypersegregation in the Twenty-First Century." *Demography* 41 (1): 23–36.

Wilson, William J. 1987. *The Truly Disadvantaged.* Chicago: University of Chicago Press.

Wirth, Louis. 1928. *The Ghetto.* Chicago: University of Chicago Press.

Wodahl, E. J. 2006. "The Challenges of Prison Reentry from a Rural Perspective." *Western Criminological Review* 7 (2): 32–47.

Woodruff, Nan Elizabeth. 1993. "African-American Struggles for Citizenship in the Arkansas and Mississippi Deltas in the Age of Jim Crow." *Racial History Review* 55: 33–51.

Wright, Erik Olin. 1997. *Class Counts: Comparative Studies in Class Analysis*. Cambridge: Cambridge University Press.

Wynn, Jonathan. 2011. *The Tour Guide: Walking and Talking New York*. Chicago: University of Chicago Press.

Xie, Min, and David McDowall. 2010. "The Reproduction of Racial Inequality: How Crime Affects Housing Turnover." *Criminology* 48 (3): 865.

Yin, Robert K. 2003. *Case Study Research: Design and Methods*. 3rd ed. Applied Social Research Methods Series 5. New York: Sage.

INDEX